SILENT VOICES

The
Southern
Negro
Woman
Today

SILENT VOICES

by Josephine Carson

DELACORTE PRESS, N.Y.

Published by Dell Publishing Co., Inc.
750 Third Avenue
New York, New York 10017
Library of Congress Catalog Card Number: 69–17530
Printed in the United States of America

DESIGNED BY *Larry Kamp*

First printing—August 1969

ACKNOWLEDGMENTS

FIRST, to Mark Rider for patience and all the rest, the author is deeply indebted.

Also, to Richard Kennedy, senior editor of Delacorte Press, for patience, imagination, and trust;

to The Division Fund of Palo Alto, California, and Mr. Robert Klein, for support;

to Richmond Neighborhood House of Richmond, California;

to Mrs. Martin Luther King, Jr., for trust and recommendations;

to Mrs. Margaret Long of Atlanta, Georgia;

to Miss Cathy Cade of New Orleans, Louisiana;

to Mrs. Christine Haynes of Washington, D.C.;

to Mrs. Ann Behlmer for thoughtful and efficient editing and typing;

to Miss Isabelle Ziegler for editorial advice;

and to all the women, young, old, hungry, rich, wise, honest and brave who opened their doors and their thoughts and who are gathered anonymously herein . . .

Annelle, Freddie, Emma, Ruby Doris (posthumously), Bernice, Mrs. Clark, Mrs. Leonard, Mrs. Roberts, Mrs. Lewis, Mrs. Scott,

Mrs. Lowe, Alma, Mrs. Brayboy, Mrs. Young, Mrs. West, Mrs. Purnell, Mrs. Hayward, Iola, Mrs. Boynton, Mrs. Harvey, Bessie, Mrs. Middleton, Mrs. Nelson, Mrs. Rolax, Sandra, Marjorie, Urlucia, Gail, Francis, Celia, Thelma, Juanita, Mrs. Holoman, Mrs. Gale, Joan, Miss Pinkett, Bobbie Jean, Kathleen, Margie, Portia, Georgia, Mrs. Alston, Mrs. Brown, Mrs. Collins, Mrs. Whitted, Mrs. Parker, Miss Ivory, Dorothy, Pearlette . . . my deepest gratitude.

JOSEPHINE CARSON

Ojai, California
January, 1969

for SEPTIMA POINSETTE CLARK
with love, admiration
and gratitude

. . . these are not your names but these are
your words and my impressions of your words
and acts and attitudes. Without intent to betray
you, I have sometimes given one of you two
voices, and I have sometimes seen you in classic
or tragic or comic pose; for that and for much
more I have presumed that you will, as is your
nature, forgive me. I sought the quick of your
life and was rewarded a thousandfold.

SILENT VOICES

"When the infinite servitude of woman
shall have ended, when she will be able
to live by and for herself, then man—
hitherto abominable—having given her
her freedom, she too will be a poet.
Woman will discover the unknown. Will
her world be different from ours? She
will discover strange unfathomable
things, repulsive, delicious. We shall take
them, we shall understand them."

RIMBAUD

The Myth

A PREVIEW

THIS WORK is an impression and the search for a silenced voice, a crucial part in the chorus of American voices.

Black woman, silent, almost invisible in America, has been speaking for three hundred years in pantomime or at best in a borrowed voice. She has moved silently through the mythological roles forced upon her—from chattel to Mammy to Matriarch. She has solaced and fortified the entire South of the United States, black and white, male and female, a South which reveres and heeds her in secret, which confides in her and trusts her to rear its children, black and white, yet which—like the rest of America —has never asked her to speak, to reveal her private history, her knowledge, her imaginings, never asked her participation in anything but maintenance of humanity by way of the back door. The few rare cases of her rise to influence have been almost entirely in the fields of service, public, private, or domestic; she is teacher, nurse, social worker, sometimes lawyer, sometimes physician, even representative in state government, but this rise

1

has occurred against great odds and in the face of a double restriction: she is woman and black.

A few have spoken as poets but—woman, black, and poet? Americans do not heed them, only sometimes indulge them. Few of us today could name even one Negro woman poet; fewer could recite her lines or define her meaning.

Who has asked for more than her body's labor and succor? Who has sought her wisdom, her ideas, her advice?

And who is this Black Woman, now, today? How did she move through these three centuries out of slavery, labeled and known mainly as servant, chick, whore, blues singer, spoiler of sons, but transcending all names and myths? (It is still more or less impossible to find reference to Negro Woman in our standard American historical and sociological works; one must still seek her by such devious headings as "rape complex" or "White Southern Womanhood," that famous exalted role in a myth that made woman, white, and purity synonymous words, a myth now in decay but still influential in Southern mores.)

Who remembers that she came here naked, shorn sometimes of royalty, of maternity; a sister severed from siblings, a peasant, a poet? Who remembers or ever knew of her as Margaret Garner, a slave caught escaping in the night, who slashed her own daughter's throat to keep her from slavery and who begged the white judge to kill her for she would "go singing to the gallows" rather than be returned to slavery?

Who remembers her as Sojourner Truth, the suffragette who, baring her breast before a convention of white male politicians who had ridiculed her femininity, asked, "Ain't I a woman?"

Chattel . . . meaning to live and die as mere bone and muscle, meaning to survive as a good body, a breeder, a worker. Chattel is some*thing*, not some*one*. The soul took exile in secret inside the naked somethingness. In Black Woman, modesty was spiritual; to survive, the body succumbed to its conquerors.

Chattel the color of black was made to work fields and to breed more marketable pounds of chattel by the plantation stud or his master, following no natural taste or cycle, following market requirements. Chattel was first like a sterile womb. Out of that sterility she managed to be reborn American and to bring forth Black America—to hold it together as a people—and to feed and solace, besides, her white masters. Cotton and tobacco and sugar fed on black sweat; children, black and white, on black milk and black love. How shall that Southern white have eaten, have strengthened his bones without this black chattel? His hardiness is still his shame.

History is drama. In the familial drama of Southern history there are four characters: two who speak in words and two who speak in action. These are (1) White Man, author, villain, patriarch; history's stud perhaps, for he fathered most of the mulatto and all the white population of the South; (2) White Woman, symbol of virtue and racial purity in whose name were committed the most perverse crimes in Western history; (3) Black Man, tragic hero and animal sacrifice; and (4) Black Woman, heir to the spoils—from the charred remains of her lynched mate or son to the living rapacious body of White Man and the mulatto generations he sired. Nothing she gave could secure the manhood, dignity, or safety of her black mate; nothing she gave could humanize his white tormentor, but she gave it all the same.

Today she has inherited this cast and the stage in the final moment of that drama and still she has not been given lines but makes her statement almost entirely by her physical presence on that stage. Plainly, if given lines, she could only use them to tell it like it is and was, and the playwright and the world do not yet want it told that way.

And so she takes a body's position in the midst of a disintegrating drama, a historical pageant. As Rosa Parks she sat on the bus and with her body said "No"; and by that she bore that thing, already buried they say, called the Movement. She bore movement silently, letting the body's *verboten* presence tell it all, where fervent speeches before her had brought no movement.

She stands there still. She is the only person in the South today who greets all Southerners. That unsolicited history of matriarchal power has cast her into confrontation with all of society where if one language does not communicate, another will. She stands there still, receiving the wounded into her care—child or man. There is no South without her. She moves as envoy in her white uniform of caretaker from her black ghetto through the neutral zone of the city to the white ghetto, in the dawn, alone on the bus, working for white families to feed black families; her business is to tend, to heal, to endure, to support, to know, and to keep the story silent. One of her daughters, the young poet, Laverne Miranda, still sees her there alone and still hears her silence:

The Moving of the Mama Out of Bed

The moving of the mama out of bed
First the body then the head
One foot
Two foot down
Three foot taken
One step ahead
The movement of the body on the feet
The leaving of the children in wet beds
Bunion footed children
Left in bed
It should be me
Mama
In the kitchen singing no song
Five o'clock
First the head on the bus
Then the body
Eyes wide open on the town
It should be me
Mama
Moving slow
Leaving man at home
Leaving son
Talking whispers
Waking everybody in the house
With whispers
To work
To factory
Army of the black headed
Black faced
Only women ride the buses in the dawn
Only women
Unseen women, hungry women
Black women ride the buses in the dawn.

But let her speak now. The houselights are already going up. That old ritual drama of race is ending in America now. Where it is resurrected there is a hollow sound. The lights go up, and we must look into each other's faces.

"Is she a matriarch?" my neighbor asks.

And I say, "Is she not a human, a woman, evolved out of tragedy and the body's inventiveness, the soul's patience? Do you still believe she has nothing to say?"

SOUTH

SPRING. A stillness here and a stifle; the air is not hot, only striated with warm filaments through blocks of cold. Her milieu is temperamental, baffled, weatherish.

Also rural. In Atlanta there are one million rural folk. In New Orleans one million village and rural folk. Her milieu, they say, is in flux, from rural to urban. Francis Simkins wrote, in *The Everlasting South:*

> Our historians should explain or justify these supposed deficiencies of the South by showing that its genius is rural, not urban; that the larger the cities grow, the more countrified they become because of the rural origin of their newer inhabitants.

Yes, something rural remains. In the city these folk keep rural time, are neighborly, have a rooster, a piece of yard, a cousin (something rural about having a cousin). And they don't support much culture. They sit on the stoop, especially Negroes. They are together, the link is not broken. Black is intimate. Whatever the broken family is, one feels unbrokenness here more than brokenness: *My sister . . . My cousin . . . My mother keeps him while I work . . . This is a picture of my son . . . My daddy was a preacher . . . My granddaddy bought my grandma . . . Listen, with a man you has to put up with a heap o' thangs to stay, like you said you would, till death . . . The chillrun stops by my aunt's place till I comes home . . .*

Unbroken among broken pieces. There is a chain of black being.

Rural and familial. A family is not two parents with children in a housing tract, in a housing project—apartment 291 B. A family is kin. All kin. The black woman's milieu is among kin. She is rural, kin, and peasant, all that, though in flux.

And she is in flux, too, from bondage to freedom, as befits a human being. Something is happening—nature's creation is being affirmed by another. There is a movement, and it dominates all of humanity in one way or another; there is a sense of it everywhere. It is a great springtime overturning of the old social earth and the hardy seed of a new perennial laid in. *Movement. Happening.* The words carry revolutionary weight.

And something more: Harriet said, "If you wanta talk about the Negro woman, just say she livin' in poverty. That's all you got to say—she livin' in poverty. Look around. Poverty." More than talk about her, I wanted to hear her out—in that speech, with its irritable fervor, or any other.

Poverty—a lake. A quicksand. A quarantine. This is Louisiana. Harriet, though not quite stricken herself, lives in quarantine with a view of that quicksand from her kitchen window in the project apartment. She looks down on a one-hundred-year-old slum house that has more board than glass at its windows; that has never been without lives in its rooms; that is condemned and that condemns those who occupy it, yet shelters them—an anonymous brood of black bodies and souls.

Harriet's apartment is three flights up, above traffic and trash, above the winter rivers of mud in the adjacent open field where boys of the project play ball and where in a year or two "they" will erect another project building and lay a permanent bandage of cement over another acre of the rural South. No, Harriet is not stricken; she has risen from that muck of poverty to the third floor of cheap-construction multiple housing—cement blocks and iron railings, painted doors, high narrow windows in the bedroom for privacy, cubicles in a maze, echoes of gymnasium. She has climbed three flights from street-level disease to the crow's-nest of convalescence. "I'd rather have me a house but houses round here that I can afford is all run down. I can't live like that any mo'. I *had* it."

But she lives, even so, within that quarantine, that zone; the heavy project building is flanked on all sides by the perpetual seep and collapse of chronic poverty. Harriet can go no place from her door except by way of it, as if treading a vast sore in the flesh of some prone creature—sick, brooding, acquiescent.

Yes, the project lies in the moat of poverty, and Harriet is incarcerated in its tower.

"But the worst one," she says, "is the rich black woman 'cause she knows what goin' on with black people. She knows it *still* goin' on—no food and just about no votin' and two percent integration in school, no jobs or bad jobs. She knows they misery—tryin' to feed they kids. You come here and ask me to say, but she don't. The point is poverty, Honey. That's the whole point and the rich black woman knows it."

Yes, she knows. Is that why she sometimes turns her head?

Now and then we collide with the floating statistics that do not define but make a silhouette:

". . . Using these criteria, the number of poor families is smaller, but the number of large families who are poor increases and the number of children in poverty rises by more than one-third—from eleven million to fifteen million. This means that one-fourth of the nation's children live in families that are poor." So says Daniel Moynihan in his famous report, "The Negro Family," prepared for President Johnson in 1965.

Harriet knows these statistics: "You know too many of those poor chillrun is black, Honey."

As reported by the last census, approximately half, 48.5 percent, of the heads of nonwhite (mainly Negro) families had not finished elementary school.

Poverty?

Forty-one percent of all nonwhite families earned less than

$3,000 in 1963, which placed them at the poverty level. This figure has changed almost imperceptibly for the better since that time.

What is poverty?

"Poverty simple, Honey," says Harriet. "It's not having no money and not eatin' too good. And no way to change it. That's all."

To know the other, one becomes the other. To find the outcast, one goes outside the magic ring of law, of logic. The position of the outcast is not logical. It breaks all law and becomes its own law.

To sink, therefore, into this milieu of rural, kin, movement, poverty, slum—and the front stoop, the kitchen, the family, black and white. The Movement, the church, the school, the bus . . .

Ride the bus when she rides the bus, where she goes.

The bus, five o'clock. A great weary band, they sit heavily, holding bundles, their black coats sometimes shabby; sometimes a white uniform hangs below the hem; sometimes they wear white nurses' shoes, more often black flats, "slippers." I heard her say, "I got to git me some new slippers. Lookit these thangs!" and laugh.

The music in the heart of the bus:

"I'm gittin' off later and later sence she have that bunch o' family visitin' ovah there."

"Shoot, she don't know if that chile be indoze o' out. She off in that big car all day."

"He don't know she drink. I haft' hide that stuff round under the dirty clothes!"

"I told 'em I'm goin' to work full time over to the motel. I makes mo' money. But she ack like she don't even hear me."

"Say, how Adele feelin'? I hear she married again. Wonder how her po' mother doin'. I haven't saw her sence Christmas or some."

Soft, idle, back-stoop talk, tinged with a faint disgust; rueful, speculative. An unwinding on a ritual ride from white to black camp, through the squalling center of five o'clock town. Atlanta. New Orleans. Charleston. Birmingham. Washington.

There is no such thing as working next door or down the block. The domestic job is suburban white residential, and that is across town. Mrs. Pennel in the Grapeland district, slum, ghetto, black, says: "Yessum, I works fo' a white lady on the othah side of town. Well, I likes the work most the time. I has to work and they good people. I cleans, cooks supper, care fo' the chillrun—she have three. Yessum, I goes to the back do'."

They flower strangely in the mannered neighborhoods at dawn —the black face, black limbs moving alone among cottonwood trees and magnolias, huge slopes of lawn, up the long drives to the back of the house. The white bus driver winds through the gardens of the lords of the earth and lets them—Bessie, Avis, Mary Lou, Pearl—off at the nearest corner. Sometimes she makes the last part of the ride alone, and he will ask, "Well, how's Mr. Willard's boy? Walking yet?" She tells a white man's news to a white man, and her own news is closeted in a patient soul.

Ride the bus home again. Half of them at five o'clock will begin another day, the evening day of the black camp where black children wait for the remainder of their energy, love, concern; or merely for their weary presence. The mass of dark faces banks the sides of the bus. Some brood. Some doze. Most will trade some talk. One hears little of major consequence—nothing of the Movement, of politics, of law, or of current news. The talk is of bargains, friends, Miss Ann (white woman). A little gossip. A wry comment. The presence of Miss Ann on this bus at this hour is enough to stop the seriousness, if there is any, of these exchanges. Miss Ann manages to break the domestic barricade, nothing more. Mr. Charley would do even less.

Ride to the end of the line. To the end of the pavement and over the rutted dirt road. Or cross that mysterious, sometimes invisible boundary line and enter, magically, that outside, that slum which is easier to enter than to leave. It is as if the city has been tipped drastically and all its loose, broken, tattered parts tumble and lodge themselves permanently in crazy juxtaposition in the slum. Suddenly the street lights are dimmer. Suddenly there is a hole in the street, an automobile cadaver in the yard, a boarded-up building at the dead end of a narrow block. It was once something else. Everything here was once something else; the people, too.

Move into the slum—Greenwood, The Willows, Vine District—and find her milieu; see if Harriet is right. And work up and out with her.

ATLANTA

Windy. Assailed by March. Everything tenuous. Today at her office I met Mrs. Charity Simmons who handles the adult literacy education program for a civil rights organization here, traveling mostly in the rural South.

She hurried in a few minutes late, offered me a casual hand-clasp and a quick intense scrutiny, then smiled and left for a few minutes to check her mail. My impression was of a squat, vital, plush, and graceful woman in her early sixties. Her face is broad, serene—an islander's face; her wide middle and large bosom are tidily swathed in hot green wool jersey; her hair hangs straight down but back from her dark gold face. It is grayish hair, but seems incidental; her face is complete without it, her rounded brow extremely bare. Her hair tucks under in a neat roll about an inch below the ears. She is like a Rousseau painting. Her voice is pleasant, dusky, streaked with the thin rasp of age, yet not definitely aged; it is also high.

When she returned I saw that her arms and legs, which are slender and shapely, youthful in appearance, have an extraordi-

13

nary grace for a heavy person. They emerge from the bright field of her green dress like lovely bronze stems.

I saw a wedding band on a long left-hand finger.

I followed her gratefully through the maze of narrow halls, feeling as if I had been thrust suddenly into the presence of the archetype of Southern Negro female. Several other Negro women had said to me, "The woman you want to talk to is Charity Simmons." The oracle. All seemed content to let her speak for them. She is calmly powerful.

I met ten or twelve employees, all Negro women, in crowded little makeshift offices. The halls were lined with cartons of printed matter stacked to the ceiling. There was a sound of machines, telephones, soft voices. I had met most of these young women a few days before. They were polite, gentle, cool, very busy but not rushed exactly. There seemed to be a long, attenuated emergency, something chronic about the tension. Their work seemed to go on in a spirit of mild trance, as if there were no end to it, as if even the most imperative deadline could not be divested of its merely relative importance. Don't know how this feeling came through so precisely. Something about the way they all moved and spoke. No doubt they are down to the bare gears of this complex operation known as The Movement.

The subject here is elusive, debatable, if momentarily absolute: a dream as old, as exceedingly exalted, as absurd and fabulous as man himself: Freedom. Freedom here is a business—office hours, board meetings, field workers, appointments with government officials, salaries, grants, publicity—Freedom! That migrating bird which has traversed its own secret routes and seasons as long as the hunter has known of it. I look around for a glimpse of it, a fallen feather. This office and its workers, its labors, its very physical existence, are dedicated to the most lofty abstraction in the history of human thought—Freedom. How shall anyone ever find it?

"Education," says Charity Simmons. "And work. And prayer. Nothing can stop the Negroes now. Nothing. They got faith and the time is with 'em."

She leans across the table, arms out in front of her, hands toying with a small pamphlet she has rolled into a kind of tube, and talks softly, candidly. We find many levels of agreement, especially about women and their future, the dilemma of their "role." What kind of women are most strongly influenced by fathers, which by mothers; whom do they choose as confidants in serious matters—a man or a woman? How do they feel about the necessity of marriage and children for a woman's fulfillment? What about birth control, love, education, religion, politics, American life? The Movement? The Revolution? Is this a revolution? What do they experience as black women in America—right now, this moment? I want to hear all that and much more.

"Well," says Charity Simmons, "I've had to change my thinking on a lot of subjects. I was forty years old before I could change my old ideas about sin and sex and all that. My mother was such a strait-laced woman, so strict and proper. She was quick to whip us and correct us. You'll find a lot of strict moral Negro women in the South yet today. She was brought up in Haiti and was free issue. Her sister, my aunt, used to say, 'I never served a white woman. I'm free issue.' Meaning she wasn't a slave, never had been. Oh, that meant a lot to her that she had never served a white woman.

"But my father was a slave as a boy, on a big plantation near Charleston. He had the job of carrying his master's son's books as the two rode on one horse to the schoolhouse. Then he would wait outside, grazing the horse, until school was out and they rode home to the plantation. He was a boy in the Confederate Army and about sixteen when the war ended. He received a pension for years after that—eight dollars a year. He became a caterer when he was a man. He met my mother and married her in Florida and they moved back to Charleston. That's still my home. Low Country, that's what we call it. I love that country and those people.

"Well, my father was a lot older than my mother. I think he influenced me more than she did. He had control over his emotions. He would say, 'Don't fuss over it. In a hundred years, nobody'll know the difference.' He didn't learn to read until his youngest child was learning and that was because he got a civil service job in a USO during World War I and he had to sign his name.

"Yes, I did understand my mother but I didn't realize it until later. She was so strict. She had some learning from books and was very proud but she took in washing for a big white family in Charleston. I remember, we'd come home from school and there would be those big tubs full of hot water in the yard and that big wash waiting to be done. Next day or two we'd come home to the ironing. There were eight of us. We all worked at it. But they always gave us time to study. Both wanted us educated. My mother was a big help keeping me in private school where I could get a good education. There were a lot of educated Negro women in Charleston in those days who would hold school in their homes. It was far better education than the public school. My parents sacrificed a lot for me to learn.

"My mother was so strict that when the grocery man came by the house with his truck of fresh things, you know, she'd come out and sit on the porch and make him bring the things up for her to look at and choose. She wouldn't go down to that street. No! It wasn't proper for a woman.

"Race was always a subject in my life. Race problems made me search. I remember seeing Negro convicts chained by their ankles cutting grass on public grounds. There was a white guard overseeing them. It made me feel terrible. I used to wonder why Negroes didn't work for themselves.

"But there was so much I didn't know about the world before I left home. We were poor, all huddled up in those rooms in the winter, keepin' warm. We had to watch our money! Whoo!

"A lot of my attitudes changed after I left home. I see I still have to change. That's why I like this work and meeting all those people."

There is an arch of the tongue on the *th* that makes it more like *d,* more like *doze* and *those.* But it isn't exactly either. She sometimes lowers her voice, reminiscently, and the speech then is more Southern Negro than otherwise; a certain sentiment comes into it then.

"People's ideas sometimes make me change mine," says Charity. "I changed my mind about birth control, too. Now I accept it, but before I was against it."

I ask about a woman's life without marriage.

"It's hard to say if she can have a full life that way. A few can, but most can't. But I know I couldn't have done all these things that I've done, my work, if I had married again. Even if the man I had had lived, I couldn't have done it."

I know little about her former life. She has a son now in his forties who has children. He was raised by an aunt while Charity worked and traveled.

She looks candidly at me. She is giving me that rare gift, her time, of which there is never enough. And she intends to say precisely what she means. This generous candor and lack of self-consciousness give me immediate peace and ease. I had forgotten, if I ever knew it, that such results come that way. Social testing is wiped out with one honest intimate exchange of glances. She is able to be intimate.

Charity's equanimity, her clear, wise expression, imply hard experience endured and resolved. She has passed through many a fire, one feels. Am I projecting? Such a force of calm maternalism and natural intimacy is irresistible. I may be in the presence of a matriarch, if there is such a thing. We shall see. Anyway, this is a very powerful woman.

I learn that this strict mother and philosophical father gave her a certain essential, not to be duplicated, self-respect. She had it free from them, and her hard work and intelligence earned it later from teachers and ministers. A lot of people responded to the child Charity and went into building her.

"There were two Negro women on our block who had families by white men who came regularly to visit them. Their children were beautiful, but I remember we had very strained relations with them. My parents were determined that my sister and I never nurse white babies. Being in a white home might lead to temptation with the white man of the house or even delivery boys. 'They might mark your legs,' my mother would say."

She worked her way through high school as companion and nursemaid to a young Negro woman neighbor and her children. She taught school after that and slowly, in night schools and through scholarships, got a college education.

"No," says Charity, "I don't think a woman can be complete without having a child. That is the greatest love. The first time a woman puts a child to her breast, that is the greatest love she can know." So says Charity Simmons, who nevertheless had to give her only child over to the keeping of another woman in order to support him and perhaps also to fulfill what she might call her own destiny. She implies that her work is no happenstance. She is deeply dedicated—always was—to educating the deprived, perhaps more than she was dedicated to motherhood.

She does not make the final statement about the ancient quandary of a woman's life—that she has no fulfillment without husband and child; yet she has no fulfillment either without work and influence of worldly significance beyond the maternal and domestic. Charity says that married she could not have lived this life dedicated to the Lord and to education, especially to the humble black people of the South.

"What's the answer to the problem? Do you have one?"

"There's going to be a new kind of woman," she says. "Maybe without all these babies. That's what changed me about birth control. One baby or two, that's different from six or ten babies. Anyway, with babies or not, there's going to be a new kind of woman. She's coming. I see it. She will be used."

"Yes," I say, "and she will have to break the rules to do it."

We laugh.

Moved this week into a boardinghouse run by a church where Charity, the only Negro resident, lives when in Atlanta. It is on the fringe of a slum area, mostly Negro. I shall travel with Charity, also. Meantime, I ride buses and walk streets, meeting with any woman who will talk to me.

How Charity lives. Charity the body, the woman at home, in private. Our room: Upstairs. Pink walls, three stern little single beds, a brick and plank bookcase under the window. A small oval-shaped rag rug. A 75-watt bulb in the ceiling fixture and no other light. A gas heater. An old brown chest of drawers, well-cared-for, with three large drawers and two small. A narrow shallow closet.

Charity had no time to unpack from her last trip. I offered to unpack a few things and hang them in our closet so she would not have to press them at the last minute. She gave me a look of amazement, very brief, and agreed, thanking me. I hung up two dark cotton suits, one navy, one black, with print blouses; a bright blue wool jersey dress much like the green one she wore the first day we met; a black crepe. She has learned to live out of these suitcases, also to handle them. She is independent and uncomplaining, seems indifferent to many physical discomforts. Her luggage, a recent gift which she likes very much, is dark blue and green plaid canvas with black plastic face and binding; zipper bags, they are very light in weight. She has several hats, one a deep cloche that lay half folded on top of her clothes. She is busy every day, all day, and most evenings. How she finds time to maintain herself physically is beyond me at the moment.

We talked late last night about women, about the Movement and what it promises for women. "We livin' in a great time." She said it with a controlled passion, and one feels that she would have said this no matter what her historical time might have been. She is living, that is more what she means, I sense. She talked about what the Movement has done for some of the women in her organization, and more excitedly, about what it is doing for Negro men: making leaders, making men. She uses words such as "know-how," mentions love often and the Lord sometimes.

I was nearly blinded by the glare of the overhead bulb and talked the last hour with my eyes shut, which made it difficult for me to stay awake, as interested as I was. But she seemed indifferent to the glaring light. She does not always remember to open out the heavy blanket that is folded at the end of her bed and that must be dead weight on her feet. She moves with the same deliberate even timing no matter what the occasion. She sighs over the mad activities of the human race but never, it seems, from fatigue.

I have fastidiously divided the top of the chest and all the drawers down the middle, my things occupying the left side. Charity, who usually lives in this room in a very transient fashion, has no more belongings with her than I have and seems to care little where her things are, but of course she would have more privacy and space if I were not here. This is the only guest room in the house. The other rooms are occupied by the young internes in service to the church who live here and work in the community, giving their earnings to the church and receiving, besides room and board, only a small allowance. We share the second-floor bath with six of them.

Supper is good, a very rich-tasting beef stew. A young boy from the neighborhood wanders in to share supper with us—as he has now and then done before. He is the only Negro besides Charity at this table. She is strangely indifferent to him except to comment on his infantilism. His mother is in the state mental institution for what the boy calls a nervous breakdown. We join hands, about fifteen of us, at the huge round table and hear, with bowed heads, a spontaneous grace from one of the group. The talk is of their work—often of the recreation center they have opened in this slum for the local kids, all Negro. It is a three-room, very modest little place, in the basement of an old apartment building a few blocks from the house. It is the first of its kind to have been used by a large number of neighborhood children, probably because it is simple and crude enough not to intimidate them. Several young people from the house maintain it. They discuss possible donors of basketball equipment. Charity makes mental notes.

Charity eats a lot, with apparent pleasure and a steady meditative rhythm, as if under a spell, and yet listens all the while. She eats bread with her supper and drinks coffee afterward, black, strong. She also sometimes drinks tea. She drinks little water. This evening meal is usually her only meal during the day unless there is some kind of luncheon meeting, which almost dictates dining.

"Don't you get hungry?" I ask her.

"No, not much. Not till night. Then I like a good meal. I need to lose weight."

But she does not lose it and does not seem bothered.

She relished the fish at supper last night. Charleston is a great town for fish. She ate a lot of it in her childhood. In our room afterward she gives me a recipe for catfish stew: "You take that, just a little bit of fish, cut it up in big pieces and brown it a little and then cook it in milk with potatoes and onions. That's *really* good!" She laughs, that is the goodness of it. She relishes with calm, with a gentle laugh. But this seems to be a creature with capacity for great passions. How does she harness them?

"That's a cheap dinner and nourishing. Family can live on that fish stew. Around the rivers a poor person can live well if he can fish a little." She has a great imagination for domestic management and is very conscious of the waste of food, time, money, or energy, yet gives all these away open-heartedly. She is not an aggressive mother but more like a plant that has grown up around one on all sides, at a respectful distance so as to give a lot of air, a lot of space, but nevertheless encircling; her maternalism somehow encircles one without either person desiring it or even allowing it. I notice this in the house. There is something quieting about her presence; a buffer, a barrier against the world is thrown like a net loosely around us by her arrival.

It is late. Charity goes barefoot down the hall to the bath but finds it occupied. She comes back to wait with no comment. It is chilly outside. Our little stove pours heat ferociously into the room and I find it stifling, but Charity is comfortable. A mockingbird has begun to sing next door in a huge peach tree. I am exhilarated by the sound. This capricious spring in the South! Cold. Sudden chaotic winds. Sudden still heat. Mad birds. A little rain. I remember it from childhood. I am lonely tonight and very glad of Charity's company. She has taken off her black clothes and put on aqua-colored nylon pajamas and a matching robe—the traveling kind of nightwear. Against her dull gold skin the color solidifies. On the bookshelf lies a pile of papers she must deal with for tomorrow's meetings. She seems unconcerned, not preoccupied with them. Also, there rests her high-crowned black hat, reminiscent of the stove pipe, a type of hat I saw on most of the Negro women last Sunday in both churches I attended. I think of native Peruvian women in their high, rounded derbylike hats.

She sits now on the end of her bed, talking, rolling up her hair in a few neat curlers, smearing it first with a kind of bluish cream from a small jar. One leg hangs over the edge of the bed—her foot, very small, neat, like that of a child, not touching the floor. The other leg is crooked up under her, a position I find uncomfortable for any length of time. Her back is straight.

"You would have liked that meeting. Those are the people

from Alabama who are running for office in the spring primaries. Some of those Negroes are going to win and they have to know something about the job before they take it over. No white person in that office is going to tell them how to do. If the sheriff wants to find a form or do some kind of routine job, you know that white clerk isn't going to help him. Won't even show him where the forms are. We got local people, some of 'em white, in the same kinds of jobs to come down and give them some ideas, tell them what the job usually entails. Oh, they are so proud! I love working with those people. They have so much faith and pride. They work so hard. It's dangerous running for office in Alabama, if you're Negro. They could be killed if they're elected, but that won't stop 'em."

"I'll go with you next weekend."

"Good."

Later. Her paper work out of the way, she sits on the side of her bed, leaning across it to read the newspaper that is spread out before her, one hand lifting it slightly, her other hand holding a cigarette. She wears steel-rimmed glasses for reading. She has just come from the bath and now feels the heat of the room. The stove is finally turned off. I have opened the window beside my bed about half an inch and am delirious with the fragrant night air.

"I didn't know you smoked, Charity."

"I like about one cigarette or two in a week. Sometimes relaxes me. You don't smoke?"

"No."

I am relieved she does not make the usual offer to deprive herself, but I know that if she did, she would mean it, which is not often true of smokers. "Mind if I smoke?"—match poised. She simply smokes her rare cigarette.

I study her face. With her hair drawn up into curlers, her face is younger, broad, clear, sufficient. Her mouth is wide, thinned by age; the few lines of aging are all in her lower face. But there is something maidenish about her, even this woman, not prudish but only a subtle remnant of the virgin. I have seen that trace of girlishness in many a black woman's face, or in a quickened coltish move, since coming South.

Charity suddenly grunts and spews a breath of scorn. "Look at that! They *still* tryin' to get to that moon!" I laugh. That moon! The condescension is profound but so kind, as if to say—poor dears, poor fools!

"You don't approve, Charity?"

"Seems like a lotta good money and time and education to get to the moon!" She laughs a little, shaking her head.

How, I wonder, would she accept the idea of fertile idleness? Of permanent leisure? Would she pass a moral judgment on all that? Progress. Education. Work. These are her subjects. And integration, in which she absolutely believes. This is a stanch Protestant and Puritan, yet one with all the instincts of a great savorer. She loves to eat, to hear country accents, to know the details of other lives, to move among people, all people. Is this mind as literal as it seems? That I must find out. It is such an integrated, logical mentality; one that wants to change, has changed; one that withholds judgment if not opinion. Nothing ordinary in all that.

"Why do you think they do it, Charity? Aim at the moon?"

"Men got to have something new all the time. They can't dig. Women dig down better."

Ah! I offer agreement even though we may mean different things by the idea.

"But maybe that's only because women feel they have nowhere else to move but inward and down in that sense. Digging. Maybe if we had the same freedom and license and power we'd spread out and adventure and experiment and go to the moon."

"Mmmm . . . maybe so. I'll have to think about that. You talk like Morris [an educator friend of hers], Jo. You'll have to meet him. He thinks in a very original way."

On my way to town today I pass the neighborhood center. It is not yet open but at the door three Negro children stand quietly, waiting to be let in. It is cold outside, but they are thinly dressed. The oldest of them, a little girl of no more than six, although so small and wispy I cannot be sure of her age, runs to me. She stands flat-footed, legs apart. The tiny body shudders.

"You got de key?"

The tone is urgent, the face too serious for six years of living.

All three are barefoot, matty-headed, in rags. The boy is holding a large box of raisins, the standard snack from government-surplus food that many families in the area receive.

"No, I don't have the key but Bob will be along pretty soon. Aren't you cold?"

She shakes her head, staring at me, a most cunning and daring scrutiny, that look by which so many slum kids indicate the early acquired jungle habit of having to make an enormous decision in the human battle on the basis of a one-glance survey. She decides and cautiously touches my hand. Two front teeth are missing; the lisp adds to the thickness of lippy Southern Negro speech.

"Whath yo' name?"

I tell her and ask hers.

"Mine's Ronelle."

"That's a nice name. I like it. Are those your brother and sister?"

All of them giggle. "Huh uh. Dey lib roun' de cornah."

She pulls me out to the street again by a sticky and boneless little hand that is more like some gift of newborn life laid bare in my palm. She looks up, taking her risk with great bravado. There is already a jaded, mocking tone in her voice as if she were ready for proud or unconcerned defeat.

"Hey, you wanta comb my hair fo' me?"

"What?"

"Can you comb niggah hair?" It is loud and defiant.

I stoop down suddenly. "Where's your house, Ronelle? Where's your mother?"

She jerks her head. "She in de baid," and pulls back from me shyly. She absolutely does not want this pity I cannot squelch. She gambled on my toughness, and she lost. I overflow with pity and that is a snare for the likes of Ronelle. I stand up, let go of her hand. Take her on her own tough terms. Am I reading her right? She slides a look over me and then stares at the ground.

"Yes, I can comb it. I've got to get a bus right now but you come over to the house this afternoon if you really want it combed. You know, where Celia and Bob live? You know where it is?"

She knows. She takes my hand again and walks me to the bus. When I enter it she raises a flat gritty little palm turned open toward me, fingers splayed out as if to say "Five." Her rueful smile is not one that belongs to a child. She could be a pretty woman one day, I am thinking, but she will not be. How can she even live that long without some drastic rescue, now, this week, *today*? My mind casts about, desperate for an answer. We move away and she runs back up the block. What does she eat? Who fixes it? Where does she sleep? Is there anything under that thin little dress? Does she also sleep in it? Does she feel cold anymore? Her hand was warm. She looked grubby. Her hair was filled with lint and dust like some bundle of wool left under a chair for a week. *Can you comb niggah hair?* I never have. What is there to it? How many of those tiny tight stiff little braids did she have?

The bus dives under a trestle and speeds up a long grade, sweeping me out of her orbit. What to do with her? Go find her again? Will she come to the house? There are thousands of Ronelles, some not so proud, in the dingy streets of these cities. I think of her nights: Is she safe? Does the door lock? Is there a mother at home? A father? Who and what are they? Has she a grown-up Ronelle for a mother? I gaze around the crowded bus. How many of you solid women began where Ronelle did?

Five hours later I remember that she said "niggah," about herself, as if that were the only word for her I would understand. Seems almost too pat. Shall I keep it in my notes? Yes, I'll keep it. I'll ask Charity about it. Even if Ronelle has been taught some jaded sardonic style, she does not know what she is saying. All she knows is what works and what does not, I tell myself. She has little time or strength for what does not work, no doubt.

Next door an old Negro woman lives alone in a big, shabby, once handsome house. She has a little money. Now and then she loses consciousness from a mild stroke and lies on the floor for a day or two before anybody finds her. She locks the doors and windows tightly at night, fearful and cunning. She roams the rooms peering through the lace curtains. On Saturdays her grandson sometimes comes to tinker with the old green Oldsmobile in the back yard. She has not driven since her husband's death five years ago, but she hangs onto the car, perhaps as a kind of memento of freer days. Her family cannot convince her to take a companion or to sell the house and move in with one of them. That, Charity says, is unusual among Negroes. Now and then one of the boys or girls here at the house checks on her but must be careful not to overdo it, not to offend her. She refuses to admit she has fainted. Such a tyranny!

All at once she comes to visit us. We serve tea in the sitting room. She is proud, quiet, vague, suspicious—a kind of fractious old bird, clawish, frumpy, and cantankerous. She begins to talk in a kind of growl.

"I remember my daddy down on Fountain Street. He was white. White man; white as you. Worked as a pharmacy. Don't find many fine men like that now." She looks away. "He have a memory in the church, down on Eustace. On the wall. He give to the colored people because of my mother. He cut off from all the whites to come to my mother."

We drink tea and make polite response, hoping she will go on talking. But suddenly satisfied, she stands and shuffles to the door, which Bill quickly opens for her, and then he follows her down the steps, ready to catch her but not touching her; she does not like to be touched or even to be aided. She makes no farewells. She is already a ghost but she rises in the morning, dresses and feeds herself—some birdish kind of food, no doubt—and stares out the windows, managing to care for her house a little. Plainly waiting to die. She used to be a singer, traveled some, even to Europe I am told. She knew Atlanta almost a hundred years ago! I wonder if she thought that was what I wanted to hear—about the white daddy?

Once when she lay unconscious, her grandson found her by breaking in the kitchen window; he called an ambulance and got her to the hospital before she regained consciousness. The doctors said she ought to stay there and thought she would probably die there. But she simply rose up one night and dressed herself, walked down the corridor, smiled at the desk nurse, and left the building. Nobody knows how she got home. She clings to her house as a dying insect clings to some twig or tree hollow that has a familiar smell.

"If you take me to any hospital," she tells her grandson, "I've got a dagger and I'll kill the nurse with it. I've got it hid away."

She has a dagger! I am acutely aware now of this old relic next door. The deep middle of the night harbors her thin cough. Her lights are out at eight-thirty, but she lets it be known that she sleeps very little. She watches through the windows for death or life or ghosts.

Old women. Remember the figures: seventy-five percent of aged Negro women live alone. Ninety-six percent have less than $2,000 a year to live on. Sixty-eight percent of those have less than $1,000 a year. Our neighbor is a rare phenomenon.

Just say she livin' in poverty, that's all you got to say.

This neighborhood is getting to me. Today Richard, the director of the house, and I go at noon to the Too Tight Barbershop, where he gets his hair cut, to find Lucy Toomis, a young Negro woman who hangs around there picking up men.

The Too Tight is on a corner, a narrow white stucco building with an undecipherable sign on the outer wall describing some business of former years. Inside there is no light, but a general mumble and shuffle takes place as we enter; and I become aware of the presence of at least six men, all black. They move to the back of the shop, whispering. It is a two-chair shop, clean but suspiciously unindustrious in atmosphere, like a front for some questionable activity; it may be just that the lights are out. The barbershop is an ideal men's club, and this slum, like all others, no doubt, breeds an idle male population. They are everywhere and when not on the street are clustered in small stores and saloons, or in cars which are sometimes long past mobility and slump on rusty rims in back yards, side streets, and alleys.

The barber, obsequious and astonished, comes forward, blocking further passage. Although he wants not to look at me he must. He stares at Richard with very wide eyes. I must be a government woman or social worker, that is the only explanation. This is holy territory that excludes women, especially white women. Who ever heard of a white woman entering this door? I feel like apologizing to him but let Richard do the talking. I hear a conniving little laugh from somewhere in the shadows of the shop as Richard states our business. The barber is very kind.

"Lucy? She done got her a job. Workin'. Her motha down the street though. You wanta talk to her?"

"Well . . . that would be nice. You think she'd mind?"

"No'm, she don't mind. I'll git her."

He goes out in such a way as to force us to do the same. Richard leaves. I stand on the street with the barber who, with two fingers in his mouth, whistles to Lucy's mother to join us. He waves then, beckoning her. "She comin'. She be right here."

First view of Mrs. Irene Williams: A short, stocky body, lean and muscular looking, in a white uniform that strikes the lower shin just above a rumpled pair of dark boys' socks with a design up the side. The feet are thrust into sneakers without laces; the arms are partly hidden in a shapeless green sweater without elbows and without most buttons. The face, light-skinned with heavy African lips, bears an expression of stupefied horror. She is drunk, a chronic sort of drunk, immediately evident as she comes close; there is the odor of saturated, sugared alcoholic chemistry—dense, fruity, rank; no chlorophyll. The mouth is open in a kind of brutish wonder. The left eye, enduring a huge purple and yellow mottled shiner acquired about two days ago, is still swollen, the cornea streaked with fine red threads; red-ringed eyes gaze as indiscriminately as those of a staring corpse. She stumbles forward, eager to oblige. Her hair stands straight up as if magnetized into an arc of gray and black streaks three inches above the face.

"Whatsa mattah?"

"Nothin'. This lady wants to talk to ya. Here . . ." He motions me toward her as if she were an object. "She'll talk to ya." His tone is sweet, paternal toward me. I feel dreadful, hysterical. Why no protest? I have invaded; yes, this whole work is an invasion. Yes, I know that it is an invasion. *Obscene*—that is how it felt to James Agee to live with and observe innocent hosts who floundered, starved, and grappled for decency in the splintered ruin of their lives.

I thank the barber with a smile. He lowers his eyes and lunges back into the Too Tight with a grunt, and enough of Miss Ann or worse. A crescendo of laughter greets him.

"What you want, Sweetheart?" Mrs. Williams stares at me as I imagine stone age woman might do. "You from Lucy's in-surance?"

"No, no." I tell her my purpose.

"Well . . . sure . . . I'll talk to ya." Incredulous. "Come on down the house. We set on the poach."

We walk down the block. "I won't take ya inside. Ain't 'cause you white, but my house a terrible mess today. I hasn't cleaned nothin' yet." Sneaky laugh. "I hates to go into it myse'f." I laugh with her, relieved.

We pass a row of slum houses, now and then a neat one, white perhaps or yellow, with a veranda and a few flower beds. Most, though, are abused, haggard, collapsing, almost clownishly de-jected structures. There is always a stoop; it is always broken. I see windows patched with board and a rooster between houses. The rooster crows suddenly, a cracked strangled cry like the wailing of an Arab. A rooster, that most rural of creatures, incarcerated in the city slum, wails for all who share his fate. This is little Ronelle's block, I remember.

"That silly thing don't know *what* time it is," says my guide.

She waves, as we pass, to a dark elderly couple who rock solemnly on a high veranda. They do not return the salute. She may be a pariah in the neighborhood if she is drunk all the time, if the black eye was produced by a domestic row.

"Doze my neighbor. Nice folks. Here my place."

Hers is a small duplex made of composition that from a dis-tance resembles brick. Up close it is just crude, cheap, ugly siding, probably durable. The porch floor is cement; it sags and has wide cracks but seems sturdy. Mrs. Williams blows on the seat of a rusted white metal porch chair and offers it to me. I sit; she, at my side, faces the street. She stares, her eyes stunned open. I doubt that she can close them; they seem sprung. She passes the limits of the pitiful and is almost ridicu-lous—yet the availability, the graciousness, and the utter im-mediacy of the innocent drunk share with the candor of ignorance the terrain of her long face, her square youngish jaw, and there is nothing in this face but sheer humility and gentleness for a stranger.

"I hope to find a lot of different women, all sorts, who will talk

and say how they feel and what they think about the world . . ."
I am telling her. It seems insane, irrelevant, but I get it out. She
nods, appreciative, patient, even eager to grasp it. She talks a
little—about an Alabama childhood, a big family, mother, grandmother, auntie, sister . . . It is a familiar recital.

"Hit's pritty there. My motha, she still there. Grandmotha, too.
Bofe."

"You ever go home?"

"No'm, not too much. My baby in school here an' I got my
husban' and he don't like to go. Don't seem to like Alabama. I
don't know . . .

"My baby? Oh, she's a big girl now, ten years old. Her name
Virginia. I git you a picture. Wait here. I ain't goin' to bring you
in . . . 'scuse me but this house a mess today . . ." She dis-
appears into it and comes out with two pictures; the first is of her
daughter, in a small gilt frame—a tinted photo of a glowing face,
all teeth and cheeks and huge radiant eyes, two braids, ribbons.
One has no difficulty in exclaiming: "Oh, she's beautiful!"

"She smart, too. Make all A's and B's. That all she bring me
home. A's and B's. Not like Lucy. She don't bring me nothin' but
trouble. Used to be me and Lucy was close but . . ." Her voice
dims. "Don't know what happen to me and Lucy. We was friends
but she run off from her husban' . . . come bangin' in here with
them three kids. She and me fightin' all the time now. My
husban' too, he fight her."

"You all live together here?" She nods. "How many rooms?"

"We gots three. The boys have cots in de kitchen. Takes 'em
out to the back poach in the mornin'."

"Oh, that's hard. How can you manage in three rooms, four
kids and three adults? I'm not surprised you fight."

"Honey, it's awful. Gets me down. I get to drinkin' . . . I don't
know . . . well, I drinks. I don't lie to the Lord, why'd I lie to
you? I tell de truth—I drinks. It heps me."

"It must be hard on your husband, too. What does he do?"

"Oh, he . . . seem like he say he paintin' now. House painter.
I don't rightly know just what he doin' now but often he'll house
paint. It wear him out, these chillrun all over him. He not so
young. Gits angry . . . commence to holler . . ." Her head
sways slowly in wonderment, as if she is just realizing it all.

"Oh, that's too hard. Any chance Lucy might move out?"

"Well . . . it be pritty bad. She might could move sometime."

I falter, having pushed too far. I ask about Virginia's school, Reed School. Is it integrated? Richard's children are the only whites there, I have been told.

"They gots three o' fo'."

"Think they'll ever really integrate it?"

"Well, scuse me, Honey, but I don't want no integration in that school." The humble honest half-drunk gaze hangs on mine. "Me and you, it different. We talk. Womens is different. But I don't want no mo' whites in that school with my baby."

"Why not, Mrs. Williams?"

"Listen . . . you ever hear of the 'inferotty compless'?"

I could weep. "Yes, I know what that is."

"Well, that what goin' to happen to my baby if they brings them white chillrun in there. She bringing home A's and B's now just fine but you git them white chillruns comin' in there and she goin' to be lookin' at them all day, say: 'What they doin'? What they talkin'? What they clothes?' No *ma'am!* Scuse me, Honey, but I don't want them white chillrun in that school. Jess what they got now is plenty."

"You really think that would bother her for more than a few days?"

"I knows it."

"I've heard from other mothers, both Negro and white, that the children get along fine if the adults leave them alone."

"Well . . ." She wants very much to allow for me and my "rational" view of things but how rational has her life been, how rational is it now? The look is patient, apologetic, firm and kind. That is character. I retreat.

"Well, maybe you're right, Mrs. Williams. I know I wouldn't want my children upset when things are going well for them in school. It's too much to ask of them, maybe."

She is relieved. She hands me the other frame, a larger one, also cheap metal, filigreed and shining. She swipes at the glass hastily with the tail of her sweater.

"This here my son, Lucy's baby brother."

I behold an adult male version of the little girl, young, heroic, innocent, beautiful, manly; a movie hero. It is a tinted sepia photo, peach-toned and glowing. The face is incredibly hand-some. He wears the uniform of a high ranking military officer. Mrs. Williams' hand hovers near the frame as if to guard or even snatch it from me.

"What a handsome man! Is he still in the service?"

"Yessum. He have a job only two Negro men in the United States have, that special kinda rate he have. Only two doin' what he doin'. He graduate Morehouse College eight years ago."

"That's a great school. You must be proud of him."

"Oh, yeah. He got scholarships. Went all thoo. Graduate honor man. He live in California now, have him a wife and two babies. He all the time callin' me: 'Mama, please don't drink no mo'. Mama, come on out here to California.' He don't understand . . . you know . . . Oh, he'd send me a airplane ticket if I wants to go. He say, 'If it git too bad, Mama, you come on out here.' But I won't fly in no airplanes! I'm too scared!" She grins but the laugh is frozen in.

"You could take the train."

"Take too long. I don't know. One o' these days I'm goin', though. When it git too bad. I might could take my baby and go." The testament of the big mottled purplish sock-in-the-eye is there. "When it git too bad." When does it get too bad? From terrible to desperate—is the transition even noticeable to the brutalized? We are silent together now. She has not spoken with self-pity. I want no trace of false self-pity to be recorded here in her words; there is none. She requests nothing from me. But we sit here together in the quiet chill, in the scuff of wind among dried leaves and dust, in the abandoned air that only the frantic displaced rooster—far off, a cockeyed lament—cares to claim; we do sit here and must therefore receive one another now, in this ragged, broken place on these cold half-rusted third-hand chairs, on this runt of a porch in a slummy street; we sit here, she and I, and all at once we are bound, wound together in that lower common being of survival to which she has carefully drawn me down, so that I see no longer these mere dismal sights but below them, deeper, to a sort of grim purity; and I understand her suddenly, not knowing how it has happened. That rare, unsum-moned series of revelations has taken place—that opening of doors—and she who has said, "I won't take you inside . . . ain't 'cause you white," has taken me inside. Or I have entered there in spite of both of us. And not because I am white or anything that I am or she is, but only because we two women talking together forgot to defend ourselves.

"When it git too bad . . ."

Someone called Irene Williams—a drunk woman on a windy street, perpetually hurled into her living, her waking and sleeping by what she cannot describe, with which she cannot cope—that someone looks at me now, decently and honestly, and I at her. Her eyes blur, drown quickly in tears without rescue. She lowers her gaze, not her head. She drowns and says, "Scuse me." And I pat her arm stupidly.

Sudden anger attacks me. Why can't she go now, today, this afternoon, on a plane to California and visit her son? Or stay there? He has the money; why doesn't he come and take her? But now, from the point of purity, I know that all that takes imagination, and hers is devoured in the process of enduring one day and then the next of self-perpetuating trouble. Beyond today there is nothing, and nothing is something like peace. And so we sit silently.

Later. The talk is easy, free, intimate.

About women: "You know what I think the whole trouble is? Them pants they wears. Can't tell the women from the mens no mo'. See 'em goin' by on the street and you don't know *what* it is. I tell Lucy them pants don't look good but she wear 'em.

"You got such pritty hair, Honey. That you real hair color?"

"Yes."

"Pritty. Well, the trouble with womens? Oh . . . mens, that's they biggest trouble. Now, I used to work and that were better. My husban' don't always git work. But I got these little chillrun of Lucy 'round here and I got Virginia, she need me 'round. But Lucy workin' now. Got her a job lass week. She goin' to do better, I know it. I be busy. Got my housework, cookin' . . . No'm, I don't so much like the house no mo'. The work too hard. And it don't only git done till they got it all tore up again.

"My neighbor? He a preacher, got him a little church down the street. Very nice man. He hep me out one time I have trouble with my husban'. He very quiet and nice. *Some* colored mens is nice, Honey, you know that?

"Me, I think I'd rather talk to a woman. I b'lieve I would. Mens, I likes 'em but not to talk." And shyly, with a kind of grimace of friendliness, "Me and you does all right.

"Oh, yeah, I and my motha, we close. Grandmotha, too. My daddy somewhere up north lass time we heard. I haven't seen him since . . . oh, 'bout forty-two. Wartime. We all come up on a farm. Alabama. It's nice ovah there."

"It seems more like home to you than Georgia?"

"Yes ma'am, it do. Alabama my true home. It the onliest place I calls home.

"Civil Right? It comin' along. But they got mo' trouble comin', if they don't know it. Lotsa mo' trouble.

"Gov'ner Sanders? I don't know too much about him. He race-minded, I hear. Don't want Negroes in anywheres.

"President Johnson? He seem like a nice fella, what he doin' for the po', but . . .

"President Kennedy? I loved him! I *loved* him! All us loved him.

"What I knows about that Vietnam, it's a big mess. I don't b'lieve in war, anyways. Well, my son got to make up his own mind. If *they* goes, *he* got to go. That's how it is.

"No'm, I doesn't vote. Maybe next time. They come thoo here wantin' me to vote. I done regiss but I haven't vote yet. Maybe I will. I know it's important.

"Oh, yes ma'm, I believes in the Lord. I loves the Lord. Wasn't fo' the Lord . . ." She shakes her head.

"You come back ovah to see me, you hear? I be round here on the street most the days. You come back."

All that in drunkenness. She stands and waves me away, her hand stiffly open, bent-fingered, frozen halfway through a wave, a grasp at nothing; only poised in the instant.

"Plenty of messes like that one, Jo," says Charity. "That boy in California is probably sending money every month. That man may not work full time. He might be a good man, even if he hit her."

She often implies that I would not understand all that—a good man hitting a woman.

"Crowded up like that they can't have any peace. What can she tell that daughter when she comes home? She may not have any place else to go. She's got to take her in, for the children."

"You know, Charity, I think a fair number of white mothers would say no; would say, 'You'll have to get an apartment or something. I'll give you money but not my home.' Because a fair number of white mothers could give her money."

"But most Negro mothers couldn't," Charity says. "But if they could, she would still come home. That's home. They wouldn't turn her away."

I sigh.

"What good does it do anybody for Lucy to bring three children there? Does Lucy a little good but that's all. And ultimately it doesn't do even Lucy any good. It's bad for her children to live like that. Seems like anything else is better. The minute Lucy's home breaks up, her mother's home has to break up."

We stab at it vaguely.

I am irritated, haunted all day by Mrs. Williams. I go for a walk. A few blocks away two older Negro women stand in front of a big settled heavy frame house of indefinite color and mood. It is modest, vast, patched; lace curtains lid its eyes; an old heavy carved door traps its mouth. The occupant in decent black wool nods at me and lowers her tone.

". . . to the cemetery after the service," I hear her say. And the other woman drives away then in a huge dark car that hums of sobriety and solidity. So much propriety, such heavy respectability mantles the comfortable people of that generation.

Twilight begins suddenly but is longer these days, a thinning out, a glow: sometimes quite warm, warmer than afternoon. On the boulevard a young Negro fellow roars through the slum in a beautiful dark red convertible with white sidewall tires, the radio blaring, his eye cruising. He is a part of spring evening as I have come to know it here, just as the sound of radios and the glow of greenish TV light through windows are a part of this lengthening evening; as are the floating crap games that suddenly flower in the alleys and collapse at the sound of a car, disintegrate, and then as quickly form again—spasmodic occurrences, parasitic, like yeasts that fly and fix anywhere, to anything solid; boys in black tight trousers, under the street lamp, are a part of evening, and that big-breasted girl of twenty who lives over the plumber's shop on the corner with her fatherless babies, who comes out at evening in her yellow sweater, tropical, perennial, and makes the scene with the boys, flouncing, loose and humorous, leaving yellow fuzz on their jackets, wanting what she wants and finding it somewhere, with someone, somehow.

And evening is the slow, careful, but somewhat erratic drive down our block of the Polish Jew, who owns the little store on the boulevard, driving in his faded blue sedan that has a suspiciously deep growl, the low grind of bearing trouble, and a very heavy white exhaust. He stares ahead, puppetlike, into the purpling sunset, driving out of the slum, doing what the myths condemn him for: making his money in the Negro slum and spending it in a white middle-class neighborhood. But not much money is lost; he seems to be far from rich.

I walk. Lights go on, dim ones, in little frame houses; one room of a huge old tattered house is lighted, a downstairs bay-windowed room; all else is dark. A Negro woman peers out the window and moves away. I hurry back home. Something is being fried furiously in a shack near the neighborhood center. The smell is tempting. I wonder which house is Ronelle's. Richard says she has begun to use the drawing materials at the center now. Before, she only stood in the doorway and watched the others. She has drawn a huge bus with people inside and out, many people, all with the brown crayon and at the bottom of the drawing she has made the letter B four times and declared that that is her name.

CHURCH AND A COUSIN

Baffled weather is no exaggeration. It rains and is cold, icy. Spring is buried.

The church is a vast, squatting stone toad on a dingy corner of Atlanta. I saw the Cousin, very black, helping a stodgy little befurred woman up the steps, holding the umbrella over both their heads, favoring the furs and the veiled hat of the other. Cousin's hat, which seems already to have withstood such tests as this weather, was a hard felt without decoration, almost without shape, and seemed to have been tossed at her head, landing there in a flump, a little too big, meant to shelter only, not to adorn. Cousin, like all cousins, is poor, and her body carries that inference of the "in-service" soul. They mounted the wet stones carefully, and Cousin shook out the umbrella, folded and stashed it by the door. Later I saw her stand to sing a hymn—tall, buxom, maidenish, with fat long loose cheeks that trembled with her whole being in this offering; she drank solace and gave praise, all in modesty. In service. Cousins are in service.

"Hello, Mrs. Smith? My cousin sick today . . . my cousin died and I'm goin' to the funeral . . . Yes, my cousin come and carried me out to the hospital the othah day . . . Well, my cousin have a car so I gits a ride . . ."

There is one in the family who is Cousin and lives the ghostly bridesmaid's life, attending, seeing by reflected light. She is alone. As soon as she takes a mate she is not exactly Cousin anymore.

The church is a broad horseshoe shape with white painted woodwork in the balconies and upper walls, dark wood pews, hissing radiators, magenta carpet; an odor of mothballs from middle-class closets pervades. Some of the congregation are in furs; more are striving upward in old well-kept wool. Cousin's black wool was once someone else's; it does not precisely conform to her big indefinite girlish shape but seems to flare behind her too fully and to close scantily in front.

There are elders and deacons and one deaconess, on the platform below the choir—an intensely black deaconess with straight waxy hair just below the ears, glasses, good posture, womanliness, and propriety. Her hands fold in her lap. Her feet are stationed as guardsmen in double file. This one lone deaconess among the Protestant patriarchs has great dignity.

We sing two hymns. All the women sing as if offering their breasts to heaven—wide-throated singing: "I'm standing in the light of love, today; O my savior, Jesus . . ." The organ drowns us, and only the women can ride the swells. The male voices sink under; the women's are like those birds that skim the waves and soar away with spray on their wings. They stay above the force of that music. I am deliriously deafened. The organ never simply stops but fades, does a dissolve, and moves into the background behind a prayer.

A guest speaker today, graduate of Vanderbilt University. He is a skinny dandy, tailor-measured and fitted, polished. The head is narrow and cunning; the face foxy and intent. He begins in that low controlled style that is destined to build to a frenetic climax; it is a musical inevitability and all know it. Beside me two brown hands clasp a small Bible, vaguely stroke it in an affirming rhythm. "Mmmm . . . Yes . . . Yes, Brother." Softly.

He begins autobiographically. He was young and callow; he did not know *the way* and had seen no light; he was full of worldliness. The stream of talk becomes a river of allusion eddying around us, a gathering in and casting out of literary flotsam, references to Ibsen, Tolstoy, Shakespeare.

"As Shakespeare said, 'The law hath not been dead, though it hath slept.' And through those student years I labored, Brethren, as you have all labored to understand my presence on this earth—in God's sight. In *God's sight,* Brothers. I was not alone . . . I was *never* alone. *But . . .*" pause, a hand thrust out to arrest us and the voice almost whispering, "I didn't know it. That's right! I didn't know it!"

And—"Tell it, Preacher! Yes, oh Lord!" The head of the deaconess nods to affirm him. "That's right!"

He goes on to Sartre, Einstein, the nature of life, man's fate, Mozart, Santayana, Chardin—now with waving arms, the beginnings of a dance, a jerk and a swing, a pounding of fists; and the deaconess drums faintly with solid Red Cross heels, a wide marish toss of the head, and louder: "Yes! Lord!"

He drags us up, calling every name. Up front an old man cries, "Well!" questioningly, confronting the Truth. The speaker shouts it now, pulling us up and pushing us over. Cascades of our cries, turmoil of affirmation. Heels pound and voices proclaim. He may take us where he will.

"I was in pure darkness of worldly pride, Brothers and Sisters! Yes, I was *wretched* with knowledge and comfort and pride but *I did not know it! GOD* knew it but I did not know it."

"Oh, yes! Amen! Tell it . . ."

The prim plump little hands next to me pound the Book and slap her thighs to drive him on. The deaconess is lost in a whirling head and drumming feet.

"You can work and study and sweat and slave; you can humble yourself before all the worldly goods—workin' to get you a big TV set, a big beautiful car; you can send your children to college and put money here in this church *ten times a day;* you can be *good to your friends and your pastor—*"

"Yes, Lord! That's right!"

"But, Beloved, if you do not have faith in *Him!—*"

"Tell it, Preacher!"

And finally we are over the rapids and afloat in a pool of general understanding, and he names now finally the Names of Names: "Gee-zuss! Geeeee-zuss!" And the deaconess cries out from a head that casts wildly about, a deranged mare, gasping for breath with which to call: *"Yes! Jesus! Amen!"* And the congregation shouts, *"Yes, Lord!"* to embrace him and receive Jesus from him, as he fades, slackens into quiet relief and takes up now his original sober, rational, and moral tone; and we sit back to ride in with it. There are sighs and hushed coughings. The organ gives a faint moan and suddenly breaks across his last word with a crescendo that draws us to our feet.

"I have put my trust in thee-eee!" we shout.

Shakespeare, Ibsen, Mozart—all are washed clean and laid away.

Suddenly I am swamped by the odor of simmering chicken. In the basement they are cooking dinner. Preacher announces it—all are welcome, one dollar a plate. The organ drifts under his words, which ride musically upon its sounds like a little boat. Preacher draws a hum from the organ and speaks along its line. The Sons of Jacob announce the results of their fund raising. The choir sings, and we sing once more. We give to the collection plate. We sing again and then we go down the aisles to give again, this time into a small oaken box on a velvet-covered table. The organ tide comes in, and finally we give for a third time, rising again and going forward, pennies now and a few dimes.

Now coffee is being brewed below us. When we file out and form little clusters in the foyer, I am quickly greeted and asked to stay. The faces around me are red-lipped and sweet, generous; the voices are melodious. Cousin takes the arm of her benefactor and guides her down the stairs. I follow with a small woman who is a deacon's wife, tiny, quick, full of grace. Below us Cousin lumbers slowly and seems more honest in that than any of us.

The long tables are covered with white cloths. Great platters of chicken, rice, and biscuits, bowls of gravy, square half-pound cuts of butter. Pies, Jello salad, coffee, tea. Six feet down the table and across from me, Cousin gratefully, joyously shovels it in. The pleasure at these tables fairly scents the air, the head spins. Here are the innards, the soul, the lining, the essentials, the metaphysical reduction of home. One finally must resign oneself to the absurd sentimentality that runs, jellyish, in the veins. It will, it must, all wash out, carrying with it a multiple sediment. I am here, in the South, among black people who receive me as a lost relation returned. I wallow gratefully in sentiment, knowing I must purge myself of it tomorrow.

Mrs. Ferrier, Cousin's benefactor, introduces herself, her husband, and Cousin. Mrs. Ferrier is somewhat affected but direct, a passionate-seeming woman with flaring nostrils and a charge in her voice. I state my business in the South upon request, and the response, as usual, is received with heart by the women and with polite suspicion by the men. Mrs. Ferrier glows. Her hand is wrinkled, the creases darker than the flat planes; her nails are bright red, curve under, and are thick and clawlike. Her red mouth spreads wide over horsey teeth; when she smiles she lifts her face dramatically. She has great style.

Cousin watches, benign, dubious, faithful. We are all standing in the middle of the room, and I am dull with the hot rich food after the purge of the service. Mrs. Ferrier asks, "Did you like owa speakah?"

"He's a very dynamic man."

Cousin gives me a look of silent placid doubt.

"Oh, he *is!* My husband went to school with him." That seems to settle everything.

Yes, I would like very much to be driven back home. I'm living on Hampton Street. Any time they are ready, I'll join them. Meantime, I stare through a maze of hats, shake hands, and exchange niceties. All is genuine. The game is a game is a real game. Under the polish and veils and plastic cherries and high felt crowns, the veritable being flourishes. The middle-class black woman is not a zombi. I have a sense of warm blood and hope that is like a chemistry itself; of passion and of yielding that are not relegated to the mind alone, not incarcerated in the ideal, but still reside at home in the flesh. This is a feeling. I try to be objective and critical, cool, aloof from sentiment. But the feeling persists.

Cousin has moved away and scrutinizes me now from across the room and seems to know that I have named her and given my sympathy, my friendliness and respect. She smiles and nods when our eyes meet and we recognize something mutually.

The women here tend to a bit of extravagance in gesture as well as, or in spite of, dress. The men lean more to profundity or quaint paternity, to sonorous patriarchal speech tones. Some few laugh with kindly Uncle Tom evasiveness. Everybody is totally respectable, except perhaps Cousin and one or two of her ilk. Suddenly I am depressed.

We leave in the rain. The car is a black Cadillac that purrs, hums, glides like a ship through the drizzly dingy streets toward the east side of town. I share the back seat with Cousin, who now, next to me, is transformed into the individual, Miss Laney. All three of them seem stuffed inside, somehow stiff and moody. Shy? Maybe. I feel shy also and drowsy from heavy dining and from the car heater, which stirs quietly the close perfumed air. No window is open. I unbutton my coat and crack a window about half an inch.

"We have a wonderful pastah but he didn't have much time today," says the benefactor.

They laugh gently. Mr. Ferrier clears his throat, moving his big ship with respect, rarely leaving second gear and 15 miles per hour. "Well, Mr. Clayton is very educated. Good speaker if you follow him."

Cousin Laney gives me an apologetic smile. "I don't doubt it he's ejucayda, but he just goes on a little *too* long fo' me." She laughs. I join her cautiously. Mrs. Ferrier smiles indulgently at her over a shoulder, her clawish hand gripping the back of the seat near her husband's shoulder. The veil of her hat as she turns her head toward us is a network of blue wrinkles over her brow. Her fur piece, a rich mink stole, glistens as if alive. Both women are heavy and corseted, cannot bend in the middle, sit erect and still at first. Mrs. Ferrier is short, but Miss Laney is big in all directions. Her corset is probably older, looser, for she begins, a few blocks from the church, to spread out, to luxuriate like some tropical plant that grows before one's eyes. She spills across the seat, sighing, and I find that she is sitting quite close to me now and I can smell talcum powder and the clean health of her body. She smells young and of a guileless chemistry. It is with purity and grace, somehow, that she is sitting; merely sitting. I look at her hands that have worked, are plain and honest and girlish. Her fingers lie open, straight as an athlete's. Her shoes are wide and ill-fitting, cheap black pumps with medium heels.

Mrs. Ferrier talks about the charitable works of the church, about the advancements being made within the Negro community. She mentions the names of civically important women I no doubt want to meet. *Names.*

Cousin rides free in this luxury ship, a first class ticket back home, probably to a pile of work, I tell myself, projecting fatally and knowing it. But cousins have another quality, and I have a stolen moment now, within Mrs. Ferrier's monologue, to observe it. There is a broad, not particular, air of defiance; general defiance. That's it. It gives her a bluntness. She will not be moved. She spreads over the seat and she will not be moved till moving time.

Her face is puffy and flat-nosed with those long sober cheeks that trembled as she emitted songs a while ago. She has a furious health and youth. She may not be out of her twenties, and the most she suffers from seems to be this glaze of propriety, the tight clothes and rich relatives. She is like the baggage of wit and honesty and health that they relinquished in order to become proper but that they do not want to part with altogether. They take it along in the back seat.

She is chewing Beeman's gum.

And so we creep through the streets, a ship full of decorated birds afloat on Peachtree Street in an icy rain.

Cousin cracks her gum and having taken her ease in her commonness among elegant relatives, says in a casual, intimate aside, softly: "You oughtta come back when we have the full choir and reg'lar preacher. It not so fancy!" She stifles a chuckle and looks me in the eye.

Well met, Cousin.

Atlanta is famous for dogwood and peach blossoms. There are no blossoming trees in this neighborhood except for a small runty early plum or two. Bill, one of the boys here at the house, takes me with him to Government Surplus, a trip taken for the sake of Mrs. Sigh who lives a block away. We pick her up about three o'clock. The name drew me into an adventure for which I had little taste, since meeting Mrs. Williams. Any woman in this neighborhood might be called Mrs. Sigh.

The building is old, tall, flat-faced, frame, two-storied. A quadruplex—two four-room dwellings upstairs, two downstairs. It was once a sand color. Mrs. Sigh and her eleven children and her husband, a hunch-backed, one-eyed little man locally famous for drunkenness and wife-beating, but gentle and paternal when sober, all live upstairs in the four rooms on the south side. There are thirteen people, four rooms.

Bill calls up the stairs, and they tumble down in a black scatter, dark slick little puppies followed by a taciturn, small, pale-skinned mother. The children are neat and explode with vitality. They dive on the car and on Bill, seizing his hands, his clothes, and become a wild smattering of little dark palms against the windows of the car. I sit inside and beam at them. They have, all but one, brilliant gleeful smiles and the ferocity of wild cubs. The doors open and they crowd in, giggling, shushing one another, shouting, in a roiling surge of out-flung arms and legs, shoes and braids and ribbons and white teeth. I turn. The dull one is doing the shushing. She appears to be about ten, perhaps retarded. She looks faintly Mongoloid. Mrs. Sigh is at the door. I move over.

We introduce ourselves. She is a dull, stunned-looking little woman with very small, dainty hands and feet, a clean housedress, and an old man's sweater hanging from her shoulders. She fingers an identification card for the surplus-center officials, does not look at me but mumbles a "how-do." Bill is casual and free with them, knows them well. I feel a hot little hand on my neck. Something touches my hair. They shriek.

"Hey, kids, sit down so I can see out the back." He drives slowly and keeps a careful watch on traffic.

"Did you tell Mrs. Waller I would drive her out to the station?" he asks Mrs. Sigh.

"I told her. She don't want to go, she say. I don't know what's the matter."

"How's she feeding those big boys since Josh left her?"

"I don't know." Mrs. Sigh's voice is flat, dull, and serenely noncommittal. "I give her some flour last month. Somebody else give her some meal. She didn't even get the welfare check this month. He come home and got it and he ain't been back since."

She answers sensibly but makes no conversation. The twittering little birds in the back seat continue to stroke my hair at the back and to touch my neck with tiny, gentle, flickering fingers like flies' feelers. There is one girl—about eight, and very pretty, electrically bright and flirtatious—who peers around close to the side of my head. I reach back, pat her cheek, and the whole gang breaks into falling giggles.

The station where government surplus food is distributed to qualified poor is far from the center of town in a warehouse area; and to complicate things further, it lies inside the forbidding-looking fence of a small industrial plant. We go through a back street, an alley, wind a bit, and finally come through the gate into the parking area of the plant.

I follow Mrs. Sigh up the ramp and inside. Bill takes the kids to the unloading area to wait for us and the goods. Inside, a pleasant, homely, fortyish white woman takes Mrs. Sigh's card, does a quick clerical job of some sort with papers, and returns it.

"There you go, Lucille. Just go on through like you always do. You with her?"

I grit my teeth. "I am." Why can she not call this dignified woman, who is at least her age and has at least as much experience in living as she, by her married name?

"Well, just take her through the line," she tells me as if Mrs. Sigh were my dog. I glare at the white woman. Pleasantly officious, she greets the next black woman who has come to be fed for free and will pay for it by enduring the condescension so common, so usual that it is not even noticed. Or is it?

Mrs. Sigh moves quietly through the line giving no indication of having heard. Young Negro boys stand above the moving belt and, taking her card and noting the type of allotment indicated, fill the maximum order, throwing onto the conveyor belt a fifty-pound bag of flour, twenty-five-pound bag of meal, ten boxes of raisins, ten pounds of sugar, five pounds of margarine, ten half-gallon cans of meatball stew, large bags of beans, rice, dried milk, chocolate, etc.

I am exhilarated by the bounty and the thought of the Sigh children being well fed for a month, even though by handouts. They are quite decently clothed, too, much of it through church charity, I am told. How often have they ever chosen and purchased their own clothing?

She moves stoically along beside the belt counting her supplies. To one of the boys she says, "No soupmix?"

"No, ma'm. They give extra yellow peas this month."

The tenderness of his voice seems lost on her.

Bill and the children load the food into the trunk and on the back seat. The children's excitement heats the car. Mrs. Sigh, noncommittal, unperturbed, is beside me again, this time with the four-year-old, Beeboy, on her lap. Beeboy's head is round, thinly matted with a gauzy brown fuzz, a golden shimmering health in its tight skin. It looks to be as hard as a marble. It is a perfect form. He and Lee Ann, the pretty eight-year-old, are the most vital of the group. They seem to be responsible for the constant gleeful agitation of these children. Mrs. Sigh holds him indifferently as he thrashes around on her lap, treading her belly as if it were the side of a hill; his shoes, sinking in and slipping down to her thighs, clamber up again so he may watch the back-seat antics. He casts me a blissful look and drops his eyes. He has learned of his charms from all these adoring sisters.

Consider Mrs. Sigh: thirty-six years old, small-boned, pale-skinned, expressionless, taciturn. Jim Sigh, Bill has told me, has been sober for six months, even through a two-month spell of unemployment. Before that he was drunk at least four days a week, peddling with a friend a home-brewed gin from an old car, driving in the evenings up the alleys of the slum to make deliveries and drinking as much as he sold. He also worked as a fill-in on city garbage pickup, and now and then, in a busy period, at his cousin's gas station across town in another slum. He beat his wife at least twice a week when drunk, several times having slept off the intoxication of that beating, and the gin, in the drunk tank at the jail.

The oldest boy at home, Purcel, now sixteen—slight in build, delicate, a heavy smoker, a floor-pacer, a picky eater, a high school dropout—fears his father and during the beatings would get help from Bill in the middle of the night. Bill would call the police first, then throw on his trousers and run around to the Sighs' to break it up. The neighbors, in spite of the screams, had ceased to interfere; the problem was no doubt too common and seemingly insoluble.

Bill says, "It's funny how nice that guy is when he's sober. He loves those kids. Really good to them."

"Are they afraid of him?"

"The girls don't seem to be. The boys are except for Beeboy. He's too little. Jim's never hurt the kids."

The police would come and go in about six minutes, usually leaving what they found—a raging little drunk demolishing his screaming wife, except that Jim would have taken time out to pay them two dollars for a quick departure. How badly do two big city police need a dollar apiece, and how little can they be pained or even offended by the sight of a small wretched woman being pounded unconscious by her drunken mate? The awful image terrifies me: Mrs. Sigh's misery temporarily halted for the purpose of a brief money exchange between the men who own her, body and soul. I see often a certain look on female faces in this slum—and all are black faces—a look I have never seen on any male face anywhere: that adamant expression of an instinctual intent to outlive the adversary; a glimpse of that which is compounded to create endurance; nothing so simple as aggression, which is the usual male answer to oppression. At its most obvious level it comes through as a kind of rapt stubbornness. She, like Cousin, will not be moved. Killed, maybe, but not moved.

Well, Mrs. Sigh has had a six-month reprieve, maybe enough time to break the pattern. Bill says in those six months her health has improved; a kidney damaged by one of the beatings has healed, so her doctor reports.

Back at the house we all carry packages up the narrow indoor stairway to her flat. Four two-pound boxes of raisins vanish from the kitchen table almost before they touch it. Beeboy stands beaming, his long, thin, bowed little forearms out tentatively, his tiny brown fingers spread to snatch what he can from the throng of older children who make off like street thieves with the raisins and two huge bars of bitter cooking chocolate. Totally outclassed in strength, if not cunning, he still seems to relish the game. Mrs. Sigh looks at me, allowing a grudging, ironic smile.

"They'll be shittin' loose all over the place tomorrow."

I laugh aloud. "How long do those raisins last?"

She shrugs. "I hides one or two boxes if I can get 'em and puts 'em in some cookies. Spread 'em out. But they gets most the first thing. Beeboy sick last month. So were Estelle. Nothin' but too much raisins." All this is said with the least possible variation in tone, as if she had the bare strength for utterance, but none for emphasis. Even the poor stunned and drunk Mrs. Williams managed a tuneful sort of speech here and there. Mrs. Sigh is on her feet; ask no more.

I make a second trip, carrying the bag of cornmeal with some enthusiastic if ineffectual help from Estelle, Lois, the retarded girl, and Lee Ann, the bright eight-year-old. We drop the huge bag on the kitchen floor. The kitchen is small, tidy, smells of old walls and bacon grease. It has only one small window opening onto an enclosed back porch, which makes it rather dark. Mrs. Sigh slowly puts away her staples. The children dive in and out in perpetual hilarity. They touch me and dart away squealing. Beeboy falls on the floor and ecstatically wets his pants.

"Beeboy! Mamma, look what he doin'."

"Git him to the toilet."

Lois lugs him away. The other girls snicker and watch my

reaction. Lee Ann takes my hand suddenly and pulls me to the front room where a girl of about fifteen lies on her back on a battered sofa and watches television, a round-faced, sober, pale baby girl in diapers crawling about over her prone body; a boy of about five sits on her feet.

"That's my big sister. That's our baby. Looky here, Carrie. Here, baby!" The baby laughs on command. The older girl smiles. I greet her. The boy is transfixed by a beer advertisement on the screen and ignores us. Lee Ann lugs the heavy baby to me and I pick her up. She is solid and docile, like the heavy bags we carried upstairs.

"You know what she likes?"

"What?"

"Coffee! She drink my brother's coffee!"

They all giggle, fondle her bare little feet, and speak tenderly to her. She looks me over calmly, laughing with the children after resigning herself to the strange arms that hold her. She is a beautiful edition of Mrs. Sigh, who has no beauty whatever.

I start to go. In another room off the hall an adolescent boy, not Purcel, lies on a cot smoking. He regards me solemnly as I move through the hall, makes a vague gesture of greeting, and looks away. Where they all sleep, how they dine, how they stay so clean, where they keep their clothes, where they wash them is all a mystery. The children look well cared for. That, in these crowded rooms, is an artful achievement.

I want to take pictures of the family. Everyone is in the act. Mrs. Sigh, pleasant, remote, sits on the front steps holding her infant image and lets the kids do the organizing. The group is large, frolicsome, one of the most animated and handsome families of children I have ever seen. Lee Ann and Estelle, both pretty and wearing more attractive clothes than the other girls, become self-conscious before the camera, preening, shushing the others, wanting order, wanting everybody to "look pritty now." They smile with alarming vitality and freeze that way, each with a tiny finger rammed into the dimple area of a cheek. I have seen the gesture somewhere—it is a kind of 1927 Hollywood darling pose.

Now Lee Ann, Estelle, the retarded sister Lois, and Beeboy

walk me home. Beeboy and Lee Ann lead me with hot raisin-smeared little hands, Beeboy's lying inside my loose grip like a newborn mouse; Lee Ann's firm, urgent, grasping. Estelle and Lois precede us and look back for attention. Lee Ann chatters.

"Daddy taken Beeboy fishin' and fell him in."

"I done drown!"

"And Mamma screamed. Ooooo!"

And later—"Lookit Estelle. She *sweet*. She awful black but she sweet."

Estelle is indeed utterly black as the others are not and has little of the general family look. I am surprised at Lee Ann's observation. Estelle is already branded "awful black" by those who care for her most.

"Lois sweet too but she a little bit sick."

"You go to school, Lee Ann?"

"Yeah, I goes. Estelle go too, sometime."

"She doesn't go every day?"

"She don't like it."

Estelle is nine years old; Lee Ann is eight.

"And Beeboy come over with Sonny and teacher send him home. Bang! She push him out. Beeboy *so* bad. He always comin' in school in the class. Can't keep him home."

"Who else goes?"

"Lois don't go. She stay home. Sonny go sometime. I goes and I show Estelle how to read. Purcel go last year but he stop. And Bernice, she go reg'lar." That's the fifteen-year-old.

Out of nine school-age children, some magic compounded of unusual intelligence and a fever for living, good health perhaps, keeps Lee Ann in school regularly. Also Bernice, the fifteen-year-old, who is in high school. The rest, Bill says, wander over when the spirit moves or Lee Ann persuades. She loves school and does well. Bernice helps some of them with reading. She herself studies in the kitchen and in bed after Lois, who shares her bed, is asleep. Mrs. Sigh, a loose and ghostly sort of force, is the anchor at the center of their random lives. Where does the happiness come from? Bill has known them three years. "The little ones," he says, "seem happy. Around twelve or thirteen they become dull and quiet. Whole family has been that way, apparently. The older boys are pretty sullen. But I know Purcel has a lot of reason. He couldn't fight his old man when he was drunk and that made him feel weak. He told me that. He says he'd leave home but he's afraid his dad will kill his mother sometime."

Mrs. Sigh, although she was quite agreeable to the meeting, had little to say except in answer to questions. She too is stunned, as Mrs. Williams was, but has far better control over her life, evidently, and is younger. She looks anemic and listless. She is from a big family herself. She met *him,* as she calls her husband, through a brother who brought her to the city from South Georgia when she was about sixteen. Her mother ran off and left her father with six children; and he, with no hint of divorce, took another wife almost immediately. But the new wife wasn't nice, had neighbor men in her bed when Daddy was working and was mean to the children.

Yes, she registered to vote, thanks to Bill. No, she didn't vote. She had three years of schooling in the country as a child; knows who the president of the United States is and who the governor of Georgia is. She is a Baptist, believes in the Lord and prays to him. Doesn't go to church much. Sometimes sends the kids. Would have preferred three or four children but the Lord gave her more. Never heard of birth control. Wouldn't like a woman preacher or lawyer but prefers and has been attended by a woman doctor, probably a midwife. Would rather talk to a woman for real confidence, whatever her color, than to a man. "Black womens is no better than whites." Her grandmother remembered "slavey times." Her grandfather was white. She loves her children; wants Estelle to be a nurse and Lee Ann a teacher and the boys whatever they want. "Lois," she announces existentially, "is a little bit crazy. She come to life that way."

"Do you like men?"

"Well, some of 'em be nice."

"What do you think is the biggest problem in a woman's life, Mrs. Sigh?"

"Well, workin' is the hardest. But mens is the worst thing to a woman. If she don't have a good man, why then she can't go ahead and raise up her chillrun good. 'Specially the boys."

She raises her boys differently from her girls. "Boys gits away and don't pay you no mind. Girls learns somethin'."

Her preacher has told her that divorce is not a good idea; it is bad for the woman and children; divorced women become prostitutes. She ought to try to stay with her husband and see him through his troubles. She lowered her head when making that report and did not look at me until the subject was changed. She thinks integration will help her children's chances in school; that they can learn something from any white children.

"What's wrong with the world, Mrs. Sigh?"

"Too much po' peoples."

"How can we solve that problem?"

"Mens has to get jobs and mo' love needs to be preach. Like this Dr. King we got in Atlanta. He doin' so much to lift the heart and burden of the peoples till you just haf to believe what he say that we goin' come out to a better time."

She knows nothing of the term "Black Power," never heard of Stokely Carmichael, and first heard of Malcolm X through news of his death.

Just say she livin' in poverty. But sometimes she lives only in material poverty. Love and family solidarity sometimes survive the siege. In this neighborhood, with all its bitter poverty, the statistics show that only one-third are broken homes. Hard to believe. Would they call Mrs. Sigh's a broken home? It depends on which day they came round to assess it. Sometimes Jim Sigh is definitely missing—sometimes in jail; often unemployed. Once for two months he lived three doors away with a bad woman. His little children stood outside her house and threw rocks at the windows. Mrs. Sigh laughs as she recalls it, the only laugh I've heard from her. But for six months he has been a sober, kindly, semiemployed father and husband. She never threw him out and never took him back. He comes and goes. This is *his* wife and these are *his* children. This is *his* apartment. He doubts none of it. Only one, Purcel, seems to hate him. Is that a broken home? Today, no. It is only desperate, overcrowded, deprived, and dependent.

I think of Mrs. Williams' son and that unlikely journey out of

slums and deprivation into Morehouse College and a very important military position. Lee Ann Sigh will make it, maybe. Already
the family spirit is strong behind her.

"What do you want to be when you grow up, Lee Ann?"

"Teacher like Miss Scott."

"You think you'll get to do it? Go to college and become a
teacher?"

"Yessum. I goin' to college. When I'm big. I love school. I can
read good."

One out of eleven. Maybe she will make it. Bernice, the fifteen-
year-old, has already accepted a part-time job as nursemaid and
kitchen helper with a white family for the coming summer, and
that may establish a new pattern in her life. She says she doubts
she will get to college. She wants to make money, soon. She is
learning typing and shorthand. Already she has some inkling of
the needs of the impatient brood that follows her. She speaks of
helping her mother and her sisters and brothers. She has been
drafted—was drafted years ago—as an assistant mother. She
cooks about half the meals, does the washing and ironing,
changes the baby, and bathes Beeboy. She tutors the younger
ones a little in school work. She has no boy friend. She is pretty, a
little sickly looking, and like her mother is laconic and slow
moving. She lay prone that first afternoon I saw her, bearing on
her own belly her mother's youngest child, on her feet her five-
year-old brother. Her body, her sap, her consciousness all com-
mandeered for service to her family—Bernice will neither get
to college nor get off the poverty carrousel. Thanks to her, Lee
Ann or Beeboy may get away. Bernice, at fifteen, already looks
doomed and fully aware of it. Well, it will take the entire soul
plasma of this family to push one member through, and probably
it will be Lee Ann. She will move into the world and that move
could exhaust and wipe out the other ten.

Meeting tonight in the church basement. The Negro candidates for city and county offices in the coming Alabama elections
were there. Neat and shining, proud, shy, determined, they stood
to introduce themselves. Before this week some of them have
never left the counties where they live. Some have never uttered

a word in public. Some have never been in an integrated gathering. The Movement seems to have touched them like a magic wand, a miracle, a grace. It has come through their lives as a great flood in a desert. It has struck them like a fabulous lightning. They glow. They radiate a hope that causes alarm in any faintly tarnished heart. Freedom! What size will the band of Pilgrims be that finally reaches Freedom? One wants to guide them over the rapids. One wants to thank them for restoring to American society something as elementary and quaint and utterly human as this faith in their future.

Many books are written these days describing the spirit of the revolution within American black people. When one speaks of poverty and dejection and misery, one forgets to say that the most humor and affection for life, the most sheer creature vitality to be found in this country are surely in the young black face. Who could look tonight into these black faces (not all young) with anything but a sense of pride and hope? Doesn't even the angry black American face deserve the risk of respect and compassion? How can those hundreds of charged faces elicit merely fear or distaste? It is difficult to receive fully the loaded knowledge of racism. One dislikes admitting to its existence in such depth. The hopeful black face wipes out the vision of the brutalized. I saw that, even in Mrs. Williams' stunned face—or maybe a projection of it. But nobody can deny the blazing passionate hopefulness that still stirs in so many of these Negro faces in the South. Every American perishes a little in the diminishing of that light.

Well, these candidates all have it. They stand up one at a time and modestly but pridefully introduce themselves: "I'm Joe Wesley from ——— county and I'm running for County Assessor." "I'm Lucille Brown and I'm running for Treasurer of ——— county." "I'm John Saunders and I'm running for Sheriff of ——— county and I'm going to win and when I do this man here next to me is going to be my Deputy."

Loud cheers. The present sheriff of that county is an infamous brute.

Charity, sitting next to me, beams. These are the cherished and chosen people. This, she knows, is the way to build.

Upstairs the somewhat wealthy and middle-class congregation of this church is having a meeting of its own. They contribute little to the civil rights group responsible for this Alabama event, although their pastor heads it. One woman, very black, perfumed, and elegantly dressed, looks in briefly as if staring into a pen of pet animals or a child's nursery, waves, and departs.

"There, you see that?" Charity's voice can take on a kind of soap opera scorn, quite dramatic. "That's a rich woman and I bet you she doesn't give five dollars a year to the Movement. She's worried all this demonstrating and running for office will give her people a bad name. There are a lot like that. But we'll get 'em all in one day. Negroes have got to work together, all together. Those are the hardest to reach, those rich ones."

Harriet said it, too. "And the worst one is the rich black woman."

Upstairs the service breaks, and the congregation departs in what Charity refers to as their "big shiny chariots."

Downstairs Reverend R. gives a heartening folksy speech. "Don't you be afraid. Whatever Mr. Charley says to you, you hold up your head and you stay in the runnin'. And if you have any trouble, you call us. We'll come over. Somebody will come over that very day." Many cheers. We sing "We Shall Overcome." There is a small tight-lipped young group from the Students Non-Violent Coordinating Committee (SNCC) sitting by the windows. They have become very antiwhite lately, and it is rumored the whites on their staff will soon be working outside the Negro community, among whites where they can be most effective and ought to be working anyway. Fair enough.

To SNCC today to meet Callie Brown. I got a tour first, the type given to visiting press. I especially admired the big printing press they had just acquired. They turn out a lot of excellent printed stuff, good neat work with wonderful photographs. Callie appeared suddenly. She is thin, light, with flat tan skin and loose, straightened or perhaps naturally soft wavy hair; couldn't tell. Her smoky eyes are like daisies, wide open, staring. She is very pretty. She was offhand but quite alert to the experience, flattered, ready to play a cool-cat role, girl guerilla for the press. She thinks of me as the press, even referred to it. We pushed through the crowded hallways where field workers moved about, slamming doors, talking mostly about money and food. "Man, you got any bread? I haven't eat nothing for three days." "Ray got some sandwiches downstairs." "Man, you got a cigarette?" And suddenly to me, "You got a cigarette?" "Sorry, I don't smoke." "Man, you got twenty cents? Anybody got twenty cents?" They mill about. The men seem perpetually to need something; the women, if they need, do not say so. There are voices calling to other voices. Phones ring incessantly. One hears machines at work, the addressograph, typewriters, the press. On the front entrance is a small sign that says, "Nitty Gritty."

We enter Callie's office and shut the door, but it blocks out little noise. Someone has left a pair of jeans on the floor here. She lifts them, shows little curiosity, and tosses them out into the hall. "Somebody been sleepin' in here, I think. There was a sleepin' bag on the floor yesterday." She's cool, Callie is. I look at her. She is flowerish, the kind that grows on a thin long stem with no leaves and a single blossom; petals that have incredible delicacy and beauty for a brief while and then thin out, drop, never fading but separating somehow. She sits and smokes, crosses her slender stockingless legs and swings one foot. Her clothes are simple, a hint of fashionable choice in them, somewhat little-girlish. Several others in the office seemed more modestly dressed, poorer and not as tidy. She does not smile. But she talks. The talk is even eager. She is young, twenty-two at the most. She is flip, waiflike, has a streak of street corner quality about her, and a look of sweet small town ingenue also. Her hairline, I notice, is delicate, high but beautifully curved, it and the brow somehow more Latin than African. She is at least one-fourth white. Her eyes are huge, cool, the expression that of a knowing, wary child put out in the jungle a bit too soon. I think with a shock of Ronelle. Same look! If this is Ronelle's future, it isn't so bad. Precarious—yes, there is something precarious here, but not desperate. But Callie is small town, grew up among trees and fields with four wild brothers; she is telling me about it just now. Ronelle is in the fields of the city—broken curbs, trash-littered streets and alleys; her caves are broken and rotten buildings, their mildewed basements; her streams are in the gutters. But Callie—she is talking in that flip, highly agile-tongued way, her notions waspish, flighty—Callie may be saved by her country upbringing.

"Well, actually, I spent most time with my brothers. My sister, she stayed around Mama a lot. I went with my brothers. . . . No, my daddy wasn't around. Oh, I mean we knew him but he didn't come around often. My mother, she worked for this white lady that is a friend of hers. She didn't have any education like the rest of us."

Callie alone has college—one year. The others have high school. That, for a Mississippi Negro, is a lot of education.

"Yes, I was close to her, in a way. But it was my brothers, you know, that I looked to. My mother's a quiet woman. I'd do different with my kids but she was good."

"Different how?"

"Well, I wouldn't whip 'em as much as we got. And I would talk to them about the ways and facts of life. My parents . . . she told us what she knew but she didn't know the ways and facts of life very much.

"Mama had a brother that was just no good. He came to the house one time and made uh . . . you know, advances to me and my sister. He was drunk. Well, that wouldn't have been so bad for us if my parents . . . if she had told us more the facts of life."

"Did you tell her about it?"

"Oh, sure, but she let my brothers take care of it. I mean, she thought this being her brother and all, she just wasn't going to throw him out. But she hated him. My oldest brother, he took him outside and knocked him out."

"How old was he?"

"My brother? Oh, then he was about sixteen."

She ran with them, as a kind of gang. She was out at night as they were, because they protected her. Her sister stayed home. Callie was a guerilla early; she had four models.

"Who makes a better confidant, Callie? I mean a person you can really talk to confidentially, a man or a woman?"

"Oh, a fella. I'd trust a fella best any time. I mean, I *do*. A woman gets into gossips and all. But I've got one good woman friend. Real close."

Her foot swings. She chain smokes. Her whole face is smoky, that lovely smoky pale brown, absolutely flat in color with a faint lavender tinge around the daisy eyes, which she bats frequently, perhaps unconsciously, to create an attitude of innocence and honesty. She is not innocent except in the final test. She is not exactly honest, either. She knows what is of use in her own being: her beauty, toughness, her cool. She's a swinger. She blows with the wind. But the soul seems to lie like a pool of uncontaminated milk behind it all, utterly formless and infantile. Where is Callie's soul?

I am struck again by her frailty. Her eyes seem to darken as we talk. She looks dissipated. She has given a lot of hard work to the Movement, playing the dangers to the hilt—jail, repeated attempts to vote, rides in cars through back country late at night in Mississippi where she grew up. And she has given as much to a burning try at living. She is a Jeanne d'Arc, a professional soldier. She has got to have a war. I am convinced of it as I listen:

". . . when I was in jail in Greenwood . . . just after Jimmy was shot . . . They got me through by goin' in the middle of the night without the car lights and I spent about a week with my mother then. . . Oh, I use our line to call Mississippi all the time, talk to Mrs. Hamer about once a week . . ."

She has a casual but very dramatic way of getting the essence of it across to me. It's funny, I see her in juxtaposition to Charity, and they emerge as the two extremes of black womanhood, both destined to solitude, somehow: Callie, a mercenary soldier, Charity, a nun whose very name is a vow.

I ask Callie the routine questions and she creates a mythology.

"No, a woman can't live a full life without marriage because if she goes a lot . . . well, a woman if she isn't careful she gets into the area of a prostitute. I mean she might be able to support herself and everything, but she might see many things that she wants and she can't afford it and then that brings her in the area of a prostitute."

I have begun to hear this a lot and am dubious.

"You think that could happen to you?"

"Well . . . I'm on the lookout, you know. I am going to marry someone, and I know I will, but if I didn't know about that chance, why then I might fall in that way, you know? I mean, by being ignorant of what I was doing. Yes, it could be possible for anybody."

"What about children? Can a woman live a full life without them?"

"Yeah, I think so."

"Well, what's the real value of marriage, in your estimation, besides avoiding prostitution?"

"Well, it's better to have sex with one man. And for companionship and a home."

"Did you get sex education at school?"

Finally I get a laugh out of her, but it is utterly humorless. "In Mississippi you don't get that in school. You don't get much else, either. But my parents—she taught me what she knew; but it wasn't like now, not like I could teach my children."

"My parents—she" has become an unvaried reference to her mother.

"Did you want to be a boy, ever? Did you envy your brothers?"

"Well . . . we played rough, you know, but I always knew I couldn't do it as rough as they could. My sister and I, we'd fight and then I'd go off with the boys. I wished sometimes then that I was a boy but in the South if you are black, you don't want to be a man. See, a Negro woman has mo' freedom. Like if I see a white fella I wanta date, why I can go ahead. But if the fellas want to take out a white girl, why outside the Movement they can't do that, you see. They be killed or something.

"I'm going to marry a Negro. I wouldn't marry a white. I go with them but I wouldn't marry one. My husband doesn't have to be in the Movement but he hafto feel something about what's happening to us. You know? In some way. Now, what's the best life a woman can live? Well, you know what I think?"

She talks as if it were a rehearsed dream to which she must cleave even while she plays about with the "fellas." She is not finished with the "fellas" yet. She has, I noted when we came through the halls, a camaraderie with the men that is essential to her character; she imitates their tone, their manner. But she is not masculine. She is more neuter.

"What I think is: A woman ought to have a husband about her age, a little older maybe but not much, and somebody she wants to talk to. He has to be serious. I like serious men. Not somebody to be runnin' off with every Sue, Sal, and Jane. And she should have two children, one girl and one boy. And both parents work."

"What does she do with the kids when she works?"

"Well, if she has something to do with them, her mother to keep them, or somebody, when they're little, she can easily work. Or she could pay somebody. But it's better if you have family to keep them. Because she ought to work. Many times, especially with Negro trouble, the man just can't make enough, you know, and she should help."

"Would your mother keep your children?"

"Oh, yes, if we were in Mississippi."

"That would be all right? I mean, her style of bringing up kids?"

"Well . . . I'd be in charge, see, of my own kids and what they were eating and all that. I'd tell 'em what I wanted them to know."

The value of working, for a married mother, was purely economic. She suggested that it would be valuable to have a goal in common with her husband, something material toward which they both worked. But no other value was mentioned. I pressed hard for it. Nothing.

"What would you do if somebody gave you a hundred dollars this afternoon, just a gift? How would you spend it?"

This seemed to please her. "Well, you wanta know about me? What I really like? I'd buy me a dress, really good lookin'. And I'd buy me some likka. And . . . well, I'd save a little."

"Do you vote?"

She emits the cynical laugh again. "I'm registered to vote. I have gone to the polls three times in Mississippi, and they've always got a good reason why I can't vote. I think I'm listed as illiterate. But I keep goin'. Some day I'm goin' to vote."

About the police she says:

"I know the best and the worst from cops. I had it plenty in

Mississippi during summer '64. They messed with me plenty. Once at the bus station when we were tryin' to go into the café, a cop grabbed me by the arm and slapped my face. I don't know why I was surprised but I really was. I never got hit before."

"What'd you do?"

"I looked at him and I say, 'Listen, Man, take another look at me. I'm a *woman!* You don't hit a *woman!* Didn't they teach you that?' He looked kinda sorry but he say, 'You're a niggah and that's all you are!'" She laughs ruefully. "But he didn't touch anybody else."

She considers herself a radical, but she disagrees with many radical points of view.

"SNCC's gettin' militant. But we're still nonviolent. A few around are talking like violence but not me. As long as you in the Movement you gotta be nonviolent."

That is the beginning of Callie. I shall see her again. She lives near our place, on the edge of the slum in one of those large old houses which she shares with two other girls.

Yvonne, one of the young girls in this house, took me around to see her Negro friend who has four little children, the one who stays in bed most of the day to keep her new baby from falling out. Yvonne believes the story. I am inclined to think the woman drinks. I would if I had four babies, no man, and lived in that hole on the boulevard, had black skin and was on welfare in America.

Yvonne is Canadian, about twenty-two years old, and very solemn, soft-voiced, and religious. She says everything as if it were "just between us," some very subtle aside reminiscent of women-talk when the men are deciding something important in the next room. She is black-haired, with rather waxy yellowish-brown skin, and looks like an alloy of dark German, Turk, or maybe Indian. Her parents are German and Russian immigrants. In Canada she lives in an area where the Indian population is large, and she is often taken for one. She is so reliable, Yvonne; she is modest and intelligent, slightly self-effacing, loving, energetic. I think she is happy. She works at a youth center in one of the local Negro churches with a group of twelve- and thirteen-year-old girls. One of them, a little Negro girl named Bonnie, had attached herself fiercely to Yvonne, calling her almost every night and confiding family troubles, her own confusions, and plans. Last week Bonnie asked Yvonne if she were the only Negro living at our place.

"Bonnie, I'm white! Didn't you know I'm white?"

The child only stared at her. She could not believe it. And the shock lasted. Bonnie had placed a familial trust in Yvonne.

Now begins a long withdrawal for her. She tests, hesitates, and dissembles. Yvonne is dismayed. The child calls but is no longer confidential. Yvonne's fidelity will probably hold her but never in the same natural way. I met Bonnie at their open house. She was charming—big smile, gay, desperate for love, intelligent. She called me ma'm and clung to Yvonne. Well, Yvonne returns to Canada in eight months. What does she expect to solve with these temporary friendships? I suppose they break some ice, form habits, perhaps. But I am inclined to believe that they are one time occasions, gathered in like mementos: *This is my white friend, Yvonne; this is my little black friend Bonnie . . .* And perhaps never repeated again, like most meetings of such strangers.

Well, Mrs. Ferris, Yvonne's friend who lives with the four babies, is another matter. She knows who's white and who's black. Yvonne is thrilled to have penetrated the dull unfriendly gloom of this young black mother. We walked to the corner and bought some grapes and apples for her from the Polish Jew. (Sometimes I am amazed to see a legend borne out; Jews, it is said, own the only white stores in Negro slums like this. And they are neither liked nor trusted exactly. In this case it seems to be a hostile familiarity.)

The store is full of very black, very lively kids, mostly girls from about five to fifteen years old. School is just out. The older girls buy soft drinks and stand whispering and giggling. One of them comments in a stage whisper on my light hair. That happens often. Can a blond white woman be that rare a sight in this neighborhood? I forget sometimes that I am in the middle of a Negro ghetto and slum. The ghetto begins here at the boulevard in a collapse: the sudden tattered, gawky, disjointed, patched and perpetually disintegrating scene faces the boulevard like some fantastic waif, brazen and ridiculous. The appearance of a house can arouse dangerous sentimentality with its touch of some destitute human whim—a freshly painted blue shutter against rotting wallboards that saw their last paint half a century ago; a straggly potted plant on the broken stoop; a picture of a white woman in a deodorant ad pasted in a window; a small cross made of pipe cleaners hanging between the front-door glass and its curtain, which is itself often a rag.

A ragged chicken scuttles under a shack. A drunken man with yellow eyeballs, dressed in overalls, slumps on the front walk. Little black children dive and dart all around him—some of them heart-rendingly clean, some heart-rendingly dirty; some have matted hair full of lint; the little milk teeth of some are brown and rotten; some are barefoot in this 46-degree temperature. One six-year-old outside the store drools snuff spittle from the corners of her mouth. I think of Ronelle who never came to have her hair combed. I know now that she plays with children who are well cared for, as well as with those neglected like herself. Some black mother will take her in and clean and clothe her, I am sure of it. My hope gives me assurance. What a trap—false hope. It makes cheap believers. But Ronelle is likely, so I am told by Negroes, to be tended eventually by a neighbor woman.

I stare out at the wreckage of this neighborhood. Windows are boarded up here and there against the wind, and what is inside can be understood even by one who has never been inside. Inside those broken dwellings—choose any one—are beds and wooden boxes and small gas stoves or kerosene heaters, and there is always, everlastingly, that dark presence—brooding, burning, desperate, hopeful, angry-hearted or stupefied—a slum woman, a mother. I talked briefly last night with Pearl of this neighborhood. She is trying to organize the women to protest for a playground. A mother of seven kids, she said, "If you a Negro woman, you a mother one way or the other by the time you are nine years old." She carried five little brothers and sisters on her own child-back through their infancies, she told me. I think of beasts, carrying-beasts. Women are all beasts of burden. These black women bear their burdens in the belly, in their arms, finally on the back, and many have that patient stupefied attitude of beasts. One sees it in the posture, in the body that asks for nothing. That's it—the hands and arms are not reaching, not aggressive. They can give and receive, that is all. They cannot ask. The bodies of white women, except for the destitute, seem to mime a thousand requests, to preen or to beg or to tease or withdraw in anguish or petulance or—what is it? These bodies, even when well fed and comfortable, rarely express want.

Suddenly the smell of imitation-grape flavoring routs the visions. I look at the pretty girl next to me. She sucks a grape Popsicle. I smile. She smiles brilliantly, almost laughing. The others smile. One says, "You live down Men'nite House?" "Yes." They giggle and shrink away except for the grape-flavored older one. Smells here arouse nostalgia: scents of overripe apples (very expensive) and bubble gum and grape flavoring. Also, there is the smell of the old waxy wooden floor of such stores. I haunted them as a child. I read a few days ago a report on food consumption differences between white and black in the United States. An estimated 49 percent of all grape soda, 39 percent of orange soda, 17 percent of all cola drinks and 25 percent of all root beer are drunk by Negroes. On the other hand Negroes, so the report stated, buy less tea and coffee than whites. Statistics! I am certain that as a child I drank 49 percent of all the nation's grape soda myself.

The Pole has the dead white face of an Oriental puppet. He looks like a man who makes nickels and dimes. He carefully examines the change they hand him. He has 100 percent Negro trade, he says, impressed by the figure if not the fact, and cannot understand why the young people at our house do not patronize his place. He does not know that they give their salaries, when they have salaries, to their church and are handed out very small monthly allowances.

Now another child gives me a huge unabashed red-lipped smile, as if handing me a fresh red flower pulled up from some stark spot. I want to return something more than my own smile, but hers was not a request. It was freely flung at me. There is that magnificent, unfaltering decision to smile instead of—what? Instead of anything else. They smile, most of them, wherever one goes. The rural world—and yes, the South is spiritually rural—includes all sides of passion. One hates and fears and suffers and does violence or perhaps receives it, and so one also loves and smiles. There is a perpetual intimacy here, especially among Negroes. There is a whelming quality. It is as if we shall all merge into one being. Well, the passion of real city life as known in the North seems to be only for brutality. I see few zombies here, whatever the reason. Even the most depressed have an occasional animated moment. In the North, in the big cities of the country, there are whole hordes of zombies with never a glimmer of life.

And so, without reason, illogically and honestly, these black children smile at me and I smile at them.

But Yvonne and I need not have bought fruit for Mrs. Ferris. We walk down the boulevard past all those falling shelters to her place. Two men, slightly drunk, are on the steps there and do not move for us. We charge through like hearty social workers and climb the stairs, a narrow wooden passage reeking of strong stale urine and general filth. Just as we enter the stair well I hear a door closing upstairs on Mrs. Ferris's side.

"I hear something. I think she's home."

But though there is no lock on the door (her means of locking up when she leaves the place is a heavy metal padlock), we get no response. Yvonne is amazed. Her pride in this contact, in which she says there is mutual interest, clouds her understanding of what I suspect is true: the probable mistrust and irresponsibility that necessarily will limit the friendship. Yvonne will be gone from here, that's a fact they both know. But Mrs. Ferris will remain. She's as trapped in this spot as the building she occupies and, like it, can only live here until she falls.

I can smell liquor as we stand there. Yvonne knocks and we wait.

"I don't understand it!" she whispers. "She wouldn't go out without putting the lock on the door. Somebody must be inside there."

Logic! I'm irritated at her but try not to show it. She knocks again, calling to Mrs. Ferris. I can smell a gas heater and somehow feel the heat of the room through the door. Behind us someone makes cautious steps beyond the door of Number 4.

"Let's try her another day, Yvonne. She may not feel like having company this afternoon. Let's leave the fruit over here at Number 4. They'll give it to her."

She is dubious and confused. It doesn't make her kind of sense but no doubt it makes Mrs. Ferris's kind.

"I've *told* her all about you and she said she'd like to meet you and be glad to talk to you." Logic industriously locks up her mind, jamming the understanding.

I knock on the opposite door, which opens immediately to reveal a gaunt, tough-faced, middle-aged black woman in a tattered housecoat. She blows smoke in our faces. I give a little laugh at the open hostility.

"Could we leave this fruit with you, please? It's for Mrs. Ferris and she doesn't answer her door. Would you give it to her later?"

"Sure, I'll keep it in the icebox. What y'all lookin' for?"

"Just visiting. Thanks a lot."

We leave, Yvonne very soberly. All the way back to the house she ponders aloud.

I find myself, since the futile visit, developing an almost sadistic desire to force Yvonne to experience irrational life, brutality. I feel conspiratorial with Mrs. Ferris. Plainly the poor woman, who is young and wretched, alone up there with four children and no man, no education, no way out, cannot afford Yvonne's tidy sanities. But I keep silence. Yvonne's world is, I observe with growing incredulity, entirely rational, to the core, and she is sublimely unacquainted with any chaos in her own being. Never heard of it. She can only see Mrs. Ferris as some kind of external phenomenon, a rational creature oppressed by degrading circumstances. She cannot comprehend the fact that Mrs. Ferris *is* her circumstances, is as wild and absurd as they are, just as Yvonne herself is as rational and tidy as her own circumstances. She would have to break some law, or imagine doing it, of her own society before she could begin to understand Mrs. Ferris and her stronghold of unpredictability. It is good strategy, ask any war veteran, to remain unpredictable to the enemy. That is sometimes the only strategy available to the outcast—unpredictability.

What's in the whole friendship, anyway, for Mrs. Ferris but to do all the creative understanding herself; what's in it for her but extra work and a little charity and a couple of flawed dreams that this contact might lead to something better?

Why must Yvonne be protected? Why can't she be allowed to know anarchy and irrational existence? Well, she was bred inside authoritarian society and that is where she will die. Mrs. Ferris, who is as anonymous as dust, lives as dust—in the universe, everywhere, anywhere, horizontally, upside down; her life is lawless, sundered, abandoned, meaningless. She lives because she was created. She *is*. Yvonne *does* life, being equipped with form and style and law. Mrs. Ferris *is* life and has and does nothing.

Later Charity, too, tries to give me rational explanations for Mrs. Ferris. "See, she may not have a mother or anybody to help out with those babies. She may not have any other company or pleasure but that man who gets her pregnant." I hear her out but feel that none of this is quite to the point. I am convinced that Mrs. Ferris is a real "outlaw," that she knows irrational life fully and therefore knows madness. I am intrigued now and really interested in meeting her. If she is intelligent—and I guess that she is, for I detect in her hostility and her dignified privacy in not seeing us today, the scorn, bravado, and courage of intelligence—if she is intelligent and proud, then no doubt she will resist me, and I cannot blame her for that. I have nothing to offer her. But I am shamelessly interested in her and think if we talked I might hear truth from her.

Think of all that is implied in that free-floating, irrational life! Commitment only to one's *being* because—if there must be a because—one is *here,* one is of this moment and this space. This is an age of trips—trips in and trips out. The laws that sustain us as landed, grounded provincials do not apply in space where Mrs. Ferris lives. Her very space and time are not what we know, not what we can use, can abide, can admit to. Ask any poet, a hobo, an artist. Ask a Negro man. Negro men, the unattached or unemployed, know this and live it more often than any other people in this land. They are really free-floating. Whatever the statistics, when one enters the slum that is the first phenomenon that falls on the consciousness: that random presence of what we call idle men. We simply say to ourselves that they live by their wits or on charity. But that is not how they *live,* that is only how they survive. Somewhere they find food and shelter; somehow there are garments covering their bodies. But how they *live*—what the psyche knows, its view of space and time and the presence of others, of phenomena—only they or their spiritual kin could tell that, and probably they would not. They probably know what James Agee discovered he knew, that:

> A good artist is the deadly enemy of society, and the most danger-ous thing that can happen to an enemy, no matter how cynical, is to become a beneficiary.

These men with at least a hundred years of isolation and irrele-vance to society behind them have become the artists of out-sideness, of isolation. They have *become* the false role and found the superreality at its core. They know all space and relationship outside the magical ring of law and logic. They knew what it means in a profound sense to act without logical result, to be without effect. Logically, action and work lead to certain limited ends such as the accumulation of some sort of possession—a day's food, shelter, a suit of clothes, a car, stature perhaps, im-provement, progress. But these isolated men know that man's meaning lies elsewhere, for they are still alive and by their labors have not purchased these things necessarily. They have pur-chased, rather, understanding, broken-heartedness, patience, an-guish, madness, perhaps wisdom and divine humor—abstracts. They have purchased abstracts. They have become philosophers. They know something and they possess something, perhaps only a shred, perhaps now and then a real root, of the great prizes after which we all scramble. The outcast, the artist of outside-ness, has purchased these prizes *before* he has purchased mere bread. Listen, therefore, to him. He knows something. Artists know something. Listen to them.

And this Mrs. Ferris who lives on the boulevard in that same severance knows or is learning it, too. I would like to know if she has a phrase for it, if there is something she might say, quite innocently, that would tell it all.

Charity's life unfolds like the classic case history. She had already taught school on one of the islands off South Carolina when she met her husband. She married and a couple of years later had a baby girl who died in infancy. Her husband, who traveled in his work, had other women and Charity knew it but kept silent. Divorce and infidelity were sins against the Lord. When the child died, Charity believed it was because of her husband's sins.

"I couldn't do anything. I went and sat by the river; I just had to be by the water, I remember. I sat there for days, all day, and just looked at the water. I said, 'I don't want *any* man,' just over and over. That made him mad—he went off but he came back."

But later she had a son and a year after that her husband died. "I always said God divorced me. I couldn't have done it myself. God did it."

There followed a long series of trial living arrangements; meanwhile she always searched for a way to keep her son with her and work. He lived with her in-laws for a while but finally Charity's aunt took him and brought him up in South Carolina. By this time Charity was traveling in her work and saw the child infrequently, although she was always in touch, always emotionally close to him.

"I never married again and I didn't want to. I couldn't take up with another man. A man fell in love with me once and I was tempted, very much. But I wanted to work more and I couldn't give it up. My son grew up easy. He was so spoiled! Oooh, my! That's the trouble right now. He's still got Auntie in his house since his first wife died."

Leroy, the son, went into the Marines during World War II. "That was the hardest day of my life, taking him to the train to say goodbye. I thought he'd be killed. I prayed so hard in the war. For all of 'em. But he was never hurt."

Leroy wouldn't go to college, wasn't interested. Charity says, musingly, "Something wrong when an intelligent man like that wants to stay ignorant." I mention the idea certain psychologists have concerning the motivations of children in relation to the presence of a father, and she gives it some thought. "Oh, he needed a man around him, all right." But I sense that the connection is loose. Charity does not look for psychological answers. In regard to motivation, she believes a person was "just weak at that time" or perhaps "just that way." She has studied psychology, but instinct, sober thought, and faith all serve her more practically. At best she may decide that an event—especially one of sorrow—is the clue to temporary disturbance in a life, an event and rarely a general condition, except the condition of poverty and even that she disregards as a major factor in character degeneration. Many poor folk do not degenerate in character as a result of chronic poverty.

Yet her mind is fluid, open to suggestion to a degree that keeps it ever altering its vision, ever demanding a new dimension. Sixty-eight years old and still flexible, still a learner.

Leroy married after the war, had three children, and held two jobs—that of headwaiter at a fashionable club for white men, and occasional outside catering. His wife died of cancer when the oldest child, Jennie, was about eight. Leroy was greatly bereaved. He kept his two boys with him, brought old Auntie back to live in and care for them, and sent Jennie to Charity who now had a house in Charleston and was living in it with her youngest sister. That is the arrangement at present: Charity travels and returns home about once a month or every six weeks; the sister cares for little Jennie; a wide variation on the natural two-parent household with Charity's role something like a man's—breadwinner who brings the world home when she returns. Her granddaughter is a late-age treasure, an apparently happy normal girl of fourteen now being reared by two older women. She sees Leroy, her father, and her little brothers on most holidays, and the families, though living three hundred miles apart, are often in touch by phone. Both households are ruled by a single or widowed woman—Leroy functioning as a kind of prince or perhaps a drone in this queendom.

In the Movement one sees apparent excessive effects of matriarchy: many of the women are single, separated, or divorced. In Charity's organization only three out of fifteen women live at home with a husband and children. The others live alone or with other women. These latter are, of course, the only women available for dedicated work, for frequent travel and unpredictable hours. "There's a lot of sex troubles around. Sometimes cause the women won't stick and sometimes cause the men won't," says Charity.

And the price paid for the relative freedom of these women, by themselves and many of their families, is very high. Often a sister or mother provides the stable home atmosphere for these workers. Charity seems to carry that quality with her, that permanence and spaciousness, that nourishment required by children and men and some women. Somehow the world seems to land in her arms. She fondles it idly, demands little, waits, receives, inspires, endures. The world gets up, staggers, finds it can walk a little; it leaves her but it will be back. One knows that some human creature will seek out this healing presence as long as she lives. One forgets that she is on the move because this sense of place in her nature is so profound.

And white people are no exception. She showed me a letter recently from a young white fellow who had worked briefly in the Movement. He is married to a white girl who is pregnant, and yet he fell in love with a very young Negro girl who was doing civil rights work during the same summer.

"Look at this: See, she believes he loves her and I don't think he does. I think he's just playin' around a little. But this child thinks he's going to give up his wife and everything for her. Read that letter. He's going to cause that colored girl a lot of pain but I believe he thinks he's serious right now. I got to wait for him to cool a little and then I'll have to tell him to stop it. But in the meantime he might get her pregnant and that's one more Negro child with no father and one more Negro girl out of school to have her baby. And one more mother to take on the girl's baby."

She corresponds with dozens of people who ask her help with job hunting, marital troubles, wayward children, and so forth. She answers them after deep consideration and with succinct candor. She writes by hand, rarely dictates anything to one of the office secretaries, reserving the last hour before bedtime (which is often one or two in the morning) for this solemn chore. She looked at my tape recorder one day and said, "I ought to learn to use one of those but I never seem to have time to buy one."

I get the feeling that Charity's life is activated by such a deep instinctual rhythm that it is much harder for her to break simple habits than it is to break up old ideas. There is rarely any change in the physical procedure of her living. She moves at one pace, emitting a quality of eternity. Nothing breaks the rhythm; there is at best only a slight acceleration in attention sometimes, in alertness. I sat with her through a long, hot, slow-moving afternoon session with field workers in a church basement recently and could have sworn that she fell asleep at several intervals. But afterward she dealt with every issue as if she had created the material herself, repeating verbatim many phrases used by other people there. She listens and broods with half shut eyes; she receives as if through the pores of her body. She relaxes. She rejects trivia. In her speech and in her letters she delineates like a master, in simple language and in the clear, neat, controlled handwriting of a penmanship teacher.

Well, Leroy has a new trouble, and she does show some irony over it, if not agitation. He has married again, this time a very young woman. She will arrive in town tonight and share our room until we leave for Alabama. Her name is Edna. And apparently she already has had trouble with Leroy.

Home late to find Edna has arrived and flung her suitcase on the floor, half unpacked; her toilet articles are strewn about the top of the chest, and she has fallen into my bed although it had obviously been slept in. The light blazes from the naked ceiling bulb, but she sleeps oblivious of it, curled away toward the wall.

Charity met her for the first time earlier in the day. She laughs now at the show of carelessness, youthfulness. I take the third bed, and we retire as quietly as possible. As I put out the light I notice a white bandage about Edna's slender brown wrist.

They move another single bed and a standing lamp into our room today. Bethel Wallace, Charity's cousin arrives this afternoon to make our trip to Alabama with us. Charity and I will rent a car, and the four of us will drive down together, taking along a girl from Charity's office as well. The room is crowded now, but it will be only for two nights. Edna awoke early and went down to fix her breakfast. One shifts for oneself in the morning in this house. Edna, although new here, made herself at home with childlike trust and impetuosity. Her immediate familial response to her new mother-in-law, Charity, whom she has never before seen, is fantastic. At breakfast, which she fixed for the two of them, she gossips about her domestic problem in an adamant, kiddish manner, oblivious of the passing of the residents through the dining room and kitchen. She has already adopted the family diminutive for Charity—"Mama-Chere." She is most splenetic about old Auntie who still dominates Leroy's household.

"You know she has *eleven* cats now. Oh, no, they not any *five* cats around there now, it's eleven! The whole place smells so bad you can't breathe. I shut my do' when I go out of the room or leave the house, but when I come home the do's open and two or three of those nasty cats up on my pritty bedspread scratchin' around. I know the baby likes me, Mama-Chere, but she's got Teddy turned against me already. She tells him lies! I mean it, just lies!"

She has found a bottomless pit of equanimity and listening patience. She pours and bleeds into it. I sit across the huge dining table and read the paper, but she makes no attempt to lower her voice. She eats six pieces of toast and fills her coffee cup four times.

"Listen, Mama-Chere, Leroy don't take up fo' me, that's all. He could stop her but he just say, 'Well, this is her home and she never had to move over for anybody before.' But that's not *my* fault. I told him when I come back she have to move out or I'm goin' back home to my Mama!"

Charity eats in an orderly silence, nodding and making mental equations. Finally she says, "Well, she's getting old. I always did think Auntie ruled 'em around too much over there but that's Leroy's problem; he's a man. He has to take care of himself." And adds very softly, "But she doesn't mean any real harm, I doubt."

"Huh!" The tigress roars and casts green glances about the room. "Harm! She wants to break up my marriage, that's all! She'll keep on till she's got me out. You wait and see. But when I go back . . ."

She settles back to another piece of toast, tearing at it with perfect square white teeth, wrinkling her freckled nose and saying "huh!" with deep scorn and suspicion.

Edna's vitality radiates in every direction. She is tall, high-hipped, snub-nosed, with a reddish freckled look, a lioness' look, and an impudently intelligent face.

After she goes upstairs, Charity says softly, "That Leroy! He sent me the first one to straighten her out and now here comes the second one." She laughs. "This one's nothin' but a baby. Just needs a little growin' up. But she's smart, I think."

That, I agree, is obvious. And her impudent charm will serve her well for a long time.

I take Edna down to pick up some baggage at the station and she tells me the story of her domestic battles as if I had not lived through it at the breakfast table. But much of this is new, and the rendition is more controlled. She has decided, perhaps, that as a sort of fixture of Charity's, I am to be trusted.

"She does all the cookin' for her and the little boys and I just say, 'Okay, go ahead and do what you want but I'm fixin' me and my husband's supper after you all done and got all that grease cleaned up in there cause I don't like that old fried liver and all that stuff anyway. You juss feed the boys and take your time and when Leroy come home, I'll fix our supper like we like it and we can eat in peace.' And that's what she does but she's got all those cats in there the whole time she's cookin'! My God! I wouldn't let *my* children eat with all those old dirty cats in the kitchen and that old woman cookin'! She touches all those cats and then cooks the food. Never washes her hands. And she tells the boys that I don't want to cook for them so they'll hate me. But, see, they can't wait that long to have supper cause they have to get to bed by eight-thirty and it's about eight by the time she gets through in there. And then I have to tell 'em she lied but they don't really believe it.

"Well, I got so sick of it one day I went in the bathroom and took one o' old Leroy's blades and cut my wrist and—" she laughs guiltily, "—she went screamin' to the phone. Call Leroy and he home in about two minutes and bringin' an ambulance. That's when he told me to come down here and see Mama-Chere. Scared him to death.

"But I told him," imagining the ferocity with which she ought to have but probably did not tell him, using it now, with a stranger, "I said, 'My God, you nothing but a *baby boy* if you can't handle that old woman and cats! I'm not comin' back till she's out. That's what I mean—*out!*' He'll do it, too. He wants me back. I know that. He had a lot of women around town. He was *something!* About six women after him and everybody in town sayin', 'Leroy Simmons never going to marry! Anybody's crazy to chase him.' But, Honey, I got my hooks in that man and I'm not takin' 'em out.

"See, I got one child but she's adopted out by my cousin because I had her so early. I was only fifteen and my mother wanted me to stay in school. But Leroy just dyin' to have a baby with me and me, too. I want about four kids if I can. *If* it's Leroy's. I know he wants 'em. And I know everything'd be all right with us if that old bitch could just be pushed out of there. That's not her house. That's Leroy's house. She makes out to the neighbors that it's her place, like Leroy gave it to her and all that, but it's not. It's in his name and that makes it part mine and she don't own a penny of it. She can get her an apartment or somethin'. Or we can move out and leave her there with all those stinkin' cats. That's what I'd like anyway.

"I told my Mama, I say, I'm not goin' back in that lousy cat house." We laugh. "I'm gonna make him burn. Honey, when I get back I'm gonna dance with every man in town and flirt till that old Leroy can't stand it anymore. I'm gonna get him *so* scared . . ."

Suddenly she wearies of it and falls silent, staring out the window, her slashed wrist lying obediently in her lap, vaguely protected by her other hand that hovers near it. Suddenly she reascends to a tenuous maturity. "Gee, I miss my man. I'm gonna talk to him tonight."

We get the bag and return to find Bethel, the cousin, arrived and sitting on her bed, smoking and talking family news with Charity.

Bethel, somewhat chic, was once a hairdresser in business for herself; she had a brief late marriage to an older man and bore him one child, a daughter who is now grown and married. Bethel looks to be about forty; very thin, of medium height, she has a big head of thick wild hair that she pulls away from her face with a ribbon at the nape of the neck. Her eyes are huge and flowerish like Callie's, but her expression is wiser and subtler—for one thing, compassion may be found there. She has the high flaring nostrils of a good horse, part of something generally horsy about her. She has a whiskey voice and a wry, slightly tough style, laughs quickly and usually with that trace of scorn I hear so often, not a personal hostility but only a slightly tarnished regard of human antics in general.

Auburn Street—midnight. Crowds of people, mostly men, leaning against the walls of closed-up shops, in doorways, against parked cars. Impatient roar of tail pipes on the slowly passing cars. Everyone is cruising, loitering, on the make for something. Edna, swaying her high hips, passes like a flame among them, followed by the various standard mating calls. Saturday night—nowhere to go. And so this is where. A smell of barbecue and carbon monoxide in the air. This market place is no different from any other except perhaps in the costumes—hard tight high narrow hats on these cropped male heads, "shades" on many faces, an abundance of black garments. There are many sports with cuff links on dazzling white cuffs, baroque hair styles and flashing teeth. A few drunks, a few toughs.

Everywhere the unimpeachable Southern Negro voice, which would have to be, to these ears, greatly distorted to lose its beauty.

Bethel pushes through and leads us into the hot white light of a short-order house—big, garish, loud, all chrome and phosphorescence. Again the clientele is mostly male and in motion, cruising, stalking, waiting. Few are merely eating and drinking in satisfactory company, it seems.

Beer is sold, no hard liquor. Louise, very black and very stoical, rubs past a young fellow who says, thickly, "Hey, Baby . . ." at her. Bethel finds us a table. Stares from all sides. I am the only white here. Edna can compete with any woman on earth and proceeds to do so with two roving eyes. She takes time out to order her usual grilled cheese sandwich, French fries, and a Coke. Charity has coffee and a ham sandwich. I drink beer with Bethel, and Louise has coffee.

"God, look at the fellows!" says Bethel.

Louise laughs. "You oughtta go out more at night when you come to Atlanta, Bethel. There are lots of men here."

"Not me, Honey. I'm through with that stuff. Men make me sick, 'specially in big bunches like this."

We laugh, eliciting attention. Edna bristles with sheer sexual vitality. A very lean and smooth young man at a table on the level just above ours passes a big-lipped kiss across the air. Edna scorns him. Louise makes a little belly laugh, trying not to show it. Usually there is a look of pained amusement on her face, her brows and forehead arched, her lips closed but drawn out in a grimace that can imply anything from commiseration to pride or pleasure. She is easily amused, seems a little hysterical, yet is altogether well controlled and staid.

Edna chews her sandwich neatly with marvelous big square white teeth, keeping her rosebud lips closed and her dainty hands arched, little fingers raised in the air like small antennae. Her eye continues to sweep the room spylike; then it rolls upward and narrows. "Mmmmm, I better call my man tonight. This too much for me."

Charity sighs and chuckles. "Oooo! Edna. You carry on!"

"Listen, Mama-Chere, I like men. Don't let old Leroy forget *that!* He don't treat me pretty nice, I got me some other ideas."

Bethel says not a man in the place is worth having. "Look at this bunch o' heads. Shoot!" She never quite says shoot, never quite shit. It is more *shhht* and delivered with profound disgust. I find Bethel fascinating and very amusing. I can imagine one might spend a great deal of time with her without tedium. She creates laughter more than she laughs herself, but her jaded view of things is not the whole creature. An animal intensity in her face and a kind of innocence and simplicity in many of her attitudes give her great charm. The perpetual struggle to control her wayward hair, her toxic, agitated and wry personality, the hoarse whiskey voice and the flaring nostrils are all attractively bizarre. As an old woman she'll be a character—I can see her smoking a pipe, cursing and laughing with wicked glee. This is not a favorable time of life for Bethel—somewhere between forty and forty-five years old. It is not for many women, perhaps. She needs to be savage, and that means young or old.

Louise comments that Bethel ought to be more patient with men. One can always get what one wants from a man by patience, she states like a little girl reciting in a third grade classroom. Edna gives her a stare of sheer horror:

"Patient! If I was patient with Leroy, nothin' would happen. *Nothin'!* I told him, I said, 'Listen, men don't get the point as fast as a woman, that's the truth.' Ha! He like to fell out." She laughs loudly and shoots a darting glance at her audience at nearby tables. Charity laughs and shakes her head. Her new daughter-in-law is a real case. Edna loves the attention. A performing child who has just captured an unpredictable audience, she aims for punch lines. "Poor old Leroy! He never even noticed how old Auntie lives till I moved in and showed him all that cat mess. I said, 'Listen, Man, you wasn't *born,* you was *invented!*' That did it! Oh, yeah!"

She breaks us up. Louise laughs weepily with a closed mouth. I watch her struggle for control. She is very black. She can hardly be seen at times—her expressions, that is. It is difficult to believe what I know of her but I caught a glimpse of it just now: She was brutally beaten by white police in a Mississippi jail at the same time Mrs. Fannie Lou Hamer was there. She sits now laughing tearfully, containing the memory somewhere inside that stoical being.

Edna's indirect hit at Charity, in the form of an attack on Leroy, passes unchallenged. Edna is flagrantly innocent of it. She sweeps aside trouble at one pole or another and never tends to the middle: she dismisses Leroy as an ordinary invention tonight; last week she slashed her wrist in a diametrically opposite challenge. Edna will never cut herself deeply, but I feel sure she will cut herself before she will cut another. That is a form of relationship, a deep recognition. I find myself stimulated by her sheer mental health, which at this moment comes through only as childish egoism. But the human, quite a whole human, is hiding there in secret patience. She can be touched. She is womanly in the elusive sense that a little girl sometimes is. Intimations of maturity lurk in her very walk. She has deftness and purpose and grace; she is neat in the animal sense—unself-consciously, simply. She has affection where she cannot rally to respect. She is not fighting Leroy for the purpose of escape, not destructively, but as an approach, for intimacy's sake, for the sake of something she *intends* to feel, some future sort of love. One suddenly sees it in her natural intimacy with Charity—that of mother and daughter, an easy confidence and a presumption that Charity understands her. Of course, with Charity, one may well presume that. How lucky Edna is with this mother-in-law! Edna attacks Leroy not as Charity's son but as an enigma, as a kind of goal or as a beloved adversary.

Wondering if these projections are valid, I ask Charity on the way to the car, "You think Edna and Leroy will make it?"

"I think so," she says quietly, confidentially. "She has to do some growin' up but with Leroy she can do that. He loves a family and kids. She get pregnant, she'll grow up. You just watch. I think she'll be good for Leroy. She's honest, you notice?"

I agree. I have an immediate pleasant fantasy of Edna as a young lioness-mother rolling about with her cubs, a little rough, very protective, happy. That is how I see her. Her mock suicide attempt does not seem to carry the warning of despair that such acts often do. It was serious but not deranged. She is just not that desperate.

Bill and I walk down to spend an hour at Callie's place tonight. She's moving out, suddenly going to New York for a rest. She is furious at the used furniture man to whom she tried to sell her stuff.

"See, that's what I mean! I call up and say I got this stuff to sell and he say, 'What stuff?' and when I tell him he say, 'Where you live?' and then when I tell him he asks me, 'You colored?' So I say that's none of his business but he knows I'm Negro now because if I was a white girl, why I'd say so in a hurry. So then he say, 'I'll give you five dollars for everything you got.' *Everything!* I got a sixty-dollar bed that's only two months old! I got the receipt. Look at this bed!"

We follow her into the bedroom and in the dusky light pretend to evaluate the bed, which is covered with sheets and spread. Callie suddenly flings herself out flat on it to indicate its fullness. Bill backs off quickly and mumbles, "Seems like a good bed," wandering away into the living room. I smile but Callie chooses not to notice. She is incensed and obsessed and wants to say so.

"I got a sofa and a good table and chairs and a good icebox and he going to give me five dollars! Cause I'm black, that's why! Shit!"

"What can you do? Can you advertise them?"

"I don't have time to show 'em. And nobody but poor Negroes would come to this address anyway. And they don't even have five dollars."

We discuss it awhile. Janice, one of her roommates who has her own furniture upstairs, will try to unload the stuff. Bill and I offer to help. But Callie is inconsolable, a show partly for my benefit, I feel, although I cannot say why. How does she manage to make a perfectly legitimate complaint seem so fraudulent?

Finally she calms down. "You want a drink?" We have brought beer, and Bill and I stick to that. She drinks a very good brand of whiskey in Coke. She puts on a jazz record and sits in a corner of the bare-floored room in an iron-legged cane chair. The other day she expressed a desire to be a jazz singer. I can feel her tightening up now to a performance. Bill seems uncomfortable, but somehow I feel that her aggressiveness is not directed toward him. After a couple of drinks she puts on a record of background blues and begins to sing with it, her style a marvelous parody of real blues singing. If something could reach and stir Callie where she lives or ought to be living, she would become a real soul singer. But I get the feeling of fragility and danger again. She is trying to live without feeling anything beyond a sort of TV-style dramatics. She sings "Terrible Trouble" with no moan, no growl, no remorse, no complaint, no threat. No guts. No soul. Good timing. The voice when high is thin but it is best there, like something delicate caught on an updraft, rising without effort.

She sits in a dark corner, the light striking her crossed legs, one swinging, the other, though straight of itself, like a reed pushed over from the root—bent to support the loose one. My imagination permanently equates her with delicate plants. Her shoe falls off. She sings in hiding. I get the impression that her mouth isn't open wide enough for this sort of performance. Her throat isn't open or relaxed. It is diction to a tune, not the music of being. It is all sterile, ludicrous, touching. This is a little girl dressed in her mama's clothes, desperate for believers. The song is thrown at us in pleading hostility.

Callie is a comic strip figure, trying to find the third dimension that the rest of the world takes for granted. She is now getting drunk and shrewish. That too seems false, a substitute for integrity or at least for some clear stance. I begin to see how badly she needs the Movement with its goals and definitions and its drama. I have not seen this in any other Negro woman, if she may be called a woman. She opens another quart of beer and serves us, Bill first, sloshing it over his hand. With mine she is careful.

Now she slams the record albums about and finds another, a jazz piano record, tells us the musician's name in a mumble, and returns to flop in the chair and swing her bare foot. Her voice loosens this time but the delivery falls apart. She leaves out a line or two and trails off as if it were done purposely.

It is dark outside. We sit, stunned by the noise of the phonograph; she has turned the volume to maximum. She sings "*You no good lowlife man!*"

Bill squirms. Suddenly the roommate stomps into the room and cuts the volume. "My God, Cal! That's too loud!" She stomps out and Callie rattles on.

When we leave she bums a cigarette from Bill and seems by that act to be asking for tolerance, for some restoration to our society. He lights it for her, gently polite. But although we make compliments, her show fell flat. And so she swaggers, coming out to the veranda and standing barefoot in her thin little-girl cotton dress. She could be eleven years old. She remains tough, blowing smoke at us. This strategic failure means little, she implies. We mean even less. We are irrelevant in fact. There are a million possibilities.

"I'll see you before I go," she assures me.

We leave early tomorrow. Now, at nine o'clock, supper done and the house somewhat settled, I hear the women—Bethel and Charity and the girl from Charity's office who has come for the evening—discussing the route.

"Where was that place you stopped for lunch? Was that a Holiday Inn?"

"It's about thirty minutes before the Holiday Inn. It's called Daniel's Cafe, I think. Right on the highway next to a gas station just after you cut into Eighty."

"Oh, I remember," says Charity. "That's a little better. Holiday Inn is pretty late for lunch. What about gas?"

"It's safe anywhere that I know except that man on this side of Montgomery that Idelle had trouble with. But why don't you take Bethel's car? You won't have any trouble with that big thing."

They laugh.

Bethel has a huge maroon-colored Lincoln that seems to intimidate cops and racists. She is cautious about speed limits and rolls solemnly through these Southern towns with her nose in the air, the hearselike car formidable, silent, a sort of specter. One of the major pleasures of her life is to create awe in the hearts of anonymous whites who watch her passing. She does field work for Charity's program and often travels through areas such as Lowndes County, Alabama.

Life for Negro travelers generally is safer this year than last. But the women must lay these plans regarding lunch and where to stop for gas. They are not afraid, even in an integrated car, even at night; but they are sensibly careful.

At this writing—1968—not one black woman has been killed in the course of civil rights work. Black women have been beaten, true. But they have not been killed. It is presumptuous to conclude that they are the darlings of some special providence, but it is clear that they are canny, courageous, reasonable, and more than all that, have no need for martyrdom, which means that they are rarely tempted into rash acts. They do not avoid dangerous work but appear to approach it artfully, with cunning and a rare sense of timing. Besides all this, they have rarely been the victims of lynchings. They have always been, if more exposed, safer from the violence of whites than Negro men.

If one may generalize, and circumstances like those in the Civil Rights Movement tend to magnify the common ground in our lives, then one may say that a very special brand of the self-preservation instinct is alive in Southern Negro women at this time, and perhaps always was. The fact that Negro people are still among us is astonishing enough. The significance of her life as worker, nourisher—as a symbol of social stability—apparently leaves a Negro woman with a minimum of anxiety over the famous identity problem that we are told plagues all Negroes and surely plagues middle-class white women. Among these Southern Negro women I just do not encounter it. They seem to know who they are and that they are of value.

Callie Brown is an exception to some of this. She is a shaky sort of character, activating the Robin Hood role for all it is worth and in the process somewhat obscuring whoever the actual Callie is. One doubts that the actual Callie is strongly affirmed in that frail soul. Also, she is the only Negro woman I have talked to who lives more dangerously than is necessary. She brags about it. Dangerous living may help to define her.

And so, we do not stop for lunch when we are ready for it on the way to Alabama. We stop when and where it is safe.

Bright day. I am in the mood for a light lunch but Bethel says, "Salad? Well, he'd probably make you one, but it might be pretty small. Negroes don't eat salad, you know, as a main meal. We like a hot meal, noon and supper, too."

Charity eats a fried steak, fried potatoes, green beans that taste like fresh ones, sliced tomatoes, four pieces of soft white sandwich bread with butter, strong black coffee, and pie.

"Well," she explains, "we might get busy and not eat at all tonight. Mrs. Clury not expecting us fo' supper and the meeting may last till late and we couldn't find a place open. Never know."

ALABAMA

BRIGHT COLD SPRING with clouds indecisively hovering in the west. It might storm, says Bethel. Our talk is of field work in the literacy program but also of clothes and hair, of bringing up children, and of men, always men.

"I knew at that last workshop if Marilee didn't watch out he was gonna get her down to the beach. She seduces men on purpose and then she can't handle it. Anyway, he's got a lot to offer her. He's got a little money, Mr. Hale has, even if he does give alimony or something to that wife he had."

Bethel, next to me in the front seat, says in an aside:

"That's why I always gave my daughter a big allowance, even when I couldn't afford it. I knew if she couldn't buy the things she wanted to keep up with the other girls, then some man would come along and buy it for her and that would do it. Next thing he'd have her up in some apartment all set up and there she goes. You got to watch out for a girl growing up alone."

"But Mr. Hale's a good worker," says Charity. "He organized Anders County. We never could get started in that county till he went in there." No human is all villain to Charity. She laughs. "I think he just missin' his wife and that Marilee is cute. I know they got all messed up together. He gave her money already, I know that."

"Well, Charity, that's bad! I think it's a bad start. You ought to talk to that girl," Bethel warns. And to me—"That's a kid from the country and she'll be in trouble in two months. Pretty soon there's nothing to do but prostitute."

"Do a lot of young Negro girls really follow that pattern?" I am dubious. I hear the ominous tone so often from mothers.

"Plenty!"

"Oh, Bethel, I think you exaggeratin' a little," Charity says.

"No, she's not either!" That is Edna, vehement and loud.

"Maybe it depends on how you define a prostitute," I suggest.

"That's right," says Charity. "You can take a lot of money from a man and not be a prostitute yet."

But Bethel settles it: "There's plenty. Too damn many. And it's young girls with no way to get money."

Charity wants to get her hair done—hot press—when we get to Mrs. Clury's house.

"I know Mrs. Carroll over there," says Bethel. "If she's closed up, she'll let me in and I can do it for you."

As is often true, we wind up talking about hair.

"You know Nell, Bethel? Well, she's wearin' hers natural now. It looks real cute."

Bethel snorts. "These kids can get away with it. Can you see me with African hair?" Everyone laughs. "Shoot! I'd look like Halloween or somethin'!"

Edna howls. "I think I'll go home to old Leroy African style. Scare him to death!"

We all break up.

"Wait'll you see Mrs. Clury, Jo," says Charity. "She's got *good* hair and she's very light. She'll show you pictures of her grandmother and tell you about her grandmother's long hair. That grandmother was three-fourths white and Mrs. Clury admired her a lot. She'll tell you how they used to comb down that long hair for her grandmother!" She laughs a little, indulgently. Bethel hisses "Shhhhhhit!" half aloud.

"That's all right," says Charity. "She's a good woman. She was brought up by a very conservative old family with a lotta money. She never worked a day in her life and then when the Montgomery bus boycott started, even with that arthritis and all, she got that big car outta the garage at six o'clock in the morning and went through town takin' all the Negroes to work in the car pool. She did that every day for three hundred and eighty-one days without stopping, sick as she was. You never know about people, see. She just saw something she could do and she got out and did it. That was brave for that old lady."

"Old lady! Charity, she's only three years older than *you!* My God!" Bethel's fury is beginning to sound like envy. I give her a quick look and see a disgruntled and confused expression.

"Well, she's a good woman. Afterward when they all came in there to organize, she let those men sleep in the house there. She took in so many she had 'em sleepin' on her good rugs in the parlor. Fed 'em breakfast. She's very careful who sits on that pretty furniture but she let 'em sleep there when they needed it. They used her phone all day—musta spent five hundred dollars calling Atlanta and New Orleans—but she wouldn't let 'em pay the bill. Montgomery bus boycott couldn't have gone on without Mrs. Clury. Don't forget it."

"Will she talk with me?" I ask.

"Oh, sure," says Charity. "She's got strong opinions."

We make a loop taking in Lowndes County and the territory west of Selma first. Late afternoon, frozen ochre-colored landscape across which swift black birds sweep and dive like bands of outlaws. "This is the road where Mrs. Liuzzo was killed. Right down here about another four miles." We are silent, all intimidated by the memory. Charity has a way of creating a sudden dramatic mood with a simple statement. Lowndes County is sobering in winter anyway—bleak, stark; the road is empty, lonely. We go slowly because ice is forming and also because we are looking for a turnoff to Tent City. Edna stares out the window and growls softly,

"I don't like this old spook place."

TENT CITY

A few muddy acres, fenced, on infamous Highway Eighty. Now a fine chilly rain falls and fills the ruts in the yellow mud of the field. The citizens of Tent City—a community of unhoused Negroes, former plantation workers, about six large families— must park their few cars four hundred feet from their tents on a little rise in the land to keep them from becoming mired in the mud. And then they must walk across that lake of mud to what is now called home.

The tents are large, faded army khaki with stovepipes jutting out the sides. One of them is full of slits; furniture legs, the corners of luggage, and boxes are exposed to the elements. That was once a storage tent, apparently, but nothing can be dry there now. The tents that are lived in are on high wooden platforms with steps and stand at random, facing all directions, perhaps for privacy from one another, against a backdrop of thin, stark winter woods in the property just to the south.

We pick our way toward them, stepping across pools and trenches of water, a sea of thick running clay. Edna mutters, amazed, "People *livin'* out here, Mama-Chere? I never saw a mess like this to live in!" Bethel's foot sinks in suddenly, up to the ankle, and she swears. Charity plows through, steady, silent.

At the end of the row an old kitchen stove, wood-burning and not large, stands on a piece of three plywood. Two women in bandana headgear are stoking the stove with wood that steams and hisses until the fire dries it. They are shabbily dressed in old sweaters, white uniforms, worn mud-caked tennis shoes, heavy dingy stockings. They smile and receive us casually. They are cooking skillet bread and "dusting" a chicken for frying. The fine drizzle has become icy. No shelter whatever covers the stove, but they continue their work unconcernedly, both cheery, modest, and rugged-looking women who are perhaps in their late thirties. One is immediately recognizable as a laugher.

Edna says, dismayed, "Y'alls' biscuit is gettin' wet!" and the cook moves to lay a piece of torn cardboard over it until the oven is ready for baking. We take pictures, Charity standing very straight and sober beside the two women. They talk.

"My husban' regiss to vote and they put him off. We never even got all owa clothin' outta there."

"How long had you lived on the plantation?"

"Twelve years."

"God!" Edna's tone is one of pure revulsion at the cruelty, revulsion and incredulity. We exchange glances, mine pained and guilty, I feel.

They have many children: one has seven with her in two tents; the other has five here and three away with relatives. Charity quizzes them perfunctorily.

"Well, some cooks indoze. This the only real stove for the whole place and if you cooks out here, sometime you don't git supper till late, waitin' on the ress to git done. So some cooks inside on those little stoves. See them pipes in the tents? Them's little stoves for heatin' the indoze. They can cook a little on them, too. One burner. Her and me cooks together—save time. We makes up a big batch o' bread and does the meat while the vegetable cookin' inside. We gits through early on account of her husban' and mine both comes in early from work, ahead of the othas, and we got the mos' chillrun. Oh, yessum, all the chillrun's in school. All but the babies."

I look around. There are a few chickens and cats scuttling about under the tent platforms. Up on a rise above the tent cluster is a ramshackle wooden structure with a partially open top: the shower. Next to it a muddy old bathtub stands completely open to the elements. Beyond that by twenty feet are two tall narrow little privies.

The laugher says with a grin: "I sponges off in the tent. I cain't take that showa in this weather! It takes a heap o' time gittin' clean and you come out in this mud, you dirty again, anyway. It's a big mess but we gettin' used to it. We been here one year. Lass winter we like to died. The ground was all ice."

She has put the chicken in the oven and sits now on an old backless kitchen chair fumbling with the sole of one sneaker.

"Lookit these shoes! Honey." She puts it to us in general after Charity has assured them we will try to raise money for them. "See can you jess git me some new sneakers. Lookit that mud gettin' in on my feet! My husban' ain't gonna let me in the baid with these muddy feet!" An explosion of high laughter affirms her.

We move away. Charity mumbles, "They can *laugh!* Whoo! All these people livin' here because somebody in the family tried to vote in the United States of America. Let's see this woman here, Mrs. Main. I think I met her last time I was through here."

Mrs. Main and her husband and her twenty-one-year-old son, who tried to vote, live here. A warm clean air hangs at the entry of the tent, which is a slit between heavy canvas flaps that are slightly folded back. Smoke spews thick and white from the stovepipe and flattens against the low heavy ceiling of storm clouds. Mrs. Main stands aside and invites us to enter. Pleasantness breaks from her round, weary, gleaming face. She is convincingly glad to have visitors: she is sociable. We duck inside and try to keep from being a burden there in the four square feet of empty floor space. There is a huge high bed against the back wall of the tent, the tent ceiling sloping to touch its outer side. It is neat, billowy, covered with clean but tattered rose-colored chenille. The little stove holds a snapping wood fire, hot and bright behind the cracks of its iron door. The tent is, nevertheless, warm only on that side.

Mr. Main, much older than his wife, seventy-one years old in fact, sits near the stove on a small straight-backed chair, his bare feet in an old roasting pan of steaming water. A piece of torn wool blanket covers his shoulders. We hesitate at the sight of him.

"Come on, come on in. Don't pay him no mind." She laughs as if he were a piece of furniture, not functional but abstractly useful. He gives us a look, sober, kindly, indifferent. His face is long, bronze, majestically quiet and handsome. His color is rich and clear and golden. He is unbelievably stately and well-made, like a work of art being transported somewhere in secret through hostile territory. Only Charity seems resistant to his magic; the rest of us stare. He continues to regard us serenely, disdaining the commonness of mere smiles, the capitulation of pleasantness.

Charity is clinical, treating them as cases, taking in the facts routinely, and unashamedly asking for rather intimate information—for instance, where do they all sleep? The son's cot, it seems, is hoisted above our heads on ropes and lowered at night after the chairs have been cleared away from this small front space. He sleeps, at twenty-one years of age, in this canvas room with his parents.

Mrs. Main cheerily gives out private details: her son has a job, showers at night after the others are all in their tents, out there in the cold. "I don't know how he do it but he goes out every night and heats up his water and gits under that showa!"

Mr. Main is still silent. I watch him. His feet, like those of the seated stone Sowekhotep in the Louvre, are perfect and straight, brown, though whitening and softening now at the edges from waterlogging, and rest in powerful immobility in the roasting pan, under four inches of clear hot water. I stare at them as if I had come upon some ancient stone god under the sea. They seem to have a life of their own submerged there; they are whole and separate from the body, eloquently fixed and present. His body and his head are perfect in simple health, innocence, and gravity. His back is straight. His hair, a thousand white wires, curls at the temples and bursts savagely from the high smooth brow. I have never seen anything like this man. He is here in his jeans with his feet in a roasting pan; that is where mankind on earth finds himself at this moment, ejected from something lowly and irrelevant—a cotton plantation in Alabama, the United States of America—for a reason that shall sound to our future as minor as an old weather report; that is, because his son went to the polls and tried to vote and did not vote. What is that? What is this? Where are we? We are in the presence of naked, self-housed, self-known, self-nourished, self-justified mankind. What else is there?

Suddenly he speaks; in a tender resolute voice he says simply, "We don't want no violence in the Alabama Freedom Party. We going to have our rights. That's what it come down to."

He turns his head again, looks down at his feet, and takes his ease. His is not an act; he is unaware of his appearance. He is the spirit of man, that's all.

Mrs. Main chats, talks about her husband's rheumatism. "He never have a sick day in his life till he come here in this wet. He seventy-one years old and worked the plantation and he never went off in his life, only over to Sinclair or Selma` once in five years or something. Our son born there, too. And they sent us off. Locked up our place and says: 'You out! Don't come back.' We got some of our things but mostly they kep' 'em."

She smiles though, when talking of her cooking, keeping house, trying to keep the mud out of the place and the clothes clean, the water hot to soak his hands and feet. She deigns to smile; she is unable not to smile. I observe that most of the children, all of the women, and hardly any of the men smile. But perhaps that is only in the presence of women. Mrs. Main plainly wishes to please, to be kind, to give, to make herself clear. *He* has no wishes; needs, yes, the fundamentals, but no wishes. He is here. That is his statement.

"Well, this year we got us a community freezer. Mrs. Bowie owns it and the boys hooked it up. It's ova there in the green tent with some storage. We all uses it and we pays the bills even divided. Thatta way you saves money, buy somethin' on special and keep it froze till come time you need it. Heap o' times you gets a good buy on you meat. We butchered us a hog here lass year and all us cut it up even. Save a lot. My son, he do all the shoppin' fo' grocery fo' me, when he come from work. I gives him the liss and he git it all. He's a good boy. Got him a good job in a garage three days after they put us out.

"My son and me goes once a week up to the laundry place and does the bedclothes and all the ress. *He* cain't do much now. He got it too bad in them feet to walk far and the doctah say don't git out in the wet. Honey, it wet here all winter. It rain and snow and freeze up by November and don't thaw out till March or some. We jess gittin' our thaw now.

"I've had me about two weeks of work since we come here. Cause my white lady that I had first, she found out I'm here and she say, 'Tent City folk is all trouble makers,' so I'm out. And then one tell another and first thing you know they ain't nobody goin' to hire you."

Someone takes Mr. Main once every two months to the clinic, an all day event.

"He set up there from nine in the morning till two in the afternoon lass time. Jess about give it out but I say, 'Now you

here, you jess as well stay and let 'em do somethin' fo' you.' But
he say he ain't goin' back."

Mr. Main is silent.

"Well, I got the hope that we be outta here befo' next winter
but I don't know how. Somebody tryin' to raise us a little money
for land lease. We got this here land leased from a colored
farmer. The SNCC peoples come help us git this."

She has heard vaguely of Stokely Carmichael, speaks of Martin
Luther King with awe and says of Black Power:

"Well, if they means gettin' owa right and keepin' outta those
mean jails, then I think it's good.

"You comes off the plantation, you has a hard time to make do.
It ain't the same way of livin'. But the Lord be good to us. We
had some white boys comin' by lass winter—thowed a big firy
stick on the tents. Coulda burnt up the peoples but they hit the
storage. We got the fire out but the weather done rot the thing
anyway. We loss some things in there." She laughs all at once.
"Nobody want to go in and see that mess! We don't know *what* it
look like. We jess leave it be. Cain't use it anyways.

"I tell you what, it the chillruns you wants to git outta here.
The big ones is in school and that beats playin' around here. But
lookit them babies out in this mud! They has a cold all winta
long."

Mrs. Main was born in Lowndes County and knows a "heap of
folks here"—good and bad. Plenty of bad in Lowndes. People get
killed often, she says.

"I tells him if I was a man, I'd run off from this place. They
hasn't much use fo' a colored man, less he work hisself to death."

Charity says the Mains are both illiterate but their son has a
high school education, probably comparable to seventh grade in
a good school system. Mrs. Main shows signs of restlessness and
boredom. She has worked hard all her life and now, although the
mere maintenance of her small family takes the whole day, she
seems confused by her life. Her husband's illness must seem very
strange in a man who has never missed a day of work before. Her
son has a girl friend. Probably he wants to marry and cannot. It
looks now as if he will be supporting these parents as long as

they are alive. The old man must know that and despise it. Neither of them could possibly take freely to the idea of dependence. These are some of her frustrations. She babysits for the neighbors when they must leave their babies, but most of the time she is trapped here in this drafty tent tending her sick husband.

All of these people are marking time and have that vague quality of transients. One is glad to see that they do not try, beyond providing the bare essentials, to make homes here.

Mrs. Bowie is younger, trim and reticent. Her four boys attend school all day, return home to do chores, eat an early supper, and then go off again to the evening tutorial school set up by Tuskegee Institute to help Negro students who are behind in some particular subject or who want to study a subject not offered in public school, such as Negro history or literature. The tutorial school, attended by all the school age children of Tent City, opens at five P.M. and closes at nine. Most of these Tent City children are in school, then, from eight to ten hours a day; but they do chores and study besides. Mrs. Bowie says:

"Well, it doin' them a lot of good. My husband and I both workin' now and in some ways our life is better since we got put off the plantation. We haven't any decent house but we do have mo' money and the boys getting better education because of the tutor school. They seems to like it fine."

The boys, nine through fourteen years old, are clean and tidy in white sweat shirts and neatly creased trousers. They sit in the dark corners of the tent on cots or stools and do their homework. They study most of the weekend, play a little ball if the weather is fine, and go once a month to see their cousins near Selma.

"Yes, *Ma'm*, they know what they workin' for! They know what they prayin' to the Lord for. I tells them. They all four goin' to college and they goin' to have freedom. Not like with us. My husband have third grade and I have tenth grade. But these boys got to study hard because they goin' all the way through and they goin' to work outside too, make a little money when they can. They'll never end up on no plantation, I see to *that!*

"Me, I never want to see the plantation again. It's nothin' but killin' work and never making a thing from it. Not even enough food. My boys eats better now."

While she talks, she turns some round, thick slabs of bread that resemble thick tortillas on the iron cover of the little stove. The tent smells of fried meat. It is as immaculate as its occupants. Across the back of the tent hangs a curtain which hides their clothes. Chairs are suspended by ropes from the tent supports. A big white refrigerator looms near the entrance, and when its motor starts the light bulb dims noticeably. The boys, holding their notebooks in hand, stand to say goodbye.

Back in the car, Edna, shaken by these sights, says adamantly, "I'm gonna get a thousand pounds of food and clothes and send 'em down here, Mama-Chere! That's the worst thing I ever saw!"

"No doubt about it," Charity says later. "These country people and farm people have a better family life. Family stays together better and the people help each other out more. They'd be dead if they didn't. See, the man always worked on the plantation or else they put him off. Both worked or if just one then it was the man. That makes a better family. Lotta strong Negroes coming up out of these farms and plantations. They learn fast and they are good people. We'll see 'em comin' out soon. Grass roots. See, that's where the strength is. You can't get the white power structure to understand that but they'll come out and then we'll see."

There was something uneasily said and newly learned about the words "white power structure" as pronounced by Charity. She would, I feel certain, use her own simple translation if she could find one. The concept itself seems new to her consciousness. She makes this adaptation to the younger generation and the language of sociology and/or radicalism quite gracefully. She picks and chooses. She is not dazzled by social change—only eager to meet it wisely.

Well, it is true according to sociologists, that among Negroes divorce and separation are much less frequent in the rural South than anywhere else.

"And even if a woman is alone on her farm, her big boys help out. Say the man dies or goes off: the boys help. Lotsa women carry a farm alone for a while till the boys get big and can work it. But that's all changing." She seems to presume there are always boys in a farm family.

"Charity, even so don't these women seem stronger to you than the men? I mean even when the family is intact."

"Yes, they are stronger. Usually. But the Movement is bringing out the men. That's one great thing about it: developing male leadership."

"And what about the women then?"

"Well, they'll be glad. They need strong men. And there's so much to do, everybody's busy. There's enough work for all."

"How do the men in the Movement treat the women, generally?"

"Well . . . some of 'em get bossy, of course. It goes to their head—the power. Now, you take even at our office: when some important people are visiting, Mr. L. will introduce all the men in the organization first. I sit there and Beulah sits there, and Louise maybe. He'll say, 'This is Mr. Caldwell, director of public relations,' and 'This is Mr. Ford, business manager.' But when he gets to me he says, 'This is Charity Simmons, Mother of the Movement.' Here I'm carryin' on this big project and he doesn't even mention it."

We both laugh. I know she has not given it much conscious thought until this moment. Now I see her pass a brief judgment and let it fall away. Her expression is one of sorrowful understanding and then she returns to more vital problems. Quick—like that—and over. That's all it's worth.

"He'll do the same thing with Beulah. There she is, manager of the whole office work force, and he'll say, 'This is Beulah Handley. She's got a beautiful singing voice.' And those men go off thinking all we can do is sing and play Mama!" We laugh again. Her understanding sinks deeper. "Seems like a man like him with all that fame and power could give the credit, but he can't. He would if he could."

"Is Beulah aware of it?"

"Oh, yes. I think that kind of treatment from men in the organization is part of her trouble. She hates men. Not like

Bethel. Bethel talks a lot but she really likes men. But not Beulah. She's living down there in Georgia and there's her husband up in North Carolina. I doubt if she'll ever get back together with him. Oh, there's a lot of pettiness. I think that's the worst thing of all—the pettiness, from men or women. I can't understand it. All working for the same goals and everybody so necessary and then all that pettiness. Just children."

"You think most people are childish?"

"Well, maybe a lot. In some ways I guess they are. People need a lot. But Bethel is right—men need the most. We got to get these colored men on their *feet*, that's all!" Resolution!

"Do you think Negro women, if they're strong mothers, are harmful to their sons and their husbands?"

"Maybe sometimes. But the trouble with Negro men is white people and poverty. Nobody black ever did to a black man what the whites have done."

The image of Mr. Main, his magnificence, lodges in my mind. He is totally exiled, I feel. His wife gave no evidence that she considered him unusual.

"Charity, what did you think of Mr. Main?"

"I think he's a very good man. You notice how quiet he was? He lets her talk but I believe he's smart. He's doing a little work for the Lowndes County Freedom Party. I don't know what. That's a man who could learn to read and write very quickly. It's too bad . . . such a waste. A smart man and he can't do much in grass roots politics without literacy. Sooner or later he has to read or write something."

"Well, I think he's one of the most fantastic people I've ever seen. I think he's extraordinary!" I tell her. "He's got the kind of dignity and intelligence and stature you very rarely see anywhere."

Charity laughs with pleased surprise. "Ha! You think so, Jo? Maybe I didn't really look at him that way."

Her look of curiosity hovers over me. I have revealed something of myself that is new to Charity. It is difficult to remain as neutral as I have vowed to do. I express some opinions but few emotions and fewer whims. She must find me a cold cat and be relieved to observe this enthusiasm.

"There are so many geniuses hidden from the world that way, Charity. Don't you think?"

"Yes. I think there are. We got to get 'em out where they can live and do something for the world. Now you got me curious about Mr. Main. I have to ask Mr. Perry about him."

Mr. Perry is probably an ordinary man who does not know a genius from a bullfrog. Sometimes Charity's humility and practicality frustrate me.

On to Montgomery.

Mrs. Clury is grave, antique, ponderous, haughty. She lives with an old, broad, toothless, bedroom-slippered black woman servant who sleeps on the back porch in a room like a gypsy tent. It is curtained off from the back entrance by a hanging bedspread, and harbors—besides her own belongings—the washing machine and dryer. This woman, whose name is Mrs. Cotton, is big, gentle and silent, the humming and shuffling sort of servant who is almost cliché. Her room, which we passed in entering from the garage, is crammed with a big high iron bed and an expensive-looking television set, two old trunks, a pole for clothes, and a chest of drawers; cutouts from magazines hang on walls and windows. The room has the tawdry and makeshift quality of a childhood game in which, on rainy days, one was permitted to make a tent by throwing a sheet over the dining room table. If Mrs. Cotton were not so totally corporeal, earthbound and slow to move, one might expect that she would break camp before dawn and vanish.

Her lips collapse together over toothless gums and curl outward. She smiles broadly like a wrinkled baby. She says, "Yethum," to Charity and is openly delighted, if politely so, to see her again. Charity always stays here as a paying guest when traveling through.

Bethel is housed in the large and formal back bedroom; it has a high wooden antique bed, heavy chests and tables, a Queen Anne chair, and a night stand with pitcher and bowl. Heavy draperies border the windows, which also have shades and glass curtains. The whole house, through which Mrs. Clury leads us in heavy formality—a mother superior guiding tourists through the convent—is packed, dense, dimly lit, cluttered, the clutter glued in place; it is scrubbed for dirt, waxed, and sprayed for moths but closeted from all natural light and air. There is no bare wall, no open window, no admission that the out of doors surrounds it. The faint odors of past meals hang here like fragments of dream in a gothic, sacerdotal head. Mrs. Clury, high priestess, solemnly reveals the bathroom Charity and Edna and I are to use as if it were a baptismal font.

Charity and Edna (because the latter is an unexpected guest) are to share a double bed in a small front room. My tiny cubicle is just off this one and is actually a walled-in end of the front porch, large enough for a bed and a chair. A gas stove in their room sputters pleasantly, and the heat is staggering. Charity and Edna seem pleased with the warmth.

Mrs. Cotton has prepared a snack of vanilla cupcakes, coffee, and cocoa. We sit at the dining table, which has three cloths on it—a plain worn white damask covered by lace covered by padding and more white, very clean damask. There are painted china, cut glass and silver napkin rings with rubbed and diminished monograms; clocks tick and chime gently in corners, in dark halls; there are antimacassars and doilies, and embroidery in frames on the wall. An overhead chandelier in the dining room provides light by which we are now boldly examined by our hostess, whose look is that of an ancient brooding cat, a transcendence to the zenith of felinity; the ultimate cat contemplates us. It may take, she implies, eons. She has escaped the movement of time. And that, I tell myself, devouring cupcakes for strength against this crushing silent scrutiny, is how she made it through three hundred and eighty-one days at six in the morning in her Cadillac. She is a woman of such expanses and patience as are implied in three hundred and eighty-one days. She is a woman who *had* three hundred and eighty-one identical days.

Her thick-lidded eyes bear down upon me. Charity, feeling the pressure, explains me, our travels, this book. The eyes slowly activate away from me. Edna receives the burden for a while. Mrs. Clury has little to offer besides her heavy purr—affirmative, negative, or more often skeptical.

"Well," she growls finally, "maybe tomorrow you have time to see the rest of my house." I feel as welcome as a snake in the robin's nest.

We are weary. Another overhead ceiling light torments the room Charity and Edna share. Edna, after a long whispery phone call to Leroy, is in bed with an arm over her eyes, gossiping at Charity who moves slowly about the room undressing, doing up her hair in the blue paste and thin curlers. She creams her face heavily with lazy affectionate strokes. It is as if she has been told to move at a certain pace and not to vary it on pain of death. She powders her body, released from the constriction of the corset, with what seems like the same deep sensual pleasure. She wears the aqua nylon pajamas and robe.

I lie now reading by lamplight the mimeographed material Charity has given me concerning local work in literacy programs; also it contains a great deal of pertinent local political information. Hopes for a large Negro voter registration here are very high because the voting-age Negro population far exceeds the white. I read, fascinated but weary and dazzled.

It occurs to me that in weeks I have not met more than one or two women who are not working desperately hard, long hours, most of them maintaining homes besides; and most are oppressed by circumstances in one way or another. Mrs. Clury's house and her life seem morbid by comparison; this is a kind of mausoleum, this old house of beloved if sometimes minor treasures. But, I remind myself, she gave her three hundred and eighty-one days. She is housing, for a small fee, a white woman because she believes it will benefit race relations and because Charity Simmons arranged it. She gives a lot of money and much quiet attention through the activities of her church to civic improvement and relations between the races. She is important.

And then again the idea of Mrs. Clury is drowned in the image of all these patient workers, these black women who seem to have the strength of ten others—just plain physical strength. Carriers . . . they are all carrying a load, carrying the major burden. I recall the back end of the Too Tight Barbershop where a half a dozen idle men spend their days. I do not see this kind of refuge for women—one sees no idle women even among the wealthy. It is true that the black woman has more opportunity to work, more contact, poses less threat to the market and the white establishment. She will not, usually, abandon a hungry baby. And so her motivation is strong. She prevails and she works. Work . . . endless, sometimes barely fruitful work. . . .

Charity comes in and sits on my bed as a grandmother might with a child—to tell me the history of the Montgomery Bus Boycott; the personal, intimate history. And especially to tell of Rosa Parks, a seamstress and former secretary for the National Association for the Advancement of Colored People in Montgomery, who refused, because she was weary, to relinquish her seat on a city bus to a white man. Out of that incident came the Montgomery Bus Boycott and subsequently the Civil Rights Movement. Mrs. Parks eventually moved away from the South after her famous catalytic act that day on the bus. She did not long involve herself in the beginnings of the Movement which some say she midwifed.

"Seemed like she just couldn't continue to take part," says Charity. "She had been so dedicated before."

"Maybe she felt her particular usefulness was all in that one moment on the bus. Maybe it alarmed her to have precipitated all this. . . ."

We discuss it for a while. Then Charity returns to her room, promising to turn off the little stove before she goes to bed as I am by this time miserably warm and breathless. I fuss with the windows by my bed but find them nailed shut. The weather has turned suddenly, capriciously, warm, and there are birds in the bush outside now, sounding out spring. There is a thin rain, a mist, settling on the leaves, and a vague smear of moon in the heavens. All the Negro homes I have been in are too warm for me. Charity complains that her house in Charleston, which she loves and has recently discovered must be razed by the city to build new roads, and which she must sell for a meager sum, is drafty. She says fervently that a warm house means a great deal to her.

She goes now to the table in her room and begins a long letter to a man in Selma, giving him information about work in Lowndes County literacy programs, a promised letter that, although it is now well past midnight, she would not fail to write and mail by tomorrow.

I turn out the light, my mind excitedly sorting and testing ideas. Rosa Parks—that one intuitive moment on the bus. . . . Hardly a word . . . Words and Acts. I wonder: What does one do when the voice is of no significance? When speech is irrelevant?

I realize all at once something that has happened in almost every conversation I have had with a Negro woman: after twenty minutes of communication each of us experiences a falling away of familiar style, defense, structure. Suddenly we are not what has ever been defined before. We seem to come to an open space where we had thought there was a wall. It is not that we become merely more intimate or trusting. Something very rash and truthful occurs, is risked. A look comes over the black face (Charity, Callie Brown, and Mrs. Clury are exceptions); it is a look of forfeit, a bold honest look from the quick to the quick—a look of the long chance taken and something profound sacrificed in the bargain. Soul victory in defeat, in deference. She defers to me for the sake of some broader goal that we had both thought was abstract, only a dream. That is the look she gives me at that time, almost invariably. Like little Ronelle's look matured—calculated risk and forfeit. She hands me the power to use the word for her.

After that curious moment, we both seem to know everything. I have a voice in the world, some basic establishment of voice, and that just might, a long shot, be useful to her. I seem to become a kind of portal through which she decides to pass for the sake of speech. Her own voice—silenced, stolen, scorned—still lives in a sanctuary of whispers, asides, fragmented damnations and assertions, mute prayers, fierce hymns of praise. Everything cached in inscrutable acts. Who has ever asked a black woman to speak, to define herself?

"Negroes," said James Baldwin, "are almost always acting."

Of course. The spurned voice is forced back into the act, there to do all its accusing, praising, wailing, explaining, pleading. The language retreats to live and strangle in the body. The life of the body . . .

Gwendolyn Brooks said, "Every Negro poet 'has something to say' simply because he is a Negro; he cannot escape having important things to say. His mere body for that matter is an eloquence. His quiet walk down the street is a speech to the people. Is a rebuke, is a plea, is a school . . ."

Rosa Parks sat on the bus one evening, said no on the bus with her body. The day before that there was no protest of bodies, no physical witness; no demonstration; no *movement*.

Vernon Johns and Claudette Colvin before her had protested, but, for history's purposes, prematurely. The speech in their acts was not yet audible, not believable. It was still an alien tongue to their own people. The time was not precisely ripe.

Rosa Parks said no in every limb, meant no with her flesh and blood and bones. She did not merely midwife the Movement; she gave birth to and is the Movement. She was tracked down "by the *Zeitgeist*—the spirit of the time," as Martin Luther King put it.

To know what this Movement is and was (they say it is dead), this revolution, this lucid, eloquent speech, this rebuke, plea, school, this never-to-be-silenced statement of denied bodies in America, one must listen to the *No* in the act of Rosa Parks's body on that bus in Montgomery, Alabama, in December, 1955. It was the accumulated *No* of Negro history in America.

The body speaking in tongues . . . speech rammed back into acts. Laws and books and long speeches in words did not awaken movement.

Stokely Carmichael once said, "We have driven ourselves nearly crazy trying to convince you that we don't want to harm you." Listen to him then, back *then*, before that speech regressed into "Burn, Baby, Burn." All black acts were once speech that went unheard, speech silenced and rammed back into history and into acts.

Yes, the woman will give me that look and then she will defer to me, not as a Negro used to defer to a white, but as a human being taking a chance on speech in a borrowed voice, a chance on the word.

Mrs. Clury, like our neighbor in Atlanta, is one of the mere 2 percent of Negro women over sixty-five with incomes of more than $2,000 a year. She is, by that fact alone, quite a rare old woman. She is about seventy-two years old, Charity estimates.

This is my first encounter with resistance from a Negro woman, and it is of a peculiarly friendly sort. She is obviously eager to talk but only on her own terms, at her own pace, and providing the information of her choice. No questions, it is implied, will be answered except the most benign and impersonal. Fair enough.

She sits on the edge of a Victorian love seat in this somber parlor; I take a chair at her side and start to put the small tape recorder on the table between us. To do it, I must move a small china figurine and an ash tray, which appears never to have known use. Since she is talking, I move these things carefully, automatically, to the back of the table to make room for my equipment. Without raising an eyebrow or changing tone and pace of her monologue, she returns them to their original places. I hold the tape recorder on my lap, therefore, and wait.

And wait.

She likes to talk. She talks about one of her grandfathers who was president of a small business college, then went into real estate and made a lot of money. After ten minutes of fluent recollection, she asks me, "Do you want to put that machine on the table?"

"Please. It works better if it stands free. I can put it here on the edge. It's very steady and won't fall."

She carefully removes the ash tray and figurine and we begin. I have been properly castigated and humbled. I recall, to comfort myself for the social blunder, that Charity told me Mrs. Clury rents two upstairs rooms to college girls, Negro, but will not let their boy friends come into this parlor when they call. They stand in the hall because, as Mrs. Clury puts it, "I don't want them sitting on my chairs with their dirty trousers." The assumption that their trousers are dirty no matter who they are is amusing to Charity. "I've seen some of those boys," she says, her literal mind at work. "They are just as neat and clean as Mrs. Clury's son. She's just worried about that pretty parlor. It's her pride, that room. She'll keep it like that till she dies and then her children will come in there and sell all that stuff . . . maybe sell the house, too."

That finicky pride of ownership entirely escapes Charity whose house is open to every creature in need. She says that months pass before she is without an overnight guest. She has housed black and white, young and old, spongers, strays and the hunted. As Charity is, herself, a kind of shelter, a place, no doubt they come there for that fastness in her nature more than for the bed and board.

Mrs. Clury, however, surprises me. She slowly reveals herself as a shy, maternal, yet open-minded, very intelligent and well-read woman with ideas of her own and a few almost radical projections. Materially she is conservative. She sits on the rosy love seat in the parlor as if holding court, her cane nearby (she is slightly lame with arthritis), her manicured hand, antique and Jesuitical, spread out on the arm of the couch as if ready to give some crucial sign or benediction. It is still yet agitated, hard to ignore.

She talks of the room, the house, her belongings—that furniture over there, those were the first three pieces she bought when she was married, over fifty years ago.

"My children used to say, 'Mama, when are you going to buy some new furniture?'" She laughs. "But I say, 'Well, I don't owe anybody anything on this that I have.' And then, I observed that after a few years all my stuff came back in style again."

The quaint irony in her voice brings a surprised laugh from me. I like this sardonic, intelligent old woman very much. She is sly but forthright, too, very honest, I feel. She has character—that old-fashioned thing that used to be called character. Now one might say that a person has soul. But Mrs. Clury has character of the nineteenth century sort.

Women? Well, we could go on all day about women. She has an opinion on most every subject.

"The Movement is doing a lot for women. There was a time when we had no reason to air our grievances; we knew they weren't going to be heard and nobody could do anything about it. So, most women kept their troubles to themselves because, as you know, the Negro man had no status whatsoever. In most families the mother had to fend for the brood. In fact, a man probably didn't make too much and what he made he would just turn over to her. As a rule the mother worked for some white person."

And then she drifts, on the thinnest thread provided by her last statement, to other matters—

"But the thing that amuses me," and here a long dramatic, ruminative pause (this is a very controlled, canny woman with a great sense of dramatic timing), "what amuses me, I tell my white friends, is that you say we Negroes can't learn enough to compete but I want to tell you you've got some awful stupid white women around. A Negro woman could bring what was left on the dishes and borrow a little here and there, scraps—they call that toting, you know—and come home with enough food to feed six or seven children and the white woman didn't even notice it! She didn't even know what she needed for cooking. That kept that Negro family alive. Half the children couldn't grow up without that extra. The white woman was awful lazy or awful stupid, one or the other. She didn't even look to see."

Or, I think, remembering my own mother and grandmother, she saw and looked the other way. It was, in fact, sometimes an act of underground collaboration between women—black and white—a spiritual bond that has always existed in the South. Sometimes, too, it was designed to keep a beggar a beggar, but not always.

"I think," Mrs. Clury drifts on, "the Movement is greatly benefiting the white woman. I knew quite a few whites before the Movement started. In fact, the high school I attended and where my father taught, had only white women and Negro men as teachers. Those women were American missionary workers who came down from the North to teach the poor Negroes, you know. Now, you can imagine they were ostracized and they had no social contact with the white people of the city at all. Even if they went to the white churches they were left alone. There they sat and I don't think anybody even spoke to them. And so they became very good friends with the Negro families. I was accustomed to them coming in and out of my mother's home. My . . ." she hesitates, not wanting the thread broken as she moves to another aspect of this thinking. Her voice is very low, slow, ponderous, scratchy with age and with the quality of confidence that reduces one's voice to a whisper. She drums on the arm of her love seat with meditative rhythm. I am forgotten. She stares into the middle of the room and across to the portraits of her ancestors on the opposite wall.

"But I say—they're always talking about not wanting us to mongrelize *their* race, but look what they've done to *ours!* You've got to get over into the Mississippi delta country way back in those woods and little Negro farms to find a real black human being anymore."

I am touched by a remote sorrow in her voice. She is far from a pure black human; half her grandparents were white. She has been mongrelized, this refined and intelligent old lady: a regrettable condition, she implies. She has lived between white and black worlds, maybe not quite at home anywhere. Wealth and unusual intelligence, very light skin, white friends, all these can still isolate a Negro woman in a Southern town.

Mrs. Clury thinks that high school education is necessary for all people but not college. "Some people," she puts it gracefully, "are . . . uh . . . skilled. They should go to vocational schools. But they should have a few college subjects. I don't think they can ever get enough English. And, in my opinion, everybody ought to study psychology. It's very important to an opening of the mind. So few people in the world know what they are doing.

"Now, I finished what was called normal school and had a certificate to teach. That's one year over high school. But I have taken a lot of night courses and attended lectures and seminars and I read a lot. What surprises me—I have gone into some of the most beautiful homes in this country and I looked around and couldn't find a book anywhere in the place. That just amazed me. I don't know what those people *do* when they aren't working. My whole family was a reading family, my children too and theirs."

"Do you know many bookish Negro people, or Negroes who read a lot, I mean?"

"Well, a few, of course. But, you know, the possession of a book is something different from reading it out of the library. If you can buy your own books then you are in a different . . . category as a reader. Wasn't long ago anyway when most Southern Negroes had no access to a library. No, I would say that was one of the most cruel punishments—not being able to use a library, not *knowing* about a library even. Think of it! If you couldn't buy them or borrow them, you didn't become a reader. But they read magazines, Negroes do."

"Yes, I've heard many Negroes refer to magazines as books."

"Yes, I hear that, too. But education being so important to a Negro family, they have a great reverence for the printed word. You'd be surprised. I see it now at these church meetings concerned with integrating the schools—the great desire of those illiterate parents for their children to have an education. They'd die for that, some of them." She gives me a look of revelation. "Some of them *have* died, just for that."

She says later, "Nothing wrong with women working. I can't believe that it hurts the family. Two salaries are necessary in the South when you're bringing up children, especially if you are a Negro. With the high cost of living, unless a man is very fortunate, he just can't make enough to support a family. The cost of sending children to school is increasingly . . . prohibitive."

All this is said in the softest, most thickly Southern speech, drawled, with a few hesitations that seem painfully long but are not made for lack of language—only for the sake of that built-in dramatic rhythm and because she is old; occasionally she must gather up her pulse again, get her breath, and, of course, not let her diction slip. It is flawless. She takes pride in language and talk. The word—her pride is a high level of that same passion she mentioned, the passion for education among Negroes. I understand more deeply than before what it must have meant to curious and highly intelligent slaves to be deprived of learning, of books and the word. All their genius went into speech and act. Their speech, which the entire South borrowed and worshiped and passed on to its children, is still inventive, acutely descriptive, and stylishly employed; individual styles abound. One feels that in Mrs. Clury a grand, dramatic, and highly colorful woman, an actress perhaps, lives and slowly dies—back inside that baroque and haughty creature. She is a complex and powerful woman. She presumes respect and receives it.

I ask her opinions about birth control, and suddenly she freezes. "I think," she says evasively and disapprovingly, "that is a matter between a woman and her private physician."

Annoyed, I push a little. "But supposing a woman is on relief, has six children, maybe she's quite young still and her husband has left or she never had one and she doesn't have a private physician? Suppose she has been delivered of her babies by a midwife and rarely even visits a clinic. Do you think some sort of publicity program concerning birth control should be aimed at her? Should society attempt to educate her with regard to birth control?"

"Well," she wavers, challenged but still offended by the general subject. "I believe that . . . yes, she ought to be made aware of it by the clinic. But you can't educate a poor illiterate woman to one thing. You have to educate her all the way around before she is going to understand just that one thing. She has to understand *why* she shouldn't have more babies."

"Don't you feel, Mrs. Clury, that in some cases she would be *glad* to stop having them? That it's a physical burden to her?"

"Oh, I know that. I don't doubt that at all. Six is too many children for any woman."

I regret my annoyance. She is plainly confused by any subject that touches on sex and I have forced her. I retreat, and almost immediately she begins to talk pleasantly about her furniture again, her plans some years ago for a sun parlor and how she changed them in order to have a larger sitting room. One large room is more useful than two small ones. The tape, which both of us have forgotten, runs out as we sit and pass the time of day a little before lunch.

I hear her on the telephone later talking to someone about plans to create a regular monthly meeting for local rural teachers to air their grievances, hopefully trying to induce white county officials to attend. She comes away from the phone chuckling and says to Charity:

"Did you see their faces when Mr. Phillips answered those questions yesterday? They've been hearing that kind of put-off for so many years they could repeat it in their sleep. He knew it. He was nervous. I spoke to him last week and he said 'Miz Clury, I'm doing what I can for them but I have a stiff board of directors to fight.' Well, I guess he does but I remember in 1940 when he beat his son so hard they had to call the sheriff because that boy went to visit a colored girl. I remember that and I don't think he's going to get better pay for those Negro teachers or even buy a new desk."

"I think he's changing," says Charity simply. "I think he sees he has to change. I talked to him and I told him I knew he was struggling and I told him I was praying for him."

In the meeting night before last, in a huge old red brick church, the young Negro assistant pastor opened with a long fervent prayer that God would help and protect and guide the whites through this hard period of change; that He would cause them to repent where they had brought pain and deprivation and that He would release them from their guilt because the world knows how they suffer. At this meeting were white men who only a few years ago would have laughed at the mere suggestion of attending a meeting in a Negro church. My own vague feelings of chagrin and embarrassment at being prayed for must have been a shallow version of what they experienced. Mr. Phillips' head, nearly bald, tasseled with white thin hairs on the sides, was very red, stiffly bowed but not low. He submitted to that strange rite in which a tyrant is forgiven and purified by his victim; when he spoke later, platitudes and perhaps shallow promises, it must have cost him a lot. I pitied him.

But all this praying is sincere, one feels. Even when the prayers are uttered by rote, there is a commitment to universal love. Love—that is the subject everywhere among Negroes. One must love his fellows and that loving, while difficult, is the only salvation. The women sing and moan and shout it. They shout where the men show more restraint. Praise in song is apparently easier for a man—that and long eloquent preaching. Perhaps the women shout and thrash and "fall out" in the service more often than men because they do not have the privilege nor the restriction offered by preaching.

At lunch we talk, Charity, Mrs. Clury, and I, while Edna takes a nap. I mention Mrs. Eleanor Roosevelt for some reason, and they express enthusiasm. About the possibility of a woman president Mrs. Clury says:

"Well, I don't think that will be soon but I think it will happen, don't you, Miz Simmons?"

"It's hard for me to say, hard for me to see," says Charity. "I feel like the more freedom in the world, the more we'll see the right kind of man in politics and that may keep the women out. We've got the wrong kind of man in politics now but it's changing."

I agree with her but am more hopeful about a woman.

"When I look at Mrs. Indira Gandhi," says Mrs. Clury, "I feel very confident about women getting more political power, but I find it difficult to believe that India would be more forward looking than America. Women kept their faces covered in India not so long ago and look at them now. They've come a long way. But . . . we've had some pretty smart American women in public life at various times."

We eat a thick chicken soup, biscuits, overcooked green beans flavored with a piece of salt pork. They drink coffee and I tea, which Mrs. Cotton has made so strong I can hardly swallow it. I suspect she has not often made tea and believes it must look as black as coffee. For dessert we have a deliciously tart apple cobbler with a perfect crust. I beam at Mrs. Cotton who gives me a shy toothless smile and fades into the kitchen.

"I've got to eat all these good things up now," says Mrs. Clury, "because she's going down home next week. Her daughter's about to have a baby and I knew she wanted to go but she wouldn't say so. I had to tell her to go." She has lowered her voice, but except for the ticking of clocks, the house is so stony quiet I cannot believe Mrs. Cotton does not hear. "She's very . . . subservient. That's the problem of this old-fashioned kind of poor Negro woman, you see. She never got out of the servant class. She could have done something else. She's intelligent. But she was illiterate and there was no place to go."

Mrs. Cotton, it seems, was a splendid mother whose children have at least a high school education; one attended college. They are proudly middle class, but she remains a servant shuffling about in house slippers, toothless and humble. Later Charity informs me that, thanks to Mrs. Clury, Mrs. Cotton has a perfectly good set of false teeth, but she finds them uncomfortable.

She will neither have them adjusted nor get new ones and really seems to prefer to leave them out. How does she eat? Sips a little of this and that, dips the biscuits in coffee. She is large, very heavy and tall. I am dubious. But she will remain a mystery to me. They cannot believe that I am interested in talking with her, and we have no time anyway.

Some women drop by, just before we leave, to bring papers and talk briefly with Charity. Mrs. Clury, I see now, is indeed somehow set apart. She is an aristocrat, and her age, perhaps her cane, and her haughtiness do not help her guests relax. They speak in confidence and even with affection to Charity whom they know very slightly. With Mrs. Clury they are formal, polite. We sit in the parlor again while Charity does business with the women. She seems to sense that I am thinking in these ways.

"I've always had a great deal of respect shown me," she says suddenly. "My daughter says it's because of my cane but I don't think so. I always had it, in the stores, everyplace. But I've noticed since the Movement that in a store, if I'm buying a piece of material or something, a white woman will say to me, 'Oh, I wouldn't get that here. It won't hold up. They have a better grade of it at ———,' some other store she went to. You know, that way women talk in a store. They try to make acquaintance and show their friendliness. But even before, I was never called by my first name or had any kind of insult personally in my whole life in Montgomery. My daughter, though, is different. She had a quick temper and I used to caution her not to make a scene anywhere. At that time we had no redress at all, we Negroes. Nothing would be accomplished by making trouble except that you'd be slapped in the face or put down on the sidewalk. Or in jail." She laughs. "I was in jail, you know. Something about my license not allowing me to chauffeur. My daughter was so upset, she took a plane here and came down to that jail so fast! They had to let her in; she would have shoved those men up against the wall. But the leaders here kept her peaceful until I was released. It didn't take long. After that, when so many of us were in jail, the jail lost its stigma." She laughs almost tearfully. "A man I know has a little boy about nine years old at that time and he said one night, 'Daddy, why didn't you go to jail? Jimmy's daddy was arrested and Peggy's mother was put in the jail. Why didn't you go?' You didn't have any prestige around here at that time if you hadn't been in jail.

"Well, the strict way I was brought up meant that I had to wait for the Movement and my old age to experience some of the most important things in my life, but I don't regret it. It thrills me to see the courage of the young people. All the people. The courage will just thrill you when you see it."

"Yes, I know."

"But, we've got trouble to come. The problems aren't much different now, there is just more hope for solutions."

"What's the biggest problem of a woman's life, Mrs. Clury?"

"Oh . . . how to hold her family together."

"What if she doesn't have a family and isn't going to?"

"Well, then that throws her with the men and she has to compete. She can compete all right, but that causes a lot of friction and heartache. I told my daughter when she divorced her first husband, 'If you have to live alone with these two babies, you'll have to work.' Now, I could have given her money but I knew she'd never have any life if she had a steady income and stayed home with those two children all alone. I strongly advised her go to work for a while after that break and she was glad. She met her new husband and they have a happy marriage now. Her first was a drinker and a weak man. A very good man but just too weak for a strong girl like my daughter. She was in a conflict for a long time over him because . . . well, she loved him. I think she loved him more than she ever will this new one.

"The worst thing that can happen to a woman is to love a weak man. If she protects him, she makes him weaker; and if she doesn't, then he'll go off and find some other woman who will. Of course, there's a lot of family trouble among Negroes because of weakness in Negro men. But they don't bother to mention that most of our families stay married. The broken family is a minority, even if it is a big one."

"Did you read the Moynihan report?" I ask.

"Yes, I did. I think it was interesting and had a lot of truth in it but the thing they left out was the value carried by the *strong* Negro family. It isn't the strong white family that is the ideal to the Negro. It's the strong Negro family. And there are a lot of them. You can see it. It's growing. The spiritual power of the Negro family is very great."

"Do you disagree with the sociologists who say that a major cause of rift in Negro families is the Negro woman's greater exposure to white middle class styles which makes her look down on her husband?"

"No . . . no, I don't disagree with that. It's true because at one time a Negro woman had almost no other . . . uh . . . model, you might say, but the white woman she worked for. She saw the way they served food and kept the house and clothed the children and she naturally learned a lot from it. Her husband might be out there plowing a field or digging a well and come home dirty. His manners wouldn't be so good. That was hard for both of them.

"Lots of healing to be done between Negro men and women. Lots of it. They need some peace and security just for that alone."

"How would you have felt if your daughter had not married?"

"I would have been worried, I believe. Because she was a temperamental person like her father and . . . well, you can't tell, any girl can get into trouble until she settles down."

"Is settling down always a matter of marriage?"

"That's the only way I see for a woman to settle down in our world today. If she works in a career that consumes all her energy, then maybe she can make it that way. But usually she can't settle unless she marries. Men and women need each other. People need a home. All people. And we need our *own* home. I could go live with my son or my daughter. They both have room for me and they want me, but I want my own home. I want to die in my own house. I'll never die in a hospital. That's one reason people die—because they put them in a hospital.

"You see, that's all part of what is meant by this Black Power talk that's got people so stirred up. Black Power means Negroes having a few choices, making their own decisions. I can make mine because I already have Black Power. I'm economically independent and if I don't want to die in some general hospital, I don't have to. I can *choose*, you see. And that's power. I can shop somewhere else if the local store is rude to me. I can go all the way to Atlanta if I have to. I can move to another city.

"I have control over my life, to a certain extent. And that's the right of every human being. That's how I interpret Black Power and I don't see what's so alarming about it except of course that white people believe that if a Negro eats well and owns his own house or his own business, then *they* are going to lose *theirs!*

"Sometimes I am amazed at how little white people know about the wealth of their own country. They don't inform themselves."

Charity interrupts us. The women speak politely to Mrs. Clury and me. She makes hardly a sound of goodbye, gives only a haughty little nod. I think of my snobbish grandmother who was actually only shy and who deprived herself of a rich life by remaining inside the sanctuary of that shyness. I sympathize with Mrs. Clury. Her ideas ought to be heard beyond this local sphere. She is growing old. Once she had all those days to give. She, a crippled old woman, came out in poignant gallantry where she was needed and gave her three hundred and eighty-one days. I take her hand when we leave and would like to kiss her cheek in the unself-conscious manner that I would with Charity, but she is formidable. She would be embarrassed. We part as strangers.

MISSISSIPPI

Mud with ice over it, a thin film, like sugar and water icing. Charity and I arrive in town late and find a Negro filling station at which to ask directions to the Holiday Inn. A man jumps in his car and leads us there, the usual kindness that never ceases to amaze me.

We go to the desk together. Although Holiday Inns are integrated, I have yet to see a Negro behind the desk there or in any but menial work. The white woman at the desk, after only a brief glance at her chart, tells us the place is full. I am dubious. The front parking lot is almost empty. Charity seems to shrink beside me. I look at her and she lowers her head, turning away slightly, ready to go, an unfamiliar attitude. She does not believe it. As an alternative I ask for a single room with a cot, but there is nothing available at all. I look the woman in the eye, finding it difficult to do. She recommends other places, her voice quiet; she is poised. Maybe Charity and I are being too sensitive and the place actually is full. Charity goes to a phone booth to call her friend Mrs. Parks.

114

"You might try Haven House Motel," the clerk suggests. "I sent some folks over there about an hour ago. Usually the management will call me if they're full and I've sent over folks we can't handle."

She's being honest, I tell myself. But I test her.

"Will they take us together?"

"We're all integrated here. You shouldn't have any trouble."

But I know what I know about Mississippi.

Mrs. Parks has given Charity the address of the new Negro motel where we decide to stay. We go to the Holiday Inn dining room after calling the Negro motel to make reservations. It is dark now. Outside thick ice has formed on the drive and heavy frost on the car windows. We sit at a corner table, Charity a touch humiliated and I, because of it, irritated. I cannot bear to see her in that attitude although I realize that her usual modesty would allow only someone close to her to notice the difference. She does not look at me. I cannot believe it.

"I think they're really full, Charity. The dining room seems crowded for this hour."

"Maybe so."

She is actually changed! Charity Simmons! I am miserable and can't squelch the annoyance I feel at her reduction. A strange veil, that old evasive, faintly sullen quality that now and then overtakes a Negro, has surrounded Charity Simmons, my stanch friend, this noble, dignified, humble, and emancipated woman. I cannot eat. She eats methodically. This is the first time I have seen her eat without pleasure. Even so she puts away half a fried chicken with all trimmings. We are silent.

"Charity . . . let's order a drink, some beer or wine or something."

She is, as usual, agreeable and gentle. Beer it is. It loosens her. By the time she gets her coffee the awful veil has lifted. A sense of rejection vanquished her temporarily, maybe because she could feel the rejection coming rather than because it actually existed. In our talk of recent doings in Mississippi we discuss the fact that a very wealthy and educated Negro woman in the area was publicly called "nigger." Charity, still not looking at me, says very quietly:

"Well, I'm not a nigger. Those things don't make a definition."

I become irrationally annoyed that she had to say it.

I want to ask her about one Negro calling another "nigger," but the idea that we are even on the subject somehow infuriates me and confounds her, I feel. We have never discussed, exactly, that ridiculous insult of "nigger." It never seemed significant enough to discuss. Now, somehow we have come upon it. It is a sort of hot potato. Did the woman at the desk toss it to us? Is Charity, in that woman's mind, a nigger and I a nigger-lover? Or . . .

All at once I feel an intense if silent communication from Charity. I feel her denying what she at first allowed herself to experience: denying the idea that *I also refused her at that desk* because the woman and I are both white, because if that woman can do it, then I can and do do it. Or something like that.

I am miserable and have a sense of betrayal.

The Negro motel is stark but clean and has good beds. The heat is not on and must be adjusted. Finally the manager, a tall, fleshy, smooth-talking, light-skinned man (I have begun to remark shades the way I hear my Negro friends do) fixes it but in order to have this heat we must endure the almost deafening roar of a blower in the machinery. The television set does not work, but except for the news, neither of us watches much anyway.

Charity usually avoids taking a bed until I choose one or bring up the subject. I cannot get her to choose. Tonight she is very tired and seems relieved to be in this hospitable place. She takes the bed nearest the window and also goes into the bathroom first, another rare move. Suddenly she comes out of the bathroom holding a small waffle-weave sort of rag in her hands, a disposable washcloth.

"Now, look at this! This is what the Negroes have to learn. We're payin' just about the same price for this place and he gives us this kinda cloth. Be better not to give one at all than this. And look at that—the TV doesn't work and the heat makes so much noise we have to shout. See, that's what they need to learn—that they have to compete with the best to stay in business. People traveling are tired and they want comfort. That Holiday Inn room would have been warm when we first went in and everything in just the right condition."

I agree but feel like defending our host who has probably embarked on a venture far removed from his usual experience and with limited finances. We were told that he had a little café and pool hall before this. I know from a small amount of travel here that compared to other Negro-owned motels this is luxurious. But Charity is hard on him tonight, her voice full of the patient scorn that bears, I suspect, an unconscious weight of anger and self-condemnation, the disgust of failure, that began at Holiday Inn earlier. That place passed its judgment on us, and she is trying to swallow that judgment in spite of her position and her wisdom and her strength. She is human, after all. I have been thinking of her as superhuman. I have done her a disservice. If she could not feel, too, then how would she know so deeply what other people suffer?

When we turn down our beds and find too few blankets, Charity finally laughs and sighs. The spell seems to be broken. I call for more blankets.

"I'm going to tell him tomorrow," she says. "He's probably never been in a good motel in his life."

We both lie awake a long time, silently, in the dark. As always, she says her quiet prayers after the lights are out. I remember her saying, "Every night I put myself in the Lord's care, in his trust." Most Negro women I meet speak with affection and without self-consciousness of "The Lord." Often I feel intrusive, but she encourages our frequent time together. She wants this book to exist. She wants us to be seen in that car together: that is education, for us and for the world. She wants us all to partake of one another's lives, intimately. She wants all the barriers down.

I tell her she has seemed too critical of this place tonight.

"Would you be so critical if you were traveling alone?"

"Well, maybe not," she says softly. "You're right. If you hadn't come in here with me, I don't know if I would have seen all these things. I'm seein' 'em with your eye in a way, I guess. I'm used to livin' with what Negroes have to put up with and maybe I wouldn't even notice."

"This doesn't seem like putting up with much to me, Charity. It's nice, really. It's very clean and new and the beds are good."

"That's not enough for Negroes now when they get into business. They got to compete with the *best*. Those big motels integrate and you'll find the Negroes will stay over there, not here, if he doesn't fix this up. You notice in the shower, he doesn't have all his tiles up yet. This place has been here ten months, maybe a year. That won't do. He'll lose out. But I'm going to tell him in the morning."

And she does. I wait in the car, warming it up. The man comes out with her, deferential and gracious. He does not know that she is in the Movement. She presents only her Homeland Ministries identification when she travels.

Mrs. Parks and her neighbor, Miss Demerest, who teach citizenship classes at night for Charity's program, have decided to take the day off to show us around town.

The decision is made in Mrs. Parks's living room where we sit in several large garish but comfortable overstuffed chairs. The little gas stove sputters and throws out an abundance of heat, and the windows steam and drip. The place smells of gas. The floors are covered with linoleum, brilliantly clean. The curtains of this tiny frame house, as well as the tablecloth, are of lace. Mrs. Parks lives here with her family. Her husband, who was beaten and suffered emotional collapse at the infamous Parchman prison during the 1964 Freedom Summer, now spends about two-thirds of his time in an institution for mental patients and cannot work. At present he is home. He moves about at the back of the house, peering at us uneasily through the rooms. This is a two-bedroom, sleeping-porch house in which seven live, including Mrs. Parks's mother.

Miss Demerest is a rugged-looking young woman with an earthy quality bursting from her countenance and her voice. "It's Miss, *not Mrs.*, please. I'm not married, thank you, Jesus!" We all laugh. "I'm gonna say I got appendicitis when I call up the lady I work for." More laughter. Mrs. Parks, very quiet and modest, laughs and offers me an apologetic look. Miss Ann is being put down.

"Why don't you tell her you just died from overwork and don't feel like coming today," I say. Miss Demerest falls forward with a roar and almost leaves her chair.

We are suddenly pals, exchanging looks of intimate hilarity; we know we can break one another up, which is enough for us. Miss Demerest is very black, blunt, heavy, sturdy, and vital—a little bit mannish and a yet little bit young-girlish. She could be any age from twenty-eight to forty.

They decide to let me listen to the phone calls to their white-lady employers.

Mrs. Parks is refined and mild, an old wisdom and maturity emanating from her tired bony face; she looks at least five years older than she is. She is not yet forty. Her voice is remote; it has the sound of an invalid's but also a sweetness.

"Hello, Miz Rine? This Emma. I have a 'pointment with my husband to see his doctor today. I forgot about it. Could I come on Friday instead? Well, all right. Thank you. Bye."

She is embarrassed and rejects our conniving laughter. Her employer knows of her husband's plight and is somewhat sympathetic.

Miss Demerest says, "She gettin' so she can lie. Took me five years to teach her how to lie without all stammerin' up."

"Okay, now, Ivy, it's your turn."

Ivy Demerest rolls her eyes. "I don't like this lady to begin with and I'm gettin' a new job in the spring. I have a friend givin' up her place that pays mo' than this one I got and twice as nice." She monkeys with the phone, indecisive. Mrs. Parks's telephone is one of three in the block; her number is unlisted since she works with the literacy program. She is a registered voter, and besides almost full-time domestic work for her white employer, she spends many nights teaching illiterate adults. She needs the phone. It is not only unlisted but a private line, although that is a pure waste of her hard-earned money. She receives threatening calls weekly, and her line is connected to at least three others in the town, busy party-liners who leave their phones off the hook. This is common. Several Negro women I have met are plagued the same way, here and in Alabama. The telephone company assures Mrs. Parks that she has a private line and that the wires must be crossed. Many times a party on the line will leave the phone off the hook all night. She is resigned to it but for the sake of a possible future legal suit she continues to pay for private service.

Ivy dials now, looking over her huge hump of shoulder at us coyly. "I can't call with y'all watchin'. Come on, turn the other way!" and giggles. Now she bends over the phone, cupping a hand around the mouthpiece.

"Hello. This Ivy. . . . Yeah . . . well, I'm sorry. I got a bad throat. . . . Yeah . . . Well, my cousin over here seein' to me. Oh, yeah. I think I be all right tomorrow, maybe next day. Yeah . . . Well, I'll see ya then. Bye."

She backs away from the phone, bent over with laughter, teary-eyed. "I forgot . . . Oh, Law, I forgot . . . I done told her some time ago I haven't got any kin in this town at all. Now I got me a cousin!"

We laugh. Miss Ann has been deceived and we can spend the day as we wish. They are very eager to take this time off with me. They want to show me the poorest woman I shall ever meet.

"She down by the rivah, that's where."

"No, I think she do better ovah in Beauford Quarter. I know it. I lived there when we first came here," says Mrs. Parks. We decide to see both places. Before we go, Ivy seizes the small bundle of laundry I had hoped to take to a laundromat and hands it to Mrs. Parks's mother.

"Mrs. Bell do it, won't you, Auntie? They have a machine." The old woman waves a dismissing finger at my protest but says nothing, as if she were mute. Mrs. Parks has arranged it already. I am embarrassed. They have no dryer and will have to hang it about the kitchen, troubling themselves and using extra gas. But they insist. Black women have washed white women's clothes here for centuries and this black woman even seems eager to do it again!

We leave in Ivy's big, third-hand, rattly Oldsmobile, a tomato-red and white car that has the deep growl of antiquity and general ague. She prefers to drive than to ride and seems uncomfortable at the idea of our car, anyway. This is a tour with Ivy as guide.

The People's Co-op Market: this new Negro co-operative grocery store, started with help from the Congress of Racial Equality (CORE), competes in prices and variety with the supermarkets that once had almost all local Negro trade. It is managed by a Negro man and two young male helpers. It appears that most projects started by the Movement, including the big civil rights organizations themselves, are headed by men, if heavily staffed by women. Fannie Lou Hamer's position in Mississippi is unusual. Tonight I will discuss all this with Charity.

Ivy shops at the Co-op once a week for herself and a crippled sister and also takes along her divorced sister-in-law, who has eight children and no car. She drives past two big white-owned markets to patronize this one.

"No trouble when you do it all at once. I'd shop here if it was fifty miles away."

She owns ten shares of the stock. Ivy, in fact, is not doing badly financially. She owns outright her little cottage a few doors from Mrs. Parks's place. The cottage and a small store building were left to her by a grandmother with whom she lived and whom she nursed during the old woman's last five years.

"My family jealous but I worked for it, let me tell you. She was on a bed pan for two and a half years! I used to wash her a change of sheets three times a week, by hand!"

During those years, she shopped, washed by hand, cooked, cleaned, kept a sizable vegetable garden, and worked as a domestic servant two days a week at thirty cents an hour, a rate that did not vary from 1950 to 1959. She now earns sixty cents an hour and hopes soon to get the new job she mentioned that pays eighty cents an hour, the pay Mrs. Parks gets. Both say this is very good money for domestic work.

I buy sandwiches and cookies, which we eat in the car, taking extras for some of the poor children we are bound to run into. I utter some objection to this sort of condescending charity, tell them I would rather give money if I dole out anything, so that people can at least buy what they like and are used to; but they silence me, seem not quite to get the point.

"Honey, don't feel bad about feedin' anybody in Mississippi. My God!" says Ivy. "We all scramblin' for food aroun' here, ain't you heard?" We laugh. Charity, excited, actually bristles with a kind of intensity and agitation. This is her cosmos—a car full of persons off to find the poorest woman in America, to get to the core of her life and her need—to touch it, bring it to light, heal it. This woman will undoubtedly be illiterate or close to it.

The river area yields little that the girls had hoped to find for my purposes. Most of the incredibly patched little hovels are occupied by poor whites who regard our invasion with hostile silence. Leaving, we pass an old black woman with a costume of patches and tatters, ludicrously colorful, and a shawl something like the Mexican rebozo. Ivy stops to talk to her for a few minutes. The woman, about sixty-five years old, would be glad to ask us inside (she inhabits half the lower floor of an abandoned and long-ago-condemned brick building which once warehoused river-boat cargo and which stands in a slouch at the top of the cement ramp leading to an old rotting dock), but she has pneumonia and cannot talk much, just went down to the corner bar for a pint of whiskey to ease her chest pain and "git up" her blood a little. Charity and I give her money. But what about next week and the one following? Charity's face is wan and pensive.

"I'm going to call Reverend K. before we leave and tell him to send somebody down here. The churches can help these people more. You see that crowd last night outside that Methodist church we passed? They all dressed up with furs and feathers!"

And so we go on to Beauford Quarter, the four of us a little depressed and our fun over the truancy of Ivy and Mrs. Parks somewhat dampened.

Movies and television have made the street familiar: a mud hole one block long, wooden shacks with holes in the sides, high covered porches or slumping stoops, the bleached antiqued wood that has never known paint—a driftwood color, beautiful, the beauty surely invisible to those who dwell within—outhouses tilted precariously away from the wind or the mudslide. Several houses have no steps and one mounts to the porch, which is as much as five feet high in some cases, by a wooden crate kept under the porch. One house is unusually neat with a supply of fireplace logs piled carefully on the porch and a line of very clean if frozen laundry hanging across the area on a line from wall to porch pillar and back to wall, blocking the front door. Ivy grabs my arm.

"My God, lookit that! How she goin' to thaw out those clothes?"

Mrs. Parks sighs, looks about in pain as we advance toward the last cottage where a woman stands on her stoop and observes the mud and rubble. Mrs. Parks lived here for two years when she was first married. This was her honeymoon street!

"Let's talk to her. Come on . . . don't be shy. She'll talk to you. I used to live across the road there." Mrs. Parks goes ahead of us. The road of which she speaks is an indefinite terrain of mud and old brush, full of pits and ruts, frozen puddles, and dead branches from the huge trees in the wood just beyond the last houses.

The poorest woman? This large erect woman stands on the collapsed stoop of her cabin and watches our careful approach through the mud. She is of powerful stature, large-breasted, wide-hipped, and tall besides. She stands with feet apart and an expression of kindly indifference on her face. She wears a nondescript collection of garments of dull brown and green wool—a long full skirt that reaches below mid-shin and a sweater with sleeves pulled up, exposing powerful young arms; beneath the sweater she wears an old cotton T shirt or jersey blouse. Hanging below the skirt hem is a garment that is more like another skirt than a petticoat—the effect is of fullness, of several skirts. The costume of the peasant has not varied much in two or three hundred years. The temperature today is not above 40 degrees, but she neither flinches nor huddles against the cold. Something of the landowner among her acres stirs in this woman.

The eyes and the lips are slow: not brooding but still; not dull but passionless. The eyebrows rise a little as we exchange glances. There is ready humor in the terse simple "Hello."

Mrs. Parks asks for an audience, and we are invited to the porch and inside.

How shall you know the dwelling of Mrs. Long unless you have crossed this threshold and absorbed it through eyes, lungs, and fingertips? Mind and heart must be ready to eschew all logic, all concept of shelter, of house. It has been home to Mrs. Long for fifteen years; her four youngest children were born here in the main room. This first room, judging by the presence of the main entrance in it and the ancient brick fireplace—falling down at the mantel, bricks askew at midpoint, and belching out sooty black smoke that has, over the years, colored the walls and the bed linen—judging by these things, was once meant to be a living room. In this front first room, just to the left of the door, two large beds with frames of chipped once-white iron are covered with lumpy fields of ragged quilts, each bearing at the head a pillow now drained of feathers and without any but yellow, stained, ticking covers, limp and slack like the drained breasts of an old bedridden woman.

A human being who came to life among the refuse of these covers stands and sinks into her mother's side, staring with big eyes and daring a smile. She is—

". . . five years old. She the baby. They won't take her up to the school till she six. That the way they does now. My boy, he seventeen, he went to the school when he were fo' years old. But that were in the country. Different here. Here, have you a chair."

She wipes at it vaguely, having pulled it from a corner, and sets it just to the side of the entrance against the open front door. Ivy and Mrs. Parks refuse the chair but I take it, feeling that someone ought to accept. The woman looks at me candidly. Charity has stayed in the car to write a letter.

There is no bathroom here. No running water. A spigot in the ground about twenty-five feet from her door serves the whole street.

I face now the back wall, just opposite the front door. It contains a door sealed by a timber nailed across its face. Against that and near the fireplace is a black kitchen stove, which is unattached to any gas line and has no ventilation pipe. A large tin can and a small deep pan rest on the hearth bricks at the edge of a sloping bank of red coals in the fireplace. Apparently Mrs. Long cooks here.

"Yeah, I does now. My stove don't work." She speaks with a thickness, a rounded loose-lipped forming of the words, with dry-mouth sounds. One feels that she never drinks water. "De kitchen fell off de house lass spring."

Ivy's eyes narrow dramatically, she squeezes back a laugh.

"Fell off?"

"Yes, ma'm. It done fell off. You can go back round there and see fo' youself. My son done broke it up after that to git me some firewood." She laughs with a wheeze. "Made a good fire!"

"So now you cook in the fireplace here?"

"Yessum, that all I got. It's a lotta trouble but my chillrun heps me. They good. All of 'em." There is no whine in her voice. She states the facts and asks for nothing. Humor and stubborn dignity, I have begun to see, are common in poor black women.

Mrs. Parks quizzes her. The block of eight houses, it seems, is owned, as it was fifteen years ago, by a Negro undertaker who has never in that time made one repair of any kind and who just recently "took and died," leaving the property in a legal mess as he had many heirs and no will. CORE members who canvassed the street a year ago to register voters encouraged the residents to stop rent payments until repairs were made. And so Mrs. Long has been fifteen dollars a month richer for one year. However, for three months before that she was unable to pay; so, she figures meticulously, she owes rent for those three months.

Her man—she does not call him husband—comes home now and then to collect a welfare check, gives her a few dollars, and takes the rest with him, disappearing until the next month. Sometimes he does not return and she gets the whole check. She averages full possession of about one-third of the checks.

Her daughter, who is the twenty-year-old unmarried mother of four, has no difficulty in receiving welfare assistance. During the period between leaving school and beginning to bear children, she did domestic work for a white family.

"I'd like to work again. Soon as these kids gits in school." She shares her welfare money with her mother.

"It the only thing we can do," says Mrs. Long. "Sometime my white lady come git me to work but she want full time and I cain't give it and see to my chillrun."

The poor fall in upon one another like the sides of a collapsing box. Statistics fail to record how many stomachs share the monthly food supply allotted for a family of four. Mrs. Long's daughter and her children deprive themselves further for the sake of hungry kin, and welfare knows nothing of it.

How to put these facts on the charts? The poor feed, clothe, house, and *know* the poor.

"Y'all live in here, you and six children now?" asks Ivy.

Mrs. Long reveals, behind another door, another room completely filled with two more double beds, one of which has collapsed at the foot. They support bare, lumpy, stained mattresses with several quilts folded at the head of the bed. The odor of stale urine is strong, although a window is open.

"I tries to air out these chillrun's baid but sometime it git so cold in here till they cain't hardly git to sleep. I be shuttin' this window 'bout three o'clock now in winter."

The "white lady," she says, is nice to her and has given her most of what she owns. Ivy shrugs that off and sighs; in ten years or so the white woman seems to have parted with little of consequence.

Mrs. Long's daughter lives next door. Her house is equipped with an oil-burning stove and as a result is cleaner than her mother's. It has one room: two double beds side by side almost fill it. We give cookies to the children, who are all under six years of age. All are barefoot except the oldest, a boy, who wears large brown hightop shoes. The young mother, Flora, lines them up for thank-yous.

"Say thank you. Whatta you say? Thank you!" holding tightly to the baby's arm and shaking him in a friendly rough manner. She almost shouts, as if they were all deaf or far away. "Say, 'My name Eddie.'" And they parrot her instructions.

"My name Eddie." "Thank you." Giggles. Beaming stares. The cookies are devoured almost desperately; the children look hungry.

They insist that I sit down. Finally, at her daughter's, Mrs. Long will also sit on a chair near me. She is totally, if indifferently, available. She will be glad to talk into the microphone and let me make a tape, but since the others stand about to observe—children, the daughter, Ivy, and Mrs. Parks—I am not to hear what I had hoped.

"I grew up over in the country, with my motha and my auntie and two brothers, five sisters. I like it over there. Yessum, it nice. My motha passed away when I were fifteen and I come here to work. I worked for a white lady. That's what I done most the time. A little spell I worked for a colored lady but mostly I worked fo' whites."

Our audience hangs on every word: spellbound children, hesitant daughter, who hopes either that her mother will not err or that she will say something cruelly true, brutal—I cannot tell which, but the daughter waits, ferociously patient, for something. Mrs. Long proceeds serenely:

"Yes, ma'm, I went to 'bout third grade. My chillrun all in school but this one. She goin' next year. They eats good. Oh, they likes beans and bread, salt meat . . . little rice or potato maybe. Yessum, they gits fruit when they be fruit: grapes, apples, pears. They has hot bread fo' breakfast. They has milk, too. Used to be we tried a garden out here but I don't know, seem like that mud won't grow nothin'. I had me a good garden in the country.

"No'm, I doesn't vote. But I think I'm goin' to vote next time they comes round. No'm, I isn't regiss yet."

"How will you know whom to vote for?"

Her eyes stray toward the door. "Well . . . I'll vote jess what they tells me, I guess. No, I don't have no paper. My neighbor lady she takes the paper. She read it. No, no radio. I used to see a little television at my white lady place, but she lookin' at those . . . stories and that stuff. No news. No, ma'm."

"Do you know who the president of the United States is?"

Ivy leans forward to urge the answer into her head. The daughter grins sheepishly, smacking the leg of a child who laughs. He laughs more, and his mother joins him. General giggles. Mrs. Long looks about, not apologetic but ruminative—indecisive.

"Uh . . . seems like I heard that name but . . ."

"It's President Johnson. Lyndon B. Johnson. He's from Texas."

"That where my son is. He playin' football in a college in Texas. Got him a scholarship, but he comin' home next year 'cause they's another college goin' to give him money. This one only give him books and school things. He don't git money. He have to work in a cafeteria so he can eat and buy his clothes. But next year he goin' to do better.

"Yes, ma'm, he do well. He very smart. All my kids is smart. I wants 'em to stay in school if I can keep 'em dress and eatin'."

"Does he vote?"

"Not yet, but he say he definitely goin' to vote when he come the age."

"Do you know who the governor of Mississippi is?"

"Uh . . ." She smiles at me and makes a long try. "President Johnson?"

Mrs. Parks moves forward to defend. "*Paul* Johnson. That's right, but they're different Johnsons."

If she were in trouble she would ask a policeman's help; any policeman, white or black. White women she trusts most of the time. "Some is bad but mos' is good." White men? There is an explosion of laughter; the daughter claps her hand over her mouth. Mrs. Long rolls her eyes. "I wouldn't know about no *white mens!* No, ma'm!"

What's the matter with women's lives, what's the hardest thing for a woman? Men. Men are not too good. Most of them are not much. Even preachers. As doctors and lawyers, women are fine. As preachers? Maybe not.

"I'll talk to a woman but not to no man, 'less he my brother."

The trouble with the world is "greedy peoples and too much po' peoples."

"What I likes? Well, I likes to eat and get me some good sleep and I likes to go to town, but I doesn't go much because it's kinda far away. And I likes my neighbors. No'm, I doesn't go to church but my chillrun sometimes goes. I prays to the Lord and that's why I'm here today.

"Well . . . what I'm goin' to do? I . . . don't know what I'm goin' to do. Git these chillrun raised and . . . maybe I work again. My lady don't need me now but might be she need me next year . . . or I need to find me a new house. My husban'? Well, he taken the welfare money. He the one asked fo' it in the first place, so they gives it to him. If I tells 'em he out of town, then they give it to me but mostly he come git it and take it away. His chillrun doesn't see much o' that money. Well, if I tells 'em how he do, then maybe they stop it all the way."

Mrs. Parks stands near her. "If I bring a school class down here in the evening, would you like to come to it? Would you like to improve your reading and writing and maybe have some kind of training? Learn more about your rights?"

"Yes, ma'm, I would. I'd come. I likes books. My white lady gives me some books, time to time."

By "books," as is often the case among Negroes I meet, she

means magazines. Her daughter proudly displays a small but tidy pile of old women's magazines on the floor under the window.

"Will you answer me if I write you a letter, Mrs. Long?"

"I sho' will. I'll answer you, Honey."

LOUISIANA

Traveling north through Louisiana. Charity talks about Plaquemines: "See, when they desegregated those public schools, they set up some quick white private schools in Plaquemines Parish. And then the people got up some protest meetings against the governor because he promised to support those segregationists with public school funds! That Leander Perez and those other men! Can you believe that—promising to use public school funds? Well, after the protest, the governor turned around and made another statement saying that he wouldn't interfere with the desegregation or use the funds after all. That protest helped but there's more to it than that. I've got to talk to Reverend S. and find out all that happened. I know they've got a lot of trouble still. The public schools are still segregated, more or less. That Judge Christenberry of Plaquemines Parish was pretty good. He asked the Justice Department to bring contempt of court against the Plaquemines School officials for trying to bring the public school teachers over to those private schools.

"That's the thing, see, those white children are being pushed in and out of those schools, out of the public into that private school that doesn't have enough teachers and their education is going to be a mess all year because of those grown men tryin' to keep little Negro and white children from sittin' in the same room! Hard to believe sometimes what a grown man will do. Deacons For Defense going to be coming in there to help integration. That city attorney over at Bogalusa is trying to get the Deacons investigated for preaching violence and arming their members, but some people say *he's* a member of the Klan. It's a mess!

"But I was in a meeting in a church not too long ago when the Klan gathered in the parking lot of a supermarket across the street. We advised the people to sit quietly in the church until the Klan got tired and left. But it was after midnight and they were still over there in their white robes and those people sitting in that hot church just as peaceful as you can imagine. We sang a lot and nobody got panicky. Finally, when we decided we had to leave the church and go home, we were going to file out quietly and try to send them home in groups when the door opened and in walk the Deacons. We didn't send for them but they got word somehow. The leader was armed and some of the others too. They led the people out and stood guard at the church. Nobody said a word but the Klan saw those big men with those firearms and they just broke up and went home. All our people got home safely. Nobody fired a shot but the Deacons carried those guns in plain sight."

She was proud and impressed by the Deacons' defense of their people, but she is troubled by the show of firearms and the implications of violence.

We cross the muddy river and enter the town of Plaquemine, finding the house of a Negro leader, Mr. Kendall, with whom she has business. I talk to two local young Negro women who come to Mr. Kendall's house from a nearby beauty shop in a neighbor's home. Their heads are under white towels, their hair long, frizzy, just clean, and not yet pressed or straightened. They look out at me from under the overhanging towels like two shy Arab girls in purdah. They are best described by that old word "countrified." They seem startled, wary, sitting with the still alertness of young deer sensing danger. Their shyness, and the fact that Charity and Mr. Kendall sit in audience, means I will not have the sort of conversation with them that I had hoped.

"I hear you've had a lot of trouble at the schools. Did either of you take part in any integration or demonstration?"

"I went to the white school. Yes, ma'm. But I come back over to the colored school again."

"Why? Was it too difficult?"

"Yes, ma'm. They was mean. And they close the school."

This girl, who is nineteen or twenty, came into town a few years ago to live with a relative and enter high school. She goes home to her family about once a month if she can get a ride and returns with farm produce to pay for her keep at the relative's house.

"Oh . . . I brings a ham and some chickens and some vegetable my sister put up. Like that. Lass time we brang in some firewood."

The other one is older, seems a bit more sophisticated. When I ask who is stronger, a woman or a man, she looks around the room in confusion, slides a glance at Mr. Kendall's feet, and says:

"Well . . . seem like you can depend on a woman mo'. Most the work in the church and integration is womens. Ain't that right?"

Mr. Kendall agrees with conviction. He says it is hard to get men involved, for a lot of reasons. "Many are working outside town; some are afraid. It is no shame to be afraid here. We have seen the threats carried out."

The girls are not Catholic but are vehemently opposed to birth control; they think of it, Charity tells me later, as a form of abortion. All Negro women I have met so far are strongly opposed to abortion, for religious or medical reasons, or both.

Both girls say education, meaning high school, is important. The older works for a white family with four children over in Baton Rouge. She lives in four days a week and dislikes it. She has a child who is being raised by his grandmother. The younger hopes to find something besides domestic work after high school but may have to return to the farm to help her mother and sisters. "I rather go up North, I got a cousin in Detroit. She say I can work in a plant, maybe." It all sounds dreamy and unlikely. They lack conviction. The older one has a quietly desperate quality and a chronically woeful expression. The younger wants to marry soon. The older is not interested. Money solves most problems. Police are to be feared, usually. Women gossip and if you can find a good man, he's the best confidant. Neither votes; the younger will when possible.

Both avidly watch television and agree that "General Hospital" is the best program. "It the most interesting and just—real-like, you know. Make me think I would like to be a nurse." The young one laughs shyly at herself. "But I hear you has to have a lot of money for the trainin'."

They like women's magazines and learn a lot from them. "I say you just as well read those books at home as go to some of these country schools, because you don't learn nothin' in those little schools. You just set over there and fool around, play in the yard."

They laugh.

Both like to cook, and the younger says she is a good cook. Both sew. Both dislike housework but try to do it well. Both are vague but somewhat skeptical about the Johnson Administration. Both cried over the death of President John Kennedy. Although neither has voted, they are somewhat interested in local political affairs; they are dimly aware of national politics.

Mrs. Kendall, who has been rattling around in the kitchen just off this room, suddenly appears with a large tray of refreshments: tea and coffee, Neapolitan ice cream, and homemade sugar cookies. Each of us is supplied with a folding table and served rather formally, a paper doily in the saucer and another on the tray itself. There are paper cocktail napkins and small wine glasses of water with shaved ice. Everything is spotless, dainty, and served with much gravity.

We eat in silence, the girls in purdah nibbling cookies very self-consciously. Charity makes a little conversation with Mr. Kendall. His family is well but his children have had trouble in town; one of them was jumped on by several large white boys. Often the girls are jeered at, and the family has resigned itself to the obscene telephone calls. His phone, like Mrs. Parks's in Mississippi, is supposedly private but is continually used by other parties.

Before we leave, his mother, who lives there also, enters the room carrying one of the children, a very large, mentally retarded girl who, although about seven years old and long-limbed like her father, is quite infantile. She wears diapers under her white cotton pajamas. She is scrubbed and soapy-smelling. She ogles us with a slobbering grin that has a mad, touching charm. She is introduced to the "folks" and gives us a kind of vague scrutiny. She is beautiful except for the idiotic expression. They obviously give her a great deal of love and care.

"We are trying to decide her future," says Mr. Kendall after the child is taken away. "When her grandmother dies it will be very hard on her. She might live to be thirty years old, the doctor tells me." He says it confidentially, without self-consciousness.

"Are there any homes in the state for them?"

He makes a wry smile. "You always wonder what will happen to your own. You know—when they can't talk and defend themselves. We are investigating all the time but Negro children are better off at home, I feel."

His wife, who disappeared briefly, is hovering now in the dining area of this large room. Suddenly she bursts into our midst:

"Oh . . ." she laughs, shakily, "I don't know why he talks like that. He *knows* I wouldn't give her up. I wouldn't put that child in a *home!* Good Lord!"

We laugh a little with her, relieved.

Later in the car Charity says, "No Negro wants to put a child in a home. Can't tell how they be treated. Most of 'em can't afford it, anyway. Some family will take care of that girl—her sisters or somebody." She shakes her head. "They just love that poor little thing. You see how clean they keep her? That grandmother is devoted to her. That's her life."

"Good people," she half whispers. "Good people." She sighs and looks out the window into the cold evening light. There is frost on the ground. Plaquemine, on the outskirts, is bleak.

"Do you sometimes lose hope, Charity?" I ask.

"I trust the Lord and he gives me strength. No, I don't lose hope. But there's so much work to do. That man's never going to see peace and integration in those schools. He isn't young. He's old to have such a young family. He won't see it. He's working for the ones to come."

I hear a new note of discouragement in her voice. I look at her profile beside me in the dim light. The same equanimity occupies her, but the tone is one of defeat.

COLLEGE TOWN

We stay with Mrs. Bradford, who is head of the English department at the Negro college here. She is an old friend and sorority sister of Charity. The sorority is a national society of Negro women in which Mrs. Bradford has held a high office for several years. Charity did not say that she was bringing a white woman along and gave Mrs. Bradford very little notice of our arrival, in any case. Charity has the habit of calling a few hours before we arrive in a town, or the day before at best, and merely states that she will be there, traveling with a friend. She is always offered a room and always made to feel very welcome. Evidently it is taken for granted that one houses Charity Simmons, not out of duty but out of love. It seems to be that simple. And Negroes, having few safe places to stay overnight, are more hospitable perhaps than most white people; a kind of frontier policy still prevails.

Our room here was once the sanctuary of Mrs. Bradford's son. There are still a few college banners and athletic trophies around.

"His daddy made him a basketball player," says Charity with quiet contempt. "He was much too smart to spend all that time playin' games but that's what he did. After the boy got away to college he did all right, though. He's an insurance man now, in the North. Makes a lot of money. They have money here. Both teaching. She's got a big salary because she's an administrator, too. And I think there is money in her family, anyway. She's very well educated."

This is a large bungalow, new, made of light brick and in a new high-grade tract where no lot is smaller than a quarter of an acre. It was supposed to have been integrated but is actually 100 percent Negro-owned, mostly by people from the college and a few prosperous businessmen. There is a large, flat, treeless back yard, fenced in and covered with thick brown wintry grass on which lie frost and patches of last week's snow. In the garage are Mrs. Bradford's Cadillac, a huge black sedan, and Mr. Bradford's Lincoln, dark green. He is a coach at a local high school; formerly, perhaps, a handsome man, he has a babyish petulant face. He wears fashionable sports clothes, is thickset, tall, pouty, and apparently drinks heavily.

We are given a late supper by a handsome woman named Mrs. Thomas, a Negro servant who is very skinny and quick moving. She serves us in a whisk as if it took no effort but perhaps a certain knowledge of magic. While we dine, she stands in the kitchen ironing, wearing a black hat and a pair of slim flat bedroom scuffs. The phone rings often, and she answers it without ceasing to iron, shouting out:

"Mr. Bee! This fo' you. Pick up the phone!" and into the mouthpiece, "Hold on. He's comin'." A red toothpick extends from the side of her mouth like a fang. She is a fiery woman, curiously similar to her employer except that Mrs. Bradford is educated, middle class, and chic and moves with more grace, if the same kind of agitated swiftness. I think of Mrs. Clury and Mrs. Cotton and wonder if women unconsciously select servants of their own temperament.

We sit after supper in the den, a general sort of room opening onto a patio; there are great piles of magazines on and under the tables, on tops of book shelves, and on a small window seat. There are books on one entire wall, crammed into the shelves; there are also boxes of puzzles, decks of cards, more athletic trophies, and two small radios. The television set and a row of file cabinets flank another wall. This is the first time I have seen more than ten or twelve books in a Negro home. Usually I see none. Mrs. Clury's books were out of sight, although I understand she has a good small library.

Mr. Bradford drinks highballs and settles with thickening speech into a sulky slump on the sofa. A young attractive light-skinned man from next door drops in, and we spend the evening and half the night talking about the South, teaching, Black

Power, which we have all begun to hear a lot of, race relations, military service, war, and marriage.

"A woman's got to be married," says the young neighbor, Mr. Prince. "I never saw a woman make it well without marriage."

Mrs. Bradford laughs scornfully. "You lookin' at one. Mrs. Simmons' husband died forty years ago and she never married again."

"Well, that's not easy," says Charity. "He's right. Most women need a man."

Mr. Bradford grunts, eyes me furtively, suggestively, and with open doubt. Mrs. Bradford mentions a friend who "cut out" on her husband and is getting along fine alone for the first time in her life. "Isn't that right, *dear?*"

She addresses Mr. Bradford with sharp bitter sarcasm, openly, as if the habit were too old to be camouflaged for the sake of a visiting stranger, or perhaps because he is giving me such dubious glances. He shrinks into his soft corner of the couch and drinks steadily, answering her with a grunt and a smeary look of hatred. Charity and I are uncomfortable, but Mr. Prince carries on with aplomb. He is intelligent, animated, and very good-looking. I am drawn to him. We begin to talk.

"I'll tell you why Negroes go into the armed services and don't fight the draft," he says. "They're patriotic. That's something a white may not know. We are very patriotic."

Mr. Bradford rises shakily and moves across the room, pours himself another drink, and continues on into the hall, disappearing into his bedroom. His wife ignores him.

"Well, Jerry, that may be true in the South," she says, "but up North our people aren't so patriotic. I think all Southern people are more patriotic, Negro and white."

"Well, my boys really want to defend the United States."

Mrs. Bradford rattles the ice in her glass. "Sure. That's one way they can be sure of steady income with family support and get out of workin' for Mama, too."

Charity laughs. Mr. Prince maintains a big flirtatious smile most of the time.

Suddenly he poses a question: if I teach college this year and find in my class an intelligent Negro student whose grammar is not on a college level, will I pass him anyway if his work is otherwise good?

"It depends. I doubt that I would ever let a semiliterate student out of a college English class, if that's what you mean."

It seems that his physical education students are weak in English but mostly quite bright.

"These boys are . . . cunning, you know? You take an athlete, he can be a cunning fellow. He knows a lot. You got to be smart to be a top player. And I hate to see all that be a waste of time because he doesn't like English."

"Depends on what he's going to do with his life. He's entering a world that reveres the word, after all. He'll be rejected from many areas of social experience if he doesn't have a decent command of the language. It may be stupid but that's how it is."

"Can't you be decent without spelling it right?"

Mrs. Bradford shouts at him: "Oh, come on, Prince! What are you doin'?" She turns to me. "Don't listen to him. *He* spells all right. He gets after his boys to learn their English. There's no reason why they can't learn it if they are so cunning. Good God! That's what's wrong now, all these spoiled Negroes running around with an education and talking like sharecroppers. I don't think it's necessary. It doesn't prove anything to me. You listen to some of those young radical leaders now: they're beginning to use worse language so the common people will think they come from the same life. That's false. All this trouble to try to get a decent education for a Negro child and then you want them to forget about the English. How's that boy going to sound when he tries to run for mayor or governor? What happens when they get up in Congress to make a speech?"

Prince is by now laughing like a prankish child. It is evident that he likes to get her ruffled, that he likes women, that he is fully engaged in the battle of the sexes and full of positive sexual tension where women are concerned. He even flirts with Charity, who is almost twice his age. He has great charm.

"The ignorant people aren't going to trust an educated leader," he says softly.

"Then they better give up Stokely Carmichael for one. He's got some education and he's gettin' more all the time." She swings her feet up over the arm of her chair, carefully pulling the dressing gown close under her knees. She gulps her drink angrily. But the irritation is friendly. There is much between them, but it seems almost familial, like an older woman with her favorite young kin. Both hold their liquor well.

Mr. Prince continually offers me questions, sounds me out. We talk of war. I am relaxed with him and rattle on, with very little censorship of ideas, something I have not done until now when among Negroes because of a need to hear them out.

"War," I declare flagrantly, "is a dying ritual and profoundly connected to the relationship between the sexes in Western society.

"Men attempt to solve the most profound problems of societies and nations with a minimum or no consultation with women who are, after all, half of society. Authoritarian military society would collapse if women had an equal share in major policy making. It's beginning to happen. In fact modern men and women are just beginning to discover the depth of their estrangement."

Mr. Prince is wide-eyed and delighted. This opens up two more hours of conversation. Mrs. Bradford agrees with me somewhat. Charity says this reflects a deeper difference between white thinking and black than she has ever considered.

"Let's face it," say I, "there is some significant position about wars and about their sons fighting them, that women have never yet taken and are increasingly pressured to take. It'll require a state of serious anarchy—a collapse of male authority in the world—to force women to take a new definite stand in regard to war."

"That's right! Now, Prince, you listen to her. That's the truth. I hear these women—they're all uneasy and they are all feelin' guilty about something. They're letting it happen." Mrs. Bradford and I exchange glances of alliance.

Suddenly Prince is sober. "I don't think a woman knows the first thing about stopping war or what war means to men. She just sees the newspaper."

"Oh, don't be ridiculous! Donny went to Korea, didn't he? I know something about war through him, my own son!"

"That's different, entirely different. Did he ever tell you much about it, real things? Did Frank ever tell you how he felt when he was in the Pacific? I mean real stuff?"

"Well, a certain amount," she says honestly. "But we aren't talking about that."

"No," I explain. "What I meant was war as a solution to political problems, war as a choice, not the experience of battle for the soldier. It's never been put on a philosophical level; the decision has never been philosophical, you know? It's been totally reactionary, whatever the leaders may tell themselves."

We carry on this way with an occasional literal interjection from Charity: "That's right. Look at all the war protests now, all those conscientious objectors. You didn't see that before."

Prince says you have to be a man to understand war, and we tell him that is exactly our point and round two begins. We all manage to laugh, Prince in that amused sparring spirit that is very seductive. We follow him like geese. I am ready to laugh aloud with him, at myself and all of us. Can't say exactly why.

He leaves at two in the morning, as animated as when he arrived. He shakes my hand and holds it in his grasp.

"I wish you were going to be around longer. You're a good fighter."

I wish the same and tell him so, very flattered. Charity stands nearby, beaming at us. The races have met in that most taboo of combinations, Negro man and white woman, and communicated! She is satisfied.

After we are in bed in the dark and she has said her prayers, she tells me suddenly:

"You had a very dramatic way of holding yourself back and then when it was just the right time, letting him see the real Jo. That was a masterpiece."

I am amazed and very touched. "How do you mean, Charity? I wasn't aware of that."

"You said what you believed and you didn't resent him when he argued. You proved to him you weren't prejudiced against him. You treated him like any man."

"But he treated me the same way."

"Yes, that's true, but he wouldn't have done that, see, if you hadn't let him. He tested you out and then he knew he could fight you."

I treasure the compliment from Charity but am disappointed at its implications. Were we playing some sort of racial game, testing on that level? I had thought our relationship was more natural, less self-conscious than that. I fall asleep depressed, having presumed that Mr. Prince responded to me as a human, a woman, a friendly adversary, and not merely as a "white woman." Every day I come to a deeper understanding of what it means to Negro people to hear themselves referred to as "The Negro." Negro writers use the term too, of course. But Negro people are people and "The Negro" is a phenomenon. I feel the positive force behind the cry of Black Power, and I know with a sinking feeling that American society will not respond to that cry; it will only react.

Charity says, as I fall asleep, "If I snore, be sure to wake me." She snores. I wake her finally. She turns over and snores again. I do not wake her again. I sleep anyway, hearing the snore through my sleep. When we wake up she says:

"Jo, you must have been restless last night. You snored. I never heard you snore before."

I laugh until I am weak and cannot tell her exactly why.

She is packed and at the little desk making some notes when I get up. She lives neatly, no fuss. How does she get things cleaned, packed, moved about, unpacked, pressed? One never notices. She is prepared. She gives functional living its due and nothing more. She lives somewhere else. She manages to concentrate well enough in the presence of others to do a lot of work while on the move. Last week we discussed privacy; the idea of a child's having a room to himself seemed to Charity like the most bizarre of luxuries, even of dubious value. I told her that sometimes I was lonely in my room as a small child and would have liked, at least when sleeping, to share it with my sister and brother. She considered my statement deeply and said it was very revealing to her. White people, she said, are lonelier than Negro people.

She stops her work this morning to chat while I am dressing.

She is still elated by our conversation of last night. She is also impressed with the comforts of this house.

"I learned something from Mrs. Bradford about fixing my bathroom. You see she has those rings with the hand towels in 'em? I wonder where she gets those?"

"I think you can get them in department stores," I suggest.

"That's one thing I don't like—having too many people using a bathroom. I don't like somebody using my towel. I was always fussy about my towel. Somebody always getting it mixed up with the others."

"Me, too. I dislike that." Privacy . . . I remember Mrs. Long in Mississippi. There was one worn and dirty bath towel hanging on her bedroom doorknob and no bathroom.

"You should see Mrs. Lee's bathroom in her apartment in New York. I stayed alone up there for five days last year while she was away. It was the first time in my whole life I could walk naked from the bathroom to the bedroom! What a feeling! And I ate alone as much as I could. But, you know, that wasn't easy for me! I liked it but a person can become very vulgar living alone."

I laugh. Sometimes she expresses herself with a succinctness that is perfect. She is profoundly just, which gives her a very clear vision. We talk more about privacy.

"I think how modest my mother was," she says. "How proper! How'd she do with all those children under her feet all the time? I never saw my mother without her clothes." She says it with wonder.

We have an early breakfast with Mrs. Bradford before she leaves for school. It is the sort of breakfast I associate with hotel dining rooms: a half grapefruit, the sections cut, served in a double glass dish with chopped ice in the lower part; ham omelet; homemade biscuits with honey; and what Charity says is the best coffee in the South, better than New Orleans coffee.

Mrs. Bradford is talking about a woman teacher at the college who lives with a local high school teacher. She suggests that they are Lesbians, and Charity says she has heard the same. The subject causes Charity to lower her voice. I ask, as I have not before, if there is much homosexuality among Negro women.

"A lot," says Mrs. Bradford, "especially among teachers. Same with men. I'd say more among men, wouldn't you, Mrs. Simmons?"

"Well, I don't know much about it with the men," says Charity, "but I see signs. But there is a lot among women teachers, that's true. I remember one time in graduate school one of them sat next to me and all of a sudden right in the class she leaned over and started to suck on my arm."

We laugh. "That's the truth! Right in the class. I pushed her away and I moved my seat right after that. I saw her around with other masculine women in the school. That's the only time I had such a thing happen. I couldn't believe it. I was so innocent."

Mrs. Bradford received anonymous love letters from a woman one time, over a period of a few months. They were very sexy, she says. "My God! You wouldn't believe some of that coming out of a woman. I know it was a teacher. It didn't sound like a student. I think I know who it was, anyway. She left this area a few years ago. But the worst thing that happened in that line was about ten years ago: someone on the staff opened a student's letter by mistake. The letter was put in his box because he had the same name as the student. This was a letter from a former student who was telling this freshman boy how to get along and make good grades through college by flirting with the right professors. He named a lot of names and told how much the boy would have to do with each one of them to get through easily. Can you beat that?"

We express amazement. I have seen so little evidence of homosexuality that I am surprised. The talk of Negro women has been of men, and the Negro men whom I have observed seem either indifferent to the world in general or very actively directed toward women. But I have not pursued the subject.

"Well, it caused a big shake-up. We had a meeting and decided that the people named would just slowly resign, over a period of two years. But some didn't wait that long, of course. One of them was a friend of ours. I was really shocked. He had been very close to Donny, my son, and helpful to him in school. I asked my son one time if he thought there was anything peculiar about the man, and Donny said it was known that the man was a homosexual but he never seemed to bother the students and a lot of them liked him."

I ask if one class of people in Negro society includes more homosexuals than another class.

Mrs. Bradford has thought it all out carefully: "It's definitely a middle- and upper-class problem; more middle, I'd say. The lower-class people—you know, the 'lowlife'—don't have the tight sex rules that the rest of us have. They don't have so many marriages. It's all looser and so the man and the woman can get together more easily and maybe they aren't so choosy. They probably have more sexual experience and easier sex than the other classes, even if the men do run out on the women. You know, Negro women have an extra—uh—*charm,*" she says it sardonically, "over white women and that is that most of us work and very often make more money than the men. And we still get more higher education; although that is changing, I just heard, and maybe beginning to even out. But women in the Negro society still make the money and get more jobs, in the North and the South. So men want these Negro women for security sometimes. A woman will support a man very often, you know."

"And that woman in bed is sometimes all the safety he's got," says Charity. "He sometimes can't feel secure unless he got that bed to come home to."

"Yes, well anyway, on the 'lowlife' level they have more access to each other. But on the upper and middle levels where the rules are tight, you just don't have the freedom. If you have a good position, you think twice about divorce or playing around. In small towns everybody knows what you're doin'. If you care, then you have to be careful. So the women are more frustrated. The men can go get what they want."

"There is really a double standard for the middle and upper classes, then?"

"Oh, Honey, is there! That's no white problem. Women have power in the Negro society, but they still have a double standard when it comes to the important things. The Movement is increasing the double standard because the men are beginning to want to order the women around."

"But I hear many women say that the Movement carries a

special possibility of new freedom for women, all women. I hear talk of that and a lot of hints. Don't you agree?"

"I don't know. I don't think so. Whatever happens in the world, I see it gives women more headaches. If there's going to be any influence against war it's going to have to be from the women. You know that. Men aren't going to do anything about war. Look at Prince: He is antiwar till one of his boys goes to enlist, and then he starts up a pep talk about the army. He talks a lot about patriotism. I admire it too but not for all wars. This war is stupid."

"Is there much talk of the war on campus?"

She laughs. "This school is a little like a country club. The students are nice, mostly middle and upper class, and they don't want to be bothered about world problems. They never were bothered before and they don't want any changes. If they had been poor like most Negroes, they might get bothered. But they are very busy finding a way to get more rich and pretend being black is no problem."

She leaves for school, and Charity and I sit talking. We lazily finish our tea and coffee and write letters.

Charity is composing her Christmas message to her many hundreds of friends and acquaintances. Every year she sends a card with a spiritual message of some sort printed on it in green on white with a simple wreath border. She gives me copies of several from past years. This is the one she calls her masterpiece:

> *The whole tone of my life gives me the equanimity to survey this situation from a vantage point. I have been through too many things. I have been too close to death too many times to find pettiness important. What interests me now is growth. I want to grow instead of just growing older.*
>
> *All I ask is a chance to express what I'm bursting with—soul. I want a chance to work under the best possible conditions, and a chance to develop and grow as a person, as an artist in the field of adult education. I must grow. Nothing can stop that. It is good to be known, wanted, loved and needed at this stage of the game.*

We drive many miles together. At night Charity writes letters, meets with teachers, ministers, in churches, in small poor homes. Sometimes I join her. The people are quiet; houses are impeccable; refreshments are served; children are introduced: shining faces, curtsies, "Yes ma'm" said softly, with wide wonder. *I'm goin' to be a teacher. I'm goin' be shrimp fisher. I gathers de wata an Otis pick de wood. All us goes to school. My teacher pritty. This owa new baby. Looky, see that? That Jesus.* A white man with golden locks. They know the words to freedom songs. They know, as one knows of birth and death, what freedom is.

Charity calls home at night. "Hi . . . how you doin'?" and has a long motherly talk with Jennie, who misses her. "Well, I thought you just bought a pair in April. Oh, well, I'll see about that when I come home on the 17th. How'd you do on that test? Don't you forget now, you write them and thank them for that present. Better do it tonight while you got it on your mind."

One feels that to Charity this grandchild is the Lord's quiet reward for whatever she has earned. Her existence is pure joy to this traveling grandmother who must hanker, now that she's in her mid-sixties, to go home for good. Yesterday she talked about retiring. "They don't believe me at the office but I'm going to do it in no more than two years." Tireless, she sometimes looks tired. And lately, I see that she is discouraged; her head is slightly bowed much of the time. Charity, I remind myself, is mortal.

Traveling on. I meet many women. The impact of racism on a Negro life is beginning to assault me.

Billie Dee, a young Negro nurse tells me of the poor but decent Negro hospital where she works. "It's very good care here. Poor but very good. They got four beds for Negroes over in the white hospital fifty miles away. In the basement. I know, I worked there. Negro doctor can't get his patient in there. They don't eat the same food as the white sick—give 'em scraps, just keep 'em alive on grits and tapioca and a little chicken in soup. Awful! *Four* beds! We had an epidemic of meningitis one time. God, I thought we would lose every colored person in this state.

"Thing you gotta understand about this race discrimination

and Negro people living in this South is: a colored got to be tough! Weak ones dies early. Negro mothers losin' one in eight of their babies and gettin' pregnant too fast again, not gettin' the right kind of care before *or* after. Prenatal care—shoot, I never heard of it till I became a nurse. I never heard of women havin' babies in a hospital. Midwife or else your own mother come around and help out. I and my sisters and my four brothers, all us born in the house or born in the field. My people 'croppers. They don't do so good, but three of us try to help 'em cause we workin' now."

She sits on an old bench in the courtyard with me, smoking furiously, checking her watch, impatient but wanting to talk, not wanting to go back on duty.

"This old place is not much but I took a lot of work and pain to get here. I'll never quit nursing, never. I had a lotta inspiration from my grandmother—my mother's mother. She was a fullblood Indian woman. Kidnapped off the reservation in Oklahoma by my granddaddy. He was a colored man. He brought her to Louisiana and they raised a big family together. She was *somethin'*, that old lady. Never wore shoes, had little gold loops in her ears. She knew root medicine, you know. You break a bone or set on a ant hill, that woman could fix you up in no time. She made boiled mixture, see. Cured up hives, cold, chest pain. She used a pack of mud and spider web on the break—thatta way. Folk medicine, they call it. She was *one* folk that knew what she was doin'. I never saw a doctor deliver a baby the way she could.

"I'm part Indian from her. See, you can tell it in my face. Lotta Indian blood in the colored peoples here. I love these country peoples but I tell you the poor, really dog poor, they don't get into no hospital. Huh uh! Not *them*. You want treat *them*, you gotta go find 'em. That's what I'd like to do: go around like the county nurse but have a bus or a wagon or somethin', maybe a doctor and two nurses. You could do more medicine in these countrysides than ever going to get to these people. Time to time, they get bad enough somebody'll bring 'em in. Children got runny sores, distended navels. Shoot! This is a filthy life for a lotta people, you know it? I mean really filthy! And they *good* people. They smart. Listen, you stay alive till twenty or some, you gotta be smart, and tough, if you colored in this crazy race-minded Louisiana, this whole South. But I hear it's the same in the North."

We discuss the problem of childbearing for rural women. Billie Dee knows many statistics—black compared to white, or just the obvious dismal figures for blacks alone.

"They lose more than a tenth of their babies around here and maybe 'bout one in fifty of the mothers. Listen, I got a cousin over in Atlanta, Georgia. She's a nurse, too. You know how many beds they got over in that city for two hundred thousand Negroes? Six hundred beds! That's the most of any city in the whole South. That city s'pose to be better on colored people than the rest but she say the care just about like everywhere else."

Billie Dee fumes smoke, disgust, righteous indignation.

"See, I wanta tell you somethin' and you can tell the world to just look it up. Don't take my word; just tell those whites to do some study 'bout these things.

"See, the Negro woman have a choice; she going to stay home and let the midwife bring her through—birth the baby, see, or she go to the hospital. Now if she don't have a Negro hospital, then she have to go into the white. And one way she going to do best in the white is not make any arrangement ahead, because mostly they won't remember that, unless she have a very good doctor there expecting her. But if she don't have a doctor to get her in the hospital, then what's she going to do? She going to get out on the street and fall down and commence to holler she's 'bout to give out that baby, or get her a taxi and tell him to get her to the hospital emergency cause she's 'bout to deliver, see. That way, she goes in as emergency in some cases. Some cases it don't do any good to do anything at all. Maybe they take you if you unconscious. But don't wake up, Honey! Ooo, no!

"But once she get inside that white hospital, her trouble just beginning. My mother's best girl friend livin' in the city and she went for her first baby 'bout twelve years ago in the city hospital. She had a very bad labor and she done an awful lot of yellin'. After she yell for fifteen hours or something, a white doctor come in there and say, 'Listen, Nigger, you yell one more time and I chuck you out the window.' And then he hit her in the stomach to shut her up! That's the God truth! He hit that pregnant woman in the stomach. And that baby born dead in a few more hours. I *know* that case. See, when you helpless like a pregnant woman, and you got that kinda race-minded mess on your hands, you better off home in the bed with your mother bringing your baby for you.

"My *God!* A woman havin' a baby—if you don't respect that, then you not human, that's all."

"So, see, that's one problem. Then she got the rest of the problems, like she didn't have no prenatal care. That's one. Twice as many Negro women as white losin' their babies today because of that. Then, she goes home, maybe she's poor, she don't eat right and she don't feed the baby right. She can't keep it clean maybe if she got to haul water from around the cornah or somethin'. Shit! They don't know nothin' 'bout what these mothers trying to do. Welfare goin' to give her some extra money for that baby but it don't get there right away. They got to come over and make sure that's a *real* baby and make sure it not borrowed offa somebody else."

She waves a disgusted hand, blunt and black and strong. She has a massive face with a tender and even happy expression most of the time. Anger and joy seem to occupy her simultaneously. She is short, stocky, built squarely with good well-developed muscles and a straight back. There is an aura of imminent explosion about her.

"Shoot! It's a mess. But the point is, Honey, you start your life out *crazy* if you a colored around here. I hear them tell it all day. I see the kids and I know what they need. What this poverty program they got goin' doin' for these hungry little children? They goin' to wait till they fifteen years old before they start eatin' good? They be dead or awful sick and messed up by that time and *then* what you goin' to do with 'em? Sometime I look at these babies and I say: 'You better off dead, little thing.'

"It may be true they a lotta things a colored don't know, but they not going to learn it off a white. Not around here noplace."

We hash it all out and she seems relieved. She jokes a little: "Country man come in the other day with a great big fish. Say: 'This fo' the doctah. He fixed up my baby.' God, we like to die tryin' to put that fish away. It was about three feet long! That's the truth! We stuff it in the refrigerator and they say all the food commence to smellin' like fish. Time the doctah got here this whole place stinkin' of fish." We howl. She is a great storyteller, fast and dramatic. Like Charity, she delineates well, as if her audience would not tarry through more than the sketchiest coverage of an incident.

I tour the hospital with her. It is quiet, with huge doors, high ceilings, ceiling fans, and old waxy wood floors; the windows are open, and curtains—stark white and simple—blow gently in some windows. It is an old-fashioned, ancient building that may soon be condemned. But it is more homelike than most hospitals, and that fact seems to register with the patients. Here are the children: beautiful tobacco- and clay-colored limbs strewn on the beds among white bedclothes, casts and bandages like dark sapling twigs upon the snow. None is fretful. One with a leg in a cast stares benignly at me and slowly reveals his thick magenta gums and square white teeth. For no reason comprehensible to me there are tears on his smiling face. Maybe he cried ten minutes ago. Elegantly and unself-consciously, with a tiny forefinger, he picks his nose.

The darkness of their faces gives them a healthier look than that of most hospitalized white children. Blue shadows and feverish faces do not show as much. Several are bloated, perhaps from hunger.

Ironically, the American child who requires the strongest psychic and physical foundations for coping with his future is still, in 1968, receiving the weakest. It still requires great cunning, fortitude, imagination, trust, and wisdom for him, being black, to move through his life to its end, which will come at least five years sooner than that of his white brother.

How much of this can black mothers and fathers allow themselves to know, to digest? The facts alone, the frightening possibilities, are enough to engender psychosomatic illnesses.

The first five causes of death among American Negro women are diseases of the heart, vascular lesions of the central nervous system, hypertensive heart disease (twice as frequent a killer as among white women), certain diseases of early infancy, and influenza and pneumonia.

It is important to note that diseases of early infancy are merely the ninth cause of death among white women. Billie Dee sees the clear handwriting on the wall: care illegally and immorally withheld begins before birth and dictates a lifetime.

Billie Dee's words, melodramatic maybe, linger with me: "You better off dead, little thing."

Maybe the fierce and tender maternalism I see everywhere here will someday stop those thoughts in her head. Few mothers, however desperate, could say that with conviction.

However, she vows to remain childless, even unmarried, to insure her future as a nurse.

"Is that really necessary—avoiding marriage?"

"Well . . . it looks like it to me. Maybe someday I change my mind."

Two weeks ago I wrote to Mrs. Long in Mississippi and sent her a box of clothes, bedding, and snapshots of her grandchildren. Today this letter was waiting for me at General Delivery, dictated, I am sure, to one of her children.

City of Love
Day of Kiss

Dear Mrs. Jo my dear frind
    recd every thing you send. you dont no how I aperciate your kindness and I will be on a lert for the new letter you send me I sure can use anything that any one give me for my family. I hope this will fine you all right—you an family. I hope you many blessing. My daughter said think you for the picture it was nice. Yes I will keep in touch with you you must not for get me.

love & Best wish to you & mr.
Lottie Long

Charity reads the letter silently, deeply touched. She looks at it for a long time. "Don't be afraid to send 'em old things. Doze women [this time it is plainly doze] can make quilts out of scraps. Anything. Send anything."

"What's the answer, Charity? Not for a few of us to keep sending her hand-me-downs and scraps."

"Send the scraps and work on the government to get rid of this poverty. The states have got to raise the welfare so people can get on their feet with it. Just eating isn't enough. Give 'em enough money to work with and they'll change their life. Why do so many people think the poor *want* to be poor?"

We drive south toward New Orleans in a kind of gloomy spirit. It is raining and chilly. Charity says:

"Twelve years pass just like that. Look at the figures—they *still* have just about 2 percent school integration. People are losing hope in some of these places where they worked so hard and still got resistance at the polls, still can't get their kids in an integrated school. Look what you got in Washington: schools started out white, then they were mixed, and now they are all Negro. That's because whites move to suburbs. And they send their children to private schools to keep 'em away from Negroes."

Slowly she releases the bitterness. It breaks from the tight pod and flowers in the safe dark of this car. She could be talking to herself; the tone is flat, sorrowful, obsessed. She cannot stop. I drive and listen.

". . . baby born in a leaky tent. What's his chance? Take him a lifetime to catch up. A third of Negroes are under fourteen years old! You realize that? That's a whole new population comin' up without any big change. They going to be so *angry*. You feel it everyplace. We're lettin' 'em down."

I can't bear it. She's doing what I remind myself cannot and ought not be done, but that I myself do sometimes: to take a stance, make a final defense, on the basis of statistics.

"But there *has* been change, Charity. That's what's happening, just what you say: they'll be angry and they'll admit it. That's change. I don't think history can be measured in those statistics. Statistics are only vague symptoms. History occurs in the unrecorded lives of the people, in the soul."

She sits solid, deaf to me.

"Twelve years and still barely 2 percent integration in schools!"

My mind scurries after means of rebuttal and some statement that will restore her hope. I have never seen her so depressed. It seems to me that our very discussion implies a social change. Lives, I am thinking. Look at them! The voice is different, the attitude. Something is happening that "two percent" can never describe. But I must let her unwind.

"Two Negro churches burned in Gillett, Arkansas," she drones. "They *still* doing it. Police just can't seem to find the arsonists. But you burn down a white church and they'll have ten Negro men suspects in jail in an hour. You know what it costs the black community to build a church again? Very few have any time or money to give. They already working twelve hours a day for thirty cents an hour. We have a teacher over in Mississippi now, teaches citizenship classes at night. She works for a white family six days a week, nine or ten hours a day carin' for those white children, scrubbing, cooking. That white woman pays her *ten dollars a week*. Today, 1968, in the U.S.A.

"Look at that racist Maddox gettin' the Georgia vote . . ."

We roll through the night, obsessed with opposing visions. We hear something behind one another's words that neither of us will heed—I, her disenchantment; she, my philosophizing.

Charity, who flatters me with these confidences, is translating into language her own sense of history and time. And I am doing the same. It comes down again perhaps to that concept of the self that one develops very early—I am "us" or I am "me." She never experienced the solitude and privacy that I did. When Charity slept it was "we" who slept, all those close little bodies like extensions of herself that clung together in sleep in one bed. She felt cold and heat with them; she shared all craving, gratification, dream, and pain with them and perhaps experienced very little of the body's singularity, the wild isolation of the self defined as "I." I slept alone in a room that was dedicated to a definition of that "I"—with *my* bed, *my* clothes, *my* toys, *my* lamp. No one shared my silence. The view from my window was unique.

Heavy rain now.

We plunge through the dark wet Louisiana night as if incarcerated in a falling burning star. We are silent, frustrated, disappointed. We have come to an impasse, not the sort created and soluble by selected attitudes, but one which is destined to rise between two persons of such estranged origins—by our very births.

"Charity," I begin once more when I ought to allow her the

grace of a real purge, "I believe that everything man is capable of—the highest understanding, the basest intention, the greatest inspiration, everything—is experienced in the individual solitary soul, any time, any place, regardless of circumstances. And no statistics can ever record what's really happening on earth: what Mr. Main knows sitting there in that tent with his feet in a roasting pan after seventy years of hard labor; or what you know from your life or what I know and suspect and feel from mine. We can't make figures of all that and then read them and say, 'That's what happened. That's how it was.' History can't be written. It can only be experienced and endured. It can only be recalled as a sort of fictional romance."

"But what they are experiencing," she says softly, "is the *same* conditions. Same as before. They don't have any history."

Ah!

Well, Charity, I am "I" and you are "us." I know that as a creature I am us; I can consciously become us again by an effort of the imagination (an act not to be slighted), but to live, to be, I shall not wait for us. And it seems you will not move on until *we* move on. Your collectivism like my individualism is not a matter of social education or theorizing; it is the body's concept of being. Here we part.

I am depressed. I look at her. Maybe it is only that she is at the end of life and I am in the middle. She sits in what seems to be relaxed immobility, but I sense that her thoughts are as distressed as mine. I see our world flung up, scattered, churned, exploded—black and white—and I know something is happening, something profound, valid, revolutionary, and hopeful. We will not fall and settle into any former molds again. Yet she sees us fall back impaled on the old rusty lethal spikes of those statistics: 2 percent. And she knows a lot that I do not know.

So intuitive is Charity that when I leave her in Baton Rouge for a few days and go on to New Orleans alone, she sits up half the night—exhausted though she is from that long stormy ride—and writes me this letter:

> We were both experiencing deep private obsessions tonight. We were exhausted and couldn't yield. I feared for your safety on

that road alone in that weather and almost called you at midnight but a grown daughter must be trusted on her own to be wise and cautious.

By that maternal assertion she acts, very successfully, to draw us back into a familial relationship where her strength is indisputable and where we have both been, though unconscious of it, very comfortable. It stems from a sort of creature wisdom, that claim on me of daughter. She transcends all intellectuality and language, all confusion. The power of family, of kinship, that is her eternal resource. She reclaims matriarchal dignity, also, and offers me the only valid communication there is: that of kinsmen, spiritual or genetic. At this point the difference is irrelevant. I am thankful.

I think rather wistfully of Charity after reading her letter and all at once am impressed by the statistics that she herself has resisted and transcended. Statistically, she had at birth only the same chance of reaching age twenty as my own mother had of reaching something like thirty and as I, in my time, have had of reaching forty-five.

In 1940 the median number of school years completed by a Negro twenty-five years and over was only 5.8, but Charity, with labor and the spiritual force of her family, with faith and cunning and sheer will, acquired a master's degree from a good university. And she went on to work in her chosen field, often against the insane discrimination that sets so many Negro people back after they have gotten their education. As late as 1962, 19 percent of the nonwhite female population with some college held jobs as private household workers, yet virtually no (about 1 percent) of white women with some college held such jobs. The percentage was lower even among white females with zero to eight years of elementary school.

In 1960, 41 percent of the dwellings in which nonwhite mothers were trying to care for their children had no bathrooms (or occupants shared a bathroom with other families).

In fifty years, during Charity's lifetime, the Negro population in America has gone from 73 percent rural to 73 percent urban, and that move is not to residential areas of cities but mainly to central cities and slums. The thought of the adjustments tried, many of which surely failed, is staggering.

The school administration, the hospital, the indifferent employment agency—none of these knows to what house and home the slum resident goes after a day's school or a day's work or a day's failure to connect. They are only beginning to discover, if not precisely to care.

Charity knows, without reading it, that 2 percent integration must become 10 percent. Many lives have been damaged and many lost altogether that this may be so.

I wonder now if she and I actually have come to an impasse, and if so, can it be transcended, that deeply implanted notion of time and self?

I reread her Christmas message: "All I ask is a chance to express what I'm bursting with—soul." That's asking everything, Charity. Is it "I" asking or "we"?

NEW ORLEANS

Mardi Gras in ten days. The Jefferson City Buzzards band parades through a Negro section of town, rehearsing with the white men's club that has hired them for carnival day. A few white men in half costume leap and whirl and dance behind them, followed and fringed by Negro children and a few adults, black and white. There is a light, warm misty rain; distant thunder growls. The great brass horns gleam and cast off our shimmering distorted reflections.

At a corner six blocks from the starting point, the band makes a sharp right and stomps full blare and beat into a small dark bar and grocery, to drink, toast, exchange laughs, and take off again. The children, licking Popsicles, waving a few tattered banners, hopping, forming circles in wild spontaneous dance, arms flying, in spasms of twitching glee, string out behind the band like kite tails in the wind.

A small Negro woman in black slacks, gray sweater, and black coat sways and skips before us, alone. Suddenly skies collapse and huge splashes wet the walks. We mush up to someone's porch. The occupant, a large black woman in an apron, opens the front door and steps out to stand before it. "Come on! Come on, git up out de rain!" We pack onto her porch in our wet steaming wool clothes like a herd of dazzled sheep. Our faces stream and our hair is misted. The small woman crushes against me.

"What's yo' name?"

I tell her and we shake hands. Her face is narrow, creased, a little crazy, formerly pretty. She is very drunk and very serious. She holds the soaked black coat open, raising her arms to spread it like a cape, like heavy black wings, and continues a vague reprise of the dancing, a tuneless hum and half-whispered babble as accompaniment. The tuba player monkeys with the mouthpiece of his instrument, which is full of water. The drummer carefully dries the tight skin of his drum with a sweater.

Mrs. Sidney, the dreaming drunken grace in black, faces me, swaying, eyes half shut. Still dancing, she says softly, "I jess got out de hospital fo' days ago. Loss my whole inside!"

A girl laughs behind us, and Mrs. Sidney swings a hip at her, whirls and puts her back to the girl.

"Thass right. Fo' days. See, I'm up and feelin' fine! Doctah say I can do anything I wants. If I wants to street dance, thass okay, too." She hums and spreads the sodden wings of black wool, one down, one up, whipped past our faces in a swoop that leaves a trail of wet wool and bacon grease smell on the heavy air.

With her permission I take her picture, from the rear by her request, and ask her to spell out her name and address.

"Listen, here my numbah. Take down my address and take my socia-curity numbah." She pops open her wallet and aims the card in its plastic envelope toward my gaze. "Here it is. We all gots to have one o' these, black or white, don't make no difference. Take this numbah!" I dutifully take the social security number, with the address, and give her my name again.

She whirls on as the parade filters down to the street again and a little sunlight comes through the storm. "I *loves* to dance! We all the same, everybody together fo' carnival. Black or white, don't mattah." She gives me a backward grimace meant as a smile. A front tooth is missing, perhaps causing the soft lisp.

"See down that street? That my house down next to the end. Lived right in this neighborhood fo' fifty years. I got six chillrun and we all loves to dance. Looky up there—see that boy? Thass my kid."

The long loose boy-body leaps and swoops low, turns, spirals on one foot, and takes flight in a leap. Then, as the band drums up, he begins a tight-footed stomp. His face, like his mother's, is naturally sober. A ring of girls surrounds him and then leaves him. Someone cries, "Bobby! Bobby!" in a high scream. A little sister in purple cotton shoots between us and finds her brother, brushes dirt from his clothes, and grips his hand, leading him into the street where they begin to dance. Mrs. Sidney moves, arms and coattails held high, up the street with her own beat and her fresh surgical scar, somber, self-surrounded, intoxicated, and empty of insides.

The Jefferson City Buzzards blast around a corner to greet a group of four men in women's dress, tight skirts and tight head-bands, outrageous rouged cheeks. Mrs. Sidney sweeps into and through their midst like a grounded bird, oblivious of them. When a few black children follow her path they are pushed back to the sidewalks and the rear of the parade. These four are white men. The parade bosses are white. Blacks keep to the sides and rear, except for Mrs. Sidney who follows her wacky muse.

Another cloudburst. We dive under a store awning and wait, mashed against one another, thirty or more of us. The band goes inside somewhere and drinks again. It goes on this way for several miles and several hours. At dusk, I wave to Mrs. Sidney, who still weaves about in the middle of an intersection entirely alone. The Buzzards have repaired to their hall, an old brick fire station. The parade falls apart in the puddled street.

Mrs. Sidney spins on, her arms spread, bearing the heavy black wings of her coat.

I've got her number and she has mine.

BECOME SOMEONE ELSE FOREVER

Read the ads this month:

"You'll love Silky Strate for the lasting care it gives your hair." And, "Enjoy the LIGHT side of life. . . . Discover how really lovely your skin can be . . . SKIN SUCCESS CREAM." And "Let Bleach and Glow Cream wake the natural beauty, the flower-freshness, of your skin."

"There are many products that straighten excessively curly hair. Unfortunately, most of them destroy hair as effectively as they straighten it. Most . . . contain alkali—a harsh chemical that is particularly hard on Negro hair. Too many women either don't know this . . . or ignore it because of their great natural desire to have smooth, feminine hair that conforms to the latest style . . . at all costs. Thus, each year, in their almost frantic efforts to look like the 'girl in the magazine,' thousands of women . . . [etc.] . . . Lustrasilk waterproofs hair by 'feeding,' literally nurturing . . . the more you use . . . the healthier it will be. And the softer, smoother and straighter . . ."

Ad in *Ebony* magazine: "PERMA-STRATE, original and world's largest selling creme hair straightener. Completely natural looking straight hair. Be sure. Go modern," etc.

"CURL FREE, new curl relaxing discovery. It's this . . . or that hot comb look. What a choice. It's awful."

"My hairdresser straightens my hair with a hot comb, but it never really looks naturally smooth. It looks straightened and . . . the more humid the air, the more it reverts. Especially in a steaming bath. Sometimes I use a hot comb on myself . . . because a press doesn't last very long. But unless you're very skilled, you can burn yourself. I've often burned the edges of my face. I've seen the Curl Free relaxer on television, and I've been hearing it from friends. I've heard Curl Free is cool . . . it doesn't burn, and it's so easy you can use it at home. I'd like to try it." Curl Free, natural curl relaxer. Complete styling freedom.

Ultra Sheen: "Let your beautician relax your hair with ULTRA SHEEN just once. *You'll become someone else forever.*" (Italics mine.)

For women who wear it like it is—Raveen Au Naturelle
"Beautiful, proud, unmistakably you. Because you're a Natural woman. Free, at last, from rollers, hot combs, sticky dressings . . ."

C. Eric Lincoln in an article entitled "Color and Group Identity in the United States" (*Daedalus* magazine, spring, 1967) says:

The white ideal of feminine pulchritude, though less stressed than formerly, is still the archetype for the persistent choice of Negro men. Cosmetic preparations for lightening skin and straightening hair represent a multi-million-dollar market among Negroes not favored with Caucasoid features. Among the less affluent and more credulous, urine rinses for the face and "mammy-leg" presses for the hair contribute to the unending search for some approximation of the white ideal. . . . A college jester put it this way: "A light woman is your passport to Negro society. I'd rather give a light woman plane fare to St. Louis than to tell a tack head what time the train leaves."

Jennifer S., a student in an all-Negro college in Louisiana, says, "If you want to really see it [the identity problem] for what it is, then you have to look at women in their relations with men because the whole thing about beauty, and how you look and all that, is all tied up with a man, and men have a lot to do with a girl's idea of what's beautiful. As long as *they* like light women, we're going to try to be light. . . . Well, no, it doesn't work the same in reverse because they get more of an idea of what *they* are and how *they* ought to look from some other fellow or just the styles that are going on around them."

"And who dictates Negro men's styles?"

Most girls agree that it is not certain who dictates men's styles but that it definitely is not women.

On identity: "I know," says one girl, "that what I really am is what's on the inside and I never had any doubts about what I was like on the inside. I never wondered who I was. I don't really think that's very prominent with Negro women. I know about that *Feminine Mystique* book but I think that it's different with Negro women than that. I don't think they understand that problem. They know who they are, that's all."

"What makes a person know who he or she is?"

Mary Beth: "Bein' loved for what you are by your parents."

Carol: "Finding a way to express yourself till you can see what you're really like by what you're doin'."

Janice: "I think just havin' a name and bein' alive in the world and seein' that people recognize you and say hello to you and all that stuff."

"Does any of that diminish in the presence of white people?"

"For some it does, but not for me. More for men, maybe."

"Not for me either, it doesn't."

"For my mother it does, but not for me."

"For me, if I be honest, a little bit it does. I mean with you here right now, why I'm interested in comin' across as somethin' big, you know? I mean I'd like you to think I'm really somethin'. And I think the rest do too if they'd be honest."

They all laugh.

"Yeah, but that's not cause she's white! That's cause she's older than we are. And she's writin' books."

"No, it's cause she's white and she's older, too."

"I don't feel it. I mean, I like to be polite but I don't care what you think of me, just that I wouldn't want to be rude or anything."

Janice says: "Listen, you know what I think? I think you hear so much about race relations now and how Negroes are treated and used to be treated till you think it is true all over and you think it's happening to *you*. But most of us here never even had a chance to get pushed out by a white. I mean how many of your mothers ever worked for a white woman?"

One hand goes up. "My grandmother, too."

And your grandmother's grandmother, too, because she was a slave. I look at them. Their great-grandmothers were chattels, bought and sold bodies. In these faces, styles, bodies, and conscious minds, the concept of ancestral chattel has been effaced. What does one retain of one's history? I ask them that in simple terms.

"You keep what your parents want to give you or what they think they have to give you. I know my father told my brothers a lot about whites and stayin' away from them and that was in 1956. And he knew what to tell them because *his* father told *him*. My father never had any trouble with whites at all but he told my brothers anyway. They tell what they think they have to."

"My mother told me to stay away from white men no matter what. If I see a white man dying on the street, I'll call the police or the ambulance or somethin' but I'm not goin' over there and help him out."

"Me, too. They told me, too."

The warning that was passed through centuries from black parent to black child is spoken now, not exactly as ritual yet. It is still translated into imaginary action: "If he's dying, I'll call the police but . . ."

"Well, as far as public, national identity, social identity goes—what do you call yourself and prefer to be called? Negro, Black American, Afro-American, just American or what?"

"Negro."

"Negro."

"I say colored people a lot. I think of my family as colored people because my mother uses that term a lot."

"I think I'm a Negro American."

"I think I'm a black woman."

"But you just started sayin' that this year after you heard that fellow speakin' here. Last year, Mary, you were a Negro girl!"

Laughter. Mary laughs at herself. "Well, *this* year I'm a black woman."

I tell them of the Negro radio station in California on which I heard a Negro male singer rendering these words in richly sentimental tones:

> A woman's mind is made to think up clever little things
> To keep her man happy.
> A woman's hands were made to rub a man's head,
> Make him some bread,
> Make him some coffee,
> And put his kids to bed.

"How does that affect you?"

"Makes me sick! I could throw up my lunch!"

"I take it as just a song. 'Old Man River' is a song too, and 'Old Black Joe.' Just songs."

"I think it's stupid and a man wrote it."

"Do you think any Negro woman would believe the ideas or like them for any reason?"

"Oh, maybe some, but not most. There's a woman in our neighborhood at home—that's down toward the coast in the country. She always talks about herself as belongin' to some man. She said to my mother last summer, 'I don't belong to Bobby Ray no more.' That was her boyfriend. She has a new boyfriend every month. I think *she'd* like to hear that song."

One small excited girl who laughed a lot says, "I'm studying sociology and . . . well, I'm a senior so I've had most the work I'm going to and I think Negro women don't want to know about some of the troubles they're going to have when the men get more . . . uh, jobs and freedom and become strong as head of the family. Because an awful lot of men and women are together with their children and still that woman is big around the house and he is just sort of quiet or acts like she's boss, you know. I mean, there is something to the idea that we have a matriarchy in Negro society, but you see that means that usually if you are a Negro girl you've got a strong mother that you can identify with and that helps you be independent. Most girls that don't have a strong mother, then if they don't have a strong father either, or maybe no father, then they aren't strong. But what I meant is, I think Negro women are going to have some troubles when there are a lot more strong men. The same as white women and they have a *lot* of trouble."

"Yes, they do," I agree. "Do you know there are approximately one million known alcoholic American housewives, most of them middle and upper class and most of them white?"

"But it's different for Negro women. I mean, some of them drink but so many of them are poor that they are always working and then when they get a husband that takes care of them they just keep on working or do church work or that way. They have a different life most of the time than white women."

They are indecisive but attack one another's arguments honorably.

"I don't think there's any difference, Janice. I mean, if there are just so many jobs and men get most, then women are going to have to stay home with the kids or . . . do some charity or something. And that's not the same. That makes them more idle."

"Do you fear idleness, any of you?"

None of them admits a fear of idleness. But the fashion-model type says, "Sometimes I have this sort of secret thing that I think about doing—I mean, a life I see myself in sometimes where

there's this guy . . . Ha!" They all break up. ". . . and uh . . .
he's my husband and he's got money and I just sort of . . . sit
around and I look good and we have parties. You know. I mean,
sometimes I dream about that and I think I'd like it. Just good
lookin' clothes and a . . . oh, a sports car or something, and we
could travel. It's . . . you know what it is? I didn't realize it but
it's just like the feeling when you're a little child. I mean, everything is nice and somebody else takes care of you."

None joins her wholeheartedly. The most any other would
allow is that very rarely she might dream of great wealth. Never
idleness.

These are middle-class, comfortable, nicely dressed girls who,
although they are majoring in fields that imply future careers,
unanimously intend to marry and raise children. While raising
their families most intend to pursue a career to some extent—
whether in teaching, social work, business, or psychological coun-
seling. None was in the arts. The fine arts department of their
college is very small and most of the students in it are men.
Several of the girls sing in school or church choirs. One plays the
piano. All but one love to dance and place it first among favored
entertainments.

The majority agree that to cook and to sew are preferable to
housecleaning. Half admit to a belief in and knowledge of birth
control. All stanchly reject the idea of abortion. Most are Catholics and most are at least resigned to if not favorable toward
universal premarital sex.

"Well," says Louella, "sex is on people's mind. That's all there
is to it. You go outdoors and look at all these students and faculty
too and they thinkin' about sex. That's the truth!"

The general feeling among these young middle-class women is
that men perpetuate the color class system and the "light" ideals.
Soon afterward I asked a group of older women, also middle
class: "Is there some voice—in fiction, advertising, Negro society
or white, or in religious dogma—some voice that describes you
and that you feel you must heed in assessing yourself, or that you
must resist?"

The answer was, in the main, "No." In about one-fifth of the cases the answer was "Yes, men." In no case was self-definition described as a serious problem.

Upper-class and wealthy women are often less willing to discuss it. They discuss everything in a less personal manner than the others. Most say, not always convincingly, that they are not concerned with identity problems. A few hint otherwise.

Mrs. Roland, a former schoolteacher, wife of a wealthy New Orleans physician, says, "There are Negro women who are afraid all the time of getting old and not being in demand in society anymore and all that. But you see, even if a Negro woman is rich now or has a big social position, she still might have a lower type of family background. Maybe very poor, you know. I know one woman who tells everybody her mother is dead but she really lives right over here on Parish Street. I've known her all my life. But she's an ignorant woman and some women think they can't be proud of their mother if she's ignorant. But she's good to her, you know, she gives her a lot. But she never takes that poor old thing out in the car. Her brother will take her out some time but not that daughter! She's afraid she'll be seen. I believe if she were to be seen she would say that that was her housemaid or something."

Mrs. Roland's own three aunts, her mother's sisters, all pass for white, are wealthy, are completely cut off from Negro society, and live with some influence in upper-class white society.

"All my cousins, too. I see them in town but we don't speak. Don't pass a word."

"How do you feel about that?"

"I don't mind. Doesn't bother me. I was darker and my mother was darker, too dark to pass. But my mother was a very unusual woman and I doubt that she would have passed if she could. She was more a mother to those sisters, being older. My cousins are all very white. We have a lot of white blood and then they married white people, of course, so their children haven't the faintest idea that they have Negro blood in them.

"There are a lot of Negro people passing in New Orleans. There's a history of it here."

The complex relations of the races in the history of New

Orleans are best revealed in the life of the quadroon woman. A quadroon is the child of mulatto and white parentage. The quadroon man generally married a darker woman since women of his own color were, for more than half a century, carefully raised to a high order of concubinage by their own mothers for the sake of possible marriage to white men. There was no protection nor any secure future for such women in marriage to colored men. The strange life of the quadroon girl, preparations for which often began in her childhood, seems to have been an accepted aspect of New Orleans society half a century ago and perhaps even more recently. The girls were educated in cultural and domestic achievements and, in what was called a "placer system," were presented to a society of wealthy white men at quadroon balls, held, among other places, at the Salle d'Orleans, which later became, ironically, a convent for Negro nuns, and where, according to one traveler in New Orleans, "various families of daughters by the same father [might] appear . . . on the very evenings when their legitimate brother is present for the purpose of following the example of his worthy father."

There were discreet houses of quadroons, and some traveling businessmen coming to New Orleans found these more choice and cheaper stopping places than boardinghouses or hotels.

Success in the role of mistress meant for a quadroon a possible marriage or at least wealth with or without marriage. But her tenure was very precarious, and there is much evidence of tragedy in quadroon histories. One writer reports, ". . . the quadroon ladies . . . rarely if ever form a connexion. Many commit suicide; more die broken-hearted."

Thousands of New Orleanians, black and white, could trace their ancestries back to these liaisons.

Mrs. Roland says, "You have to remember that in New Orleans especially it is probable that a Negro woman has a prostitute in her recent past, that is in the last one hundred years, which isn't so long ago. If not a prostitute then maybe an unmarried grandmother. They still talk and think about it, you know. They worry about their daughters."

"Well," I say, "I think all women worry about their daughters. But I have heard a lot of discussion from Negro women about the threat of prostitution. Do you think it's a hangover or is it a plausible threat of the present day? Or both, maybe?"

"It's both. Negro women's lives are still unprotected, you know. I mean the large number of them. Most have no money to buy legal representation. If they are ever put in jail in a small Southern town, they are likely to be raped by the sheriff or a policeman, and they never in the world could prove it. If they are married, that doesn't mean their husband's word can serve them anything, or his social power, because that power is only real in Negro society, not white, even today. Get him in a white court and he has no power no matter who he is. Then, this Movement is opening up again the idea of advancement for some Negro girls in marriage to a white man. You see, for a while there wasn't as much advancement as there was trouble for a Negro girl in a mixed marriage but now it may be she can have a better life that way—if she moves out of the South, that is. By better I mean economic security. Maybe you don't realize what economic security means to Negroes."

"Do you rely on your own economic security? Is it *real* security?"

Her economic security consists in an inheritance on both hers and her husband's side in the form of real estate holdings, in good education, and in her husband's profession.

"Well, yes, I do. But there are women in my same position who don't. You get a kind of life going, you grow up in it and you are accustomed to it, yet you always know that something, just . . . some crazy thing can happen in the race relations that can strip it all away. I think maybe it is that any colored man, I don't care who he is, lives in danger in the United States and all colored women know this. We rely on our menfolk in a different way maybe from white women. It's something like that. Security comes from money and money in my class comes from a man. But most of us Negro women have worked and can work again. But in my case, a woman my age would have a hard time going back to teaching after twenty-five years out of the field. Education has changed and young people are getting the jobs first."

Mrs. Roland has more security than most Negro women, and yet she keeps that margin of imagination for disaster. She has two sons, one an ordained minister who abandoned preaching for civil rights work, which once caused a deep rift between him and his parents and resulted in his having no contact with them for over two years: Dr. Roland, perhaps in a seizure of terror and disappointment after the long investment in the boy's education, became violent and fought his son, threw him out of the house, and severed relations with him. Mrs. Roland, slowly, with much subtle psychological work, managed to bring them together again. Now their son's work is a source of reluctant pride, if perpetual anxiety, to them.

"We were lucky to have enough money to educate our boys," she says. "To give them some experience. Experience—that's what young people need. And Negroes get so little of it, even today! We were comfortable; my husband's practice was good. We took the boys to Europe twice, knowing they couldn't travel far in this country without running into prejudice.

"We thought a long time about sending them out of the South to white schools. We wanted them to be loyal but finally we decided that Negroes need the best education they can get, so we sent them North. Our oldest went first to military academy in the North, very early. He was only fifteen. You don't know what it meant to give up our children so young, knowing what kind of hatred they could run into. We were very lonely but I don't regret it."

At fifty-six she does church work and most of her own housework except for heavy cleaning. Also, she works part time at her husband's office. She has a propriety and grace that are common to middle-class women of this area, black and white; it is a kind of unself-conscious style and womanliness that are very appealing.

She believes in birth control and accepts the idea of divorce if there is no alternative. "Marriage working is more up to the woman than the man. She has the power to make it work, usually, unless she's married to a no good man." She says that she is not exactly typical of her own society, that generally the women she knows are more conservative than she.

She shuns civil rights work and talk of the Movement. "I don't think I will see integration in my lifetime and that doesn't trouble

me. Negroes can do a lot for each other besides civil rights work."
She contributes money and hours of work to a free, church-
sponsored nursery school for the children, including babies over
six months old, of poor working mothers. "We've changed the
whole social life of the community where we have the nursery.
The whole economy is improving because of this nursery. It is
very gratifying."

After we had seen one another a few times, I dared a more
personal question:

"Does the passing into white society of your aunts and cousins
have anything to do with your resistance to integration and civil
rights work, Mrs. Roland?"

She thinks it over for a long time. "Yes, I believe that influenced me. But there are a lot of factors. Do you know what a
Negro family has invested in sons? Do you know the great risk in
their lives if they become leaders or . . . do anything radical? A
Negro mother especially is in a trying situation with a son. If she
can afford to educate him, she wants him to be a professional
man, have a good education and become a responsible man, you
know? She wants him strong. But if she helps him become strong,
then she's going to see him take leadership and that's when he
gets into danger and trouble. And heartache. Many Negro
leaders started out as strong men and fell away because they saw
they couldn't do much good for their people after all. They could
soothe them but not push them out, you know? They had no
place to move to . . . in the world.

"But . . ." she adds reluctantly, "that's changing. I see it. For
Negroes living in the South is now no more dangerous than living
in the North, but living is dangerous every day for Negroes."

"How did you feel when your grandchildren entered a white
school?"

"I was just sick. Very worried. My husband has heart trouble,
you know. And he developed an ulcer during the period of
trouble with his son, our oldest. He's never gotten over it entirely.
It troubles him still. He has to rest a lot and I try to keep our life
peaceful for him. But my son and his wife wouldn't listen to us
about the school and now . . . well, things seem to be all right.
The children don't know the difference while they are in school.

They are beginning to see the difference outside the school, though. They are troubled too, a little.

"I know white schools are better. I was a teacher in the South for many years, remember. Negro schools are run down and crowded, lots of them, even now. Teachers getting low pay. You don't have much equipment in Negro schools. Education is the only hope for Negroes in this country, and they still have to put up with the equipment and books cast off by white children as worn out or out of date."

Mrs. Roland takes me to an excellent Negro-owned-and-frequented restaurant, a luncheon date at which we are joined by her husband. The proprietor deluges us with appetizers and sample portions of their specialties: a creole stuffed lobster, a crab pudding, and a very exotic gumbo.

I meet two Negro lawyers, a real estate man, and an elderly couple just retired from the funeral business. Mrs. Roland describes them variously as wealthy, conservative, important in civic affairs. She is eager to acquaint me with the quality of Negro upper-class activity in New Orleans. She is very objective about it, acting as a good informant—impersonal and mindful of minor events or qualities that are revealing.

"The money in New Orleans, among Negroes that is, has helped attract Negroes back here after they leave for an education. And, of course, the schools here—the colleges—are pretty good. And natives are drawn back here to the life that is so much more interesting and—oh, I would say, sophisticated than it is in other Southern cities. This gives us a strong upper class. There's more movement back and forth with white power, too."

I have been told that New Orleans is considered by many in the Movement to be closed territory, hardly available to civil rights activity. I ask her about it, and she seems to dislike the question.

"Yes, but this city is unusual. You have to have grown up here to understand it. It's very complicated socially. There's more family structure among Negroes, going back over the generations, you see. And a history of more money handed down. We had many rich Negroes a hundred years ago. New Orleans Negroes don't want that changed."

She hints often at some equation between the Movement and a breakup of family structure, understandable in her case.

Charity arrives and we share a room at the Holiday Inn. Edna is with friends in downtown New Orleans. Charity and I are shy with one another. We go to a modest café, where the beans and rice are the best to be had, I was told recently. It is down at the wharf, not far from the Morning Call. The day is beautiful and sunny. I take pictures of the great bins of fruit and the crates of oysters, the ships. We feel very much like tourists this morning. I notice that Charity is as relieved to have a casual meandering morning like this as I am.

We sit in what is obviously the white section of the café. There is a rear door and a rear room where several Negro men are having lunch, workmen from the docks. Charity is superficially relaxed but, I feel, acutely sensitive to the surroundings. Her eye takes in every other customer, every exit, the waitresses, and all the rest like a roving but hidden camera. The waitress is friendly, but Charity says little, orders in a soft voice, and then attempts to concentrate on me and our talk.

"I forgot about beans and rice in New Orleans," she says. "Last time I was here I ate a lot of seafood but didn't get the beans and rice." Her eye strays; she cannot give me full attention. To see the entrance she would have to turn her head and that would be too obvious. But she is like a nervous cat; I feel the radiation from her antennae.

"I'm sure they haven't been integrated long, if ever," I say.

"That's right. See that back room full of Negroes? Five or six men in there right now." She almost whispers it.

It is early and the room where we sit is empty except for one customer at the counter.

"Are you too uncomfortable, Charity? Shall we go?"

"Oh, no. My, no. I been in worse situations than this!"

Quite true. She left a church in Mississippi five minutes before it was destroyed by a bomb. She was in an airplane accident and, although injured enough to be in a wheel chair, nevertheless went on into Chicago to deliver a speech where five hundred people waited an hour for her.

At this moment the door bangs open and two young men enter, both skinny and somehow rough looking; they are workmen, but out of work today, perhaps. Their clothes look old. One wears an indefinite sort of black hat with a Western brim. He is taller, very gaunt, not over thirty. His face is lined and tense in expression. His chin is long, his mouth full of jagged teeth; it forms a cruel half-sneer that is apparently permanent.

They move toward the table between ours and the counter, and then this taller one freezes. He stands, feet apart, and stares in disgust at us. Charity looks at the bottle of Tabasco sauce. I return the stare coldly. I fully expect him to spit violently; his lips are working toward it. The heat of Charity's tension, her intense stillness, burn at my side.

We maintain this pause for about a minute. I do not drop my eyes but observe him as calmly as possible. Now he moves and slouches into a chair opposite his companion. He mutters something partly audible to us; the predictable word "nigger" and a few obscenities are the most we get. He grips the pepper shaker on the table in a fist that turns white at the knuckles. The other man gives us a quick look and goes back to his menu.

"Do you think we can see Mrs. Steele tonight?" I say it loudly enough for them to hear, and say it casually.

Charity lets out her breath. "I think so. We'll call her when we get back."

The beans and rice are unbelievably good, but neither of us can relax her stomach enough to finish the plate. Charity's is half eaten, although she manages to consume all the sausage on the side, a piece of bread and butter, and her coffee.

The men leave before we do, hastily, the tall one banging, actually almost throwing, his chair backward to hit the empty chair at our table. We pause again like two deer in a bush. I look down at Charity's beautiful hand on the table—the simple, elegant, graceful long fingers lie as if carved of wax. Her faith, her courage and humility and wisdom dwell in that hand.

The men are gone.

Charity raises her head. "Mmmm! You see him grab that pepper shaker?"

"Yes. I thought he might actually throw it."

"He could have. I think being women and you being very proper looking is all that kept him from it."

"Charity, I could never be nonviolent and go through an encounter with a madman like that. I couldn't do it. I'd fight him. If he had made one move toward us, I would have stood up and fought him."

She laughs wryly, resignedly. "You would be on the floor with your head open in a minute! Don't you know that?"

"Yes. But I would have fought anyway. I can't suppress hatred for that kind of ignorant, crummy tyrant. I'd hate him. Don't you actually feel any hatred?"

"Well, I have felt it a few times, a long time ago. But it was never very . . . well, not severe with me. All I can feel is sorry for him. He must be in misery to be so full of hate. And ignorance. Ignorance is the worst. No, I can't hate him. Wouldn't last more than a minute."

We ride up Royal Street and down Chartres, cruising the Quarter. Charity has not done this before. The shops intrigue and intimidate her. She comments that they are probably very expensive. The figures of Old Slave Mammies are still perched on the doorsills of the praline shops, just smaller than life size, holding signs, their ghoulish grins and round eyes a mockery. Old Mammy in effigy, caretaker of a dead and moldy white dream. I wonder how the proprietors feel about it at closing time when they lift her and haul her inside, prop her against a wall? Do they even question the old, tawdry myth that dwells in that figure? I think the dolls are newly made every few years. They seem to be quite fresh looking. It would be bad for business if Mammy looked shabby.

"Had enough of this scene?" I ask Charity.

"Plenty," she says. We laugh, tired of it.

Edna and I take Charity to her bus. She's off to South Carolina to do some dickering on a new house. Her beloved old home is to

be sold and then torn down in about six months. She is concerned about money for the new one, loans and interest. She has
mentioned the matter several times. Since she never complains
nor worries out loud, I know this is a deep concern.

I carry her small suitcase and Edna carries the large one into
the bus station, to the utter amazement of the whites who mill
around the ticket counter. When we put her on the bus, Edna
kisses her goodbye, and they repeat the arrangement made for
meeting in a few days in Atlanta. Edna kisses her again and hugs
her. She really loves her new mother-in-law.

Then I kiss Charity's cheek and promise to meet her for the
workshop in South Carolina in three weeks. She will travel a lot
in that time. The bus driver, who stands ready to help her on,
stares and blinks his eyes as if in a parody of surprise. Several
other whites are openly aghast. I cannot believe this mime of
horror, thinking we were a little past that stage. Edna stifles a
laugh and swings off toward the car, laughing aloud once outside
the terminal.

"God! Did you see that man's face? He couldn't believe it
when you kissed Mama-Chere. He thought he was seein' stars!
Shoot!" She smiles and literally twitches with delight. I seem to
have gained a little respect from Edna, who, if she felt it for me
before, was careful not to show it. She may have been regretting
her earlier confidences.

I am sick of "the problem" and look forward to spending two
days with white friends from Washington. I feel a shameless
desire to wallow in comfort and obscurity in some good hotel,
luxuriate in my whiteness, assume my privilege to wander this
town on my own terms. I am too weary to feel guilty. I have been
away from my own world for a long time and lived more or less
incognito. When my friends arrive from Washington I am super-
animated and we start making the rounds like innocent tourists.

But it does not last long. The Negro people I have met are so
real—it is that simple, *real*—they remain with me. I am dis-
tracted by thoughts of them. Will Edna and Leroy get back
together? Can Charity afford a new house? What is Mrs. Long

eating today? Who tends to little Ronelle these days? Has she discovered that BBBB does not spell her name? Has Mrs. Ferris opened her door?

A card comes from Bill. Mrs. Sigh is pregnant again! The old lady next door with the dagger suddenly died! The neighborhood kids are breaking into the recreation center at night, but they do not steal nor damage anything; they only want to be inside it. It has become their place, a success, therefore. Bill must be proud of that.

MARYLAND

A LETTER ARRIVES FROM CHARITY TODAY.

Spent a week in Wilcox County, Alabama, getting out the vote. Many Negroes panicked on election day. It was hard for them to come off a plantation and be sworn in by the plantation boss who was a poll watcher. Both Negro and white poll watchers sitting side by side were very nervous. Their hands shook as they tried to check the rolls. Many good things occurred for the first time. A white farmer having to stand in line with Negroes voiced his disgust.

A great force was at the polls because we had no bloodshed but two white men in their early forties committed suicide in Perry County, Alabama, when they counted the ballots and found that the Negro running for sheriff was ahead. We have twenty-four Negroes in the May 31 runoff. Keep your fingers crossed for all of us. Someone must start teaching love to hostile whites.

Wilcox County, Alabama, has a grant for $350,000 for basic education, Head Start and Day Care Centers. The people will be given $30.50 a week to attend school. I feel superbly happy about it.

I had sent her a copy of *Doctor Zhivago*, which she had expressed a desire to read because of Pasternak's difficulties in the face of a restrictive government. "Think what that man went through," she said with awe. She wrote of it:

> I have the book and am nearly through reading it. It is a great novel, just fascinating. I can hardly sleep at night for reading it. It is very hard to put it aside and turn out the light. Many many thanks. Lara and Tonia and Yura will live with me forever.

St. Marys County is quiet. Something about it elicits the word deep, as in deep woods or deep silence; it also has a forgotten quality, that of a memory. Perhaps that is because I once lived here, briefly, and fell into its time patterns.

Gussie is still alive. I found her in a new little house, a green wood box of three rooms, built by her own and Henry's hands. She's in her sixties now. We talked of Aunt Lonnie who had taken in washing for a long, sober, quaint lifetime: from the age of fifteen to the age of seventy-eight.

"Well," Gussie said, "she died, Honey. She did. She were . . . oh, about seventy-eight when she die. You remember her, do you?"

I did, right then, intensely. Aunt Lonnie had seemed old even when I lived down there. She was stoical but always gentle, remote but kindly; not merely polite but sternly sweet.

Oh, I remembered her all right . . . how she stood in her doorway, her limbs long and stringy like strips of jerked beef; the narrow composure of that face, the ferocious intelligence of expression; how she spat her tobacco juice at least two yards out onto the dirt, where the chickens scattered after it and then veered away before sampling it. Her house of one room was clean and bare like the palm of her old washer hand, and fragrant with the clover air that wafted in through the open front door and out the back, which was directly opposite, only ten feet away, and fragrant with tobacco and a pot of simmering rabbit or "oshter" stew or a skillet of pone on the one-burner iron stove at the foot of the bed.

Aunt Lonnie. Both Negroes and whites called her Auntie. I am embarrassed that I never knew her last name. Hard to believe that she had died. She had fallen out back in the ravine, breaking her hip, and was just passing away when a neighbor child found her. This long poor life and this lonely death would not have pleased her mother, who had been freed from slavery.

Aunt Lonnie's brother Clinton had built, forty years ago, that crude, stanch, celibate bed in which she, a maiden of thirty and then fifty and then sixty-four, had slept her calm, just, God-granted virginal sleep. When I lived down there she did ten hours or more over the wash tubs in the back yard, stoking a fire that kept the water boiling for her all day in what was sometimes 104 degrees of clammy heat. But when I used to go over at evening for the laundry she was always there in her doorway staring, spitting tobacco juice, suspended in what seemed to be an unworried realm of pause, of question, as if having labored without doubt all day in her back yard at the laundering of white folks' bedding and intimate clothes and having driven the heavy, hard, stove-heated iron over them and made the tidy bundles of them—as if then she had come to the stoop to savor the evening and to confront her Lord in whom she ardently, undeviatingly, believed and who authored her labor and her solitary sleep; to wait, perhaps to request blessing, reprieve; to confess in this confrontation her piety and her sin of weariness, of meek anger that sometimes must have flickered in her heart. "The Lawd tell me," she sometimes said. "He tell me."

And I suddenly remembered her neighbor Inez, a much younger woman; I remembered how they looked—old Aunt Lonnie in a straight, chaste black dress and black-felt stovepipe hat with a wide, stained red band, and men's shoes (her brother Clinton's), and Inez, shorter, just ripe, heavy, in a white-eyelet cotton dirndl dress spread over the broad dark field of her young body, a dress given her by a white girl who was ten pounds thinner than Inez and lived over in Leonardtown—those two, marching single file along the edge of Newhill Road to Mass on Sunday morning and again at evening, dividing between them the cluster of small birdlike children Inez, unmarried, had borne; Aunt Lonnie had become virgin grandmother to them and formed the habit of telling them (since she did not read) stories from the Bible and even, when Inez was on hard times, feeding them from her iron stew pot, but making them eat in the yard so as to preserve the chapel cleanliness of her one-room, eight-by-ten cottage.

A few months before Aunt Lonnie's death one of Inez's daughters had taught her to write, and she had written JESUS on the wall over her bed in large careful letters with a blue crayola. It is still there, fading. The cabin is now a kind of dormitory for three of Inez's children.

"I'm so glad she learned to read and write a little," I said to Gussie. "She should have had a good education. She was a very intelligent woman. She would have enjoyed reading a lot."

"Oh, she were, Honey," Gussie affirmed it with a sober shake of her head. "Very intelligen'. She commenced to sayin' the Bible out a lot, you know. She made out like she could read it, but she never got that far. But, Honey, she were good. Ask Jesus if that woman weren't good! My God, she was!"

Aunt Lonnie had told me once that most women, including a white like me, ought to take a steady man, but that the Lord wanted her to remain pure and besides she did not really like men. She had never liked any man but her brother Clinton, whom the Lord had also wanted to stay clean. But Clinton, she explained, had stabbed a woman and was in jail for life before I ever came to that place.

"He willin'," she had said adamantly. "He willin' to be right where he be. She tempt him and he stab her off. He know de debil when he see it. He wasn't free no ways. Isn't inny black mens got freedom round here. Dey always got de law follerin' after 'em. He say de prison not so bad. He learnin' up there, some kinda work on machines. He send me a nice lettah time to time."

The priest, white, had told her that she pleased God and was a very good colored woman. That priest, I remember her saying, never said "nigger" or anything nasty. But one priest, when she was a child, had said "nigger" all the time, an old nice priest "but igrant." But most men were "igrant," she said, even rich whites. Never a white man approached *her* or came snooping around, and if he ever did the Lord would strike him down. But a white boy, and she knew who, had "laid up" with Inez, and one of her children was his, a very light little girl. "But the Lord know what he doin'." That was Aunt Lonnie: one heir, her brother, an old black man in prison for life.

While we talked I looked at Gussie and recalled her, too, standing at evening in her front door as if in that same patient quest for blessing and also looking out over the creek where her man, Henry, who worked as a handy man around the dry docks, would soon come paddling home in an old skiff if he was sober enough. That was over twenty years ago.

And I remembered how two of Gussie's kids, Sonny and Puddin, would go like two fawns on their bare delicate child feet down the mud path to the creek at summer dawn and pull the skiff free from the bank, and with their nets on long poles and wearing wide straw hats they would stand, one in each end of the boat, like small dark-stemmed upright straw flowers and glide silently along the edge of the creek hunting the big blue soft-shelled crabs; suddenly with silent swift easy aim they dipped the net, scooping up a struggling crab; no fuss, only the occasional knock of a pole against the side of the old wood boat and a soft-slurred drowsy syllable of comment between them that we, asleep in our houses on the opposite bank above the docks, grew to relish as part of summer awakening. Crabs, even then, had brought $1.75 a dozen. Sonny and Puddin that summer had earned more than half the family income. I wrenched myself out of the memories.

"Gussie, remember how Sonny and Puddin went crabbing in the mornings in that old skiff?"

"Oh, Honey, thank God, they loved that crabbin'! Made all that money! Shoot! Sonny, he come down here from Wash'ten now on a weekend, he be out there crabbin' five o'clock in the morning. He love it today. He take his little boy and they *gone*. You don't see them till supper."

"You remember Henry?" she asks me.

"Sure. How is he?" Her husband was a chronic drunk in those past days.

"Well, he doin' fine. Just fine. He stopped his drinkin'."

"He *did?*"

"Plum stop! The whole thing. Haven't took a drink since 1957." Her long horsy jaw clamps on the absolute miracle of it. Her new teeth are big and white, square, handsome young horse teeth, ludicrous in her old woman's jaws and her bloodless, gaunt convalescent face. She has cancer now and is up from surgery only two months. Can't work anymore, ever again in her life; she had a heart attack, too.

"I been awful sick, Honey. Awful sick. I tell the Lord he just about didn't git Gussie off that operatin' table. I could feel it— fallin' out."

These cautious movements of Gussie's that I see now, this quiet sitting with one of her new grandchildren in her lap—a pale-skinned lovely little girl in whose soft neck wrinkles bands of dried milk and puke and general baby dirt lie stiff, cracking, and one of whose feet is bare, the other socked in dingy white, a battered sock, much too large—this quietude of Gussie's is unfamiliar and unsuitable. She was once powerful. This is a large long noble face, a bony brow, a horse face with astonished, tragic and pained eyes, dark-ringed, sunken. I stare at her. She is dying of cancer and probably knows it; she looks it. They have taken out plenty, Louella, her daughter told me: "Some gut and all the woman organs."

"I don't move aroun' much inny more. Used to keep this place nice, too. But the kids bang it up. Can't keep my do' on straight. No use to wash the walls cause they messin' it up again in no time."

"It's a very nice house, Gussie. I remember the old place. This seems a lot more comfortable. You and Henry build it?"

"We built it. We owns all that prop'ty over to them trees, see? And down to the road. That's Louella's trailer. Welfare give it to her. That how they does now. Welfare give you the trailer and it up to you to find you a place to set it. Louella use the privy with us but the chillrun do they business in the woods. Hard to get them kids into a privy. That's a pretty trailer but it ain't big enough fo' all them."

"How many children does Louella have now?"

"She got six? . . . no, she got seven. This here one make it seven."

"Oh, that's hard. That's a lot of children, Gussie."

"It *be*, Honey! It be a lotta chillrun fo' a single girl!"

I could laugh and cry.

So Louella has seven now; she is on welfare, and most of the kids have different fathers. My thoughts begin to organize: don't they tell her about birth control down at the welfare office? Louella, I quickly tell myself, is too young.

Then I remember her twenty years ago, a little girl, maybe twelve years old, rowing the skiff across the creek in her white Sunday dress with Puddin and Sonny and Moselle sitting quietly on pieces of butcher paper so as not to soil themselves on the way to Mass. This is Catholic country. No birth control so far. No mention of it. Yes, even then, with Henry drunk and Moselle always in trouble, and Puddin and Sonny earning most of the money for summer on crabs, even then Gussie got them off to Mass. She held them together and to some notion of their own spirit. The Lord here, and the priest, the father, all males in fact, have authority. In any other part of the South except some of Louisiana, Gussie might very well have become husbandless and head of her family. But she has come through, deferring to time and trust and a father god. Henry is, in his late days, sober—a figurehead. I wonder.

No, nothing says that Louella will not have ten more children. I look back at Gussie.

"This baby is adorable. What's her name?"

"Uh . . ." she laughs. "I never kin git that name right. Lou-ella!" She calls, hoarse, weary-voiced, out the open door toward the trailer. "What the name o' this baby? Come here a secon'."

Louella is sturdy, quick, and irritable but gentle. She is short, lean, and commonly pretty. She has a truant quality, very subtle, like Moselle had. She would like to be obedient to these rules that Gussie has always taken for granted, but she cannot. One can see that rules make no sense to Louella. She walks out in the woods at night with her men friends and comes back pregnant. She is never long away from the trailer now that Gussie is so weak. Louella gives me a knowing look. I lived briefly in this area once when I was young, and black or white, everyone knew everyone else's business.

"Her name's Stephany Yvette." She snatches up the baby. "Oooo she dirty! What you showin' off this dirty baby?" She laughs scorn at her mother.

The phone rings and she goes into the bedroom to answer it, then flounces out to deliver a message to a neighbor, hip-riding the baby. Gussie's is the only phone in the neighborhood, and it is understood that everybody is served by it. All at once Caroline, a mentally retarded daughter who has been sleeping in the bedroom, stumbles out, as if drugged, and slumps on the couch. She looks kiddish but is about twenty-five by this time. I have forgotten her, saw her only once in the old days. She was the baby.

"Maybe she go back to sleep," Gussie says softly. "She git a lot o' sleep. She do a lotta work, too, since I come from the hospital. Henry, too. They all workin' my work now."

"Well, tell me about Henry. I think it's just wonderful that he's not drinking. How'd he ever stop?"

"Well, you know Moselle, my oldess? He died, in de watah. Fell out de boat and drown."

"I heard, Gussie. That was so awful. Moselle was a wonderful boy."

And he was, except that he drank like his daddy and remained at home until he was twenty-five years old, unemployed, tormenting his family. He was like Gussie—tall and elegant, but blacker and gleaming, with carved features in a fluted sensual relief like those of a young Buddha. He had none of the commonness of Henry and Louella and Sonny. He and Puddin were Gussie's to the bone—aristocrats. Moselle spent all his evenings in town at the clubs in Blister Alley with a whore he liked and sometimes at the Moonlight Club out at Newhill. He was sweet and rotten but never fought, never cut a man nor even carried a knife. Just drunk all the time. None of them, the Gaines family, had ever learned to swim although they were obliged to cross the creek in a skiff to get to work, to town, to church, and to visit most of their friends. They lived then on a relatively uninhabited neck of land across from Newhill and the yacht harbor and the dry docks. The summer I lived there we tried to teach the younger ones to swim, but they disliked the feel of the water: their hatred of it was a kind of taboo. It was assumed that some Gaines child would drown in that creek one day. And then Moselle came home one night some years after I left the area, too drunk to stand, and tried to cross the creek in the dark. Next day the skiff was seen in the channel, beached on a sand bar, the oars missing.

"Oh, Honey, that were bad. That hit his daddy bad. He love

Moselle so much. Oooo, I tell you, he cried his eyes blind, old Henry. We never found the body. Scrape that creek and never come up with nothin'. He got sucked out to the river, I 'clare."

But Henry was by then pretty terrifying himself, even more drunk and wicked and mean. He beat her sometimes, although he was sloppy drunk and a good foot shorter than she. Yes, Gussie deferred to men. She could have killed him with a well-placed blow, but she endured him instead.

"I went home to my daddy and he say, 'Go back and try one mo' time and if he don't commence to do better, you come home with de kids.' That were about twelve years ago."

I make mental note that she did not go home to mother, although she had a mother. She went to daddy. This is a more purely patriarchal Christian country. The virgin mother is obscured by God the Father, and the Son. The priest has a sacred role behind robes and the confessional, behind white skin and Latin invocations; he is unavailable to the casual exchange of the black Protestant preacher.

To make things worse, she says, Henry had by that time taken up with another woman—"dat bat" as Gussie calls her. And then one night he too crossed the creek, drunk, late in winter. There was frost on the ground. Gussie kept a wood fire banked in her stove all night.

"Honey, 'bout three in de mornin' I hear dis cryin' outside and carryin' on and I thought it's a dog or somethin', freezin' up out there. I went to the do' and there's Henry, down on his hands and knees crawlin' up de bank, wringin' wet and sobbin', moanin', just carryin' on like a baby! He have on his big wintah coat, that army coat Cap'n Ruley give him, and that thing so wet you can't *liff it up!* Well, he fell in de watah. Loss de boat, everything."

"My God! How'd he ever get out? He doesn't swim."

"God knows, Honey. He walk out on the crick bottom, that's what he say. Oh, he like to drown, don't doubt. He *cry,* Honey. Just as well be a six-month-old baby the way he cry. He come rushin' on me; I say: 'Don't look to *me!* Not *me,* Henry. Wasn't *me* rockin' dat boat. Lord knows. He givin' you hell now, Henry Gaines! Don't look at *me.* I be *glad,'* I told him. Well, he sob all night and *sick* . . . My God, he were *so* sick. He lay there and shaken for a whole week! Couldn't do nothin'. Couldn't eat only a little soup."

"Oh, Gussie! That must have frightened him half to death."

"Tell it! Fright him *sober,* that's what it done. You tell it!"

And Henry never took another drop nor ever saw "dat bat" again as far as she knew. He worked steady after that. Gussie prevailed; she endured. And now she lives in this house with him, keeping to the same bed, and watches her little grandchildren, fatherless weeds, grow. Wild, cunning, full of glee, they are slowly demolishing the proud little house she and Henry built in his late sober days. The one clean prideful thing she has owned in her life will, after her death, perhaps fall to them as to barbarians. Louella expects a certain amount of destruction. My mind, accustomed to reason, casts about: how can the morality and decency and forbearance of Gussie's generation have been so quickly wiped out? Her grandchildren are fed and that is enough. They go to school; they are clothed, on welfare; they continue to cram together in the trailer to accommodate a new arrival: Louella continues to walk the woods at night with her men friends. And to drink. She drinks heavy now, as Gussie puts it. It is a worry to Gussie, the drinking. Gussie sits in her big chair near the door and watches a slow disintegration of her labors.

But perhaps she does not think in these ways. Sonny and Puddin are flourishing up in Washington, both married, employed, parents of well-cared-for broods. Not a bad average. One is dead, one retarded, and one, Louella, breeds the masses. Gussie will die before she can influence these grandchildren with more than love. She holds them quietly. At least they will have known that. They come and go from her lap and her cabin as if from a mainspring. Louella is not still; they cannot fix her anywhere as they can Gussie; she is busy combing hair and shopping for bargains, rearranging beds, goading welfare for another trailer, scratching after a little pleasure in this bare life. She is pregnant again, perhaps.

I am stunned, stupefied. I want Gussie to rise and go off to some wild solitary spot to die alone like a noble beast and not to disintegrate amid this rabble of new generation.

Maybe these little girls (most of them are girls) of Louella's will be able to say with equanimity, with that total modesty and compassion and dignity of Maddie, the old nurse up at the local hospital who told me a few days ago: "No, I lived with my mother alone. I didn't know my father. My mother was not married," just as if she had said, "This morsel has been blessed, has been purified by divine judgment. Here, take it, swallow it with trust, with comfort." And I did, I do. Maybe these wild little children of Louella's will stay in a society that forgives them their conception in the woods by anonymous fathers. I cannot hope that they do, for that may mean that they will take all the rest of the second-rate offering of that society: mediocre education, shambling surroundings, outhouses, all the trimmings of poverty whose sole grace is tolerance. They will be tolerated, perhaps. The word illegitimate is being struck from their records at the courthouse but the fact is not so easily struck from their lives. They have no father.

Psychologists have lately dwelt upon the idea that the presence of a father in the home is essential to the development of "achieving qualities" in the child. Dozens of studies indicate a far greater tendency to immature, submissive, dependent, and effeminate behavior among fatherless boys than among those with fathers. Daniel Moynihan in his work "The Negro Family," says, "Negro children without fathers flounder and fail."

Yet 6 out of every 100 Negro females are in professional jobs, a figure substantially similar to the rate of all females in such jobs. Approximately 7 out of 100 Negro women are in technicians' jobs, exceeding the proportion of all females in such jobs.

Seventy percent of Negro employees in the United States Department of Labor are women, but only 42 percent of white employees are women.

Negro girls in these fatherless families identify with their mothers, so says Thomas Pettigrew in his book, A Profile of the Negro American, and model themselves after their mothers, preparing "to assume male as well as female responsibilities." And my observations lead me to believe that this assumption of both roles is the essence of stability and strength in Negro women. They are strong not only as women but as human beings, conditions having forced them to transcend to some degree the old rigid concepts of male and female roles, to see beyond these sometimes limiting definitions and to dwell in a dual humanity from which far subtler resources may be drawn. The adaptability of Negro women is well known but perhaps less celebrated than their capacity to endure.

A peculiar combination of forces has led to today's adaptive Negro woman—a history of slavery and service, within which she had certain privileges if she was lucky or light-skinned, handsome or a good breeder or a good nurse, a womanly woman. Negro men, however manly, in the days of slavery still had more or less the same futures ahead of them. But there was a chink in the heavy wall of slavery for Negro women, a little glimmer of a way out through a certain kind of being if not doing. Slavery, while the most degrading of conditions, can be, as most women know, a kind of refuge, albeit a dangerous refuge. There is something preservative in the very nature of existing with the body's life as the principal experience. The value placed upon one's very physical presence and performance may constitute a powerful substructure for a human being if there is some means of proceeding from that point to higher levels of living.

The degree to which she was needed—as nurse, breeder, bearer of slave population, mulatto and black—no doubt constituted a positive filament in character development, or ego development, one might say, in a black woman. Divested of its brutality and degradation, its limitations to mobility, slavery in some benign form—a life of service with some care and gratitude as recompense (and this sometimes existed)—might have created a huge population of saints in America. Even in the face of brutality and degradation, many a saintly black human being emerged to refine the American soul. The hard school of service and sacrifice did not serve her completely ill. If she had to bear children of her white master, they, at least by virtue of their lighter skins, would have the better of two slave existences: that of household instead of field slave. At least she could hope for that. White patriarchy rendered innocuous and even taboo the whole parental role of the black man. He was most often a stud who never saw his child. Even when he acted as father to his children, often he could not influence their lives or natures. She could.

And so she is first that stanch chattel—servant, mother, nurse, roles that in themselves are not destructive. And worker. She was often obliged to transcend the whole idea of black and white for the sake of nursing a white infant and giving it love. That infant made a saving lie of the whole delusory system of one human being owning another. She must have seen beyond the despised white countenance to mere frail humanity. These things must have brought her wisdom and patience. She had these virtues before and seems to have them full-blown now.

But it was that added complexity of having to be both father and mother, transcending both roles, to another order of human experience, that seems to me the final strengthening elixir. All this is no doubt bitter. Self-denial must begin early, carefully, must be grafted in slip by slip in order not to distort, or possibly destroy, the human character. But there are saints among us, and they are made in somewhat this fashion, tempered by humor and a lust for the mere fact of existence upon earth, for love and sleep and food and allowing the body expression of its own peculiar grace. If she had nowhere to go in so many steps, she had at least that inward way to go—that way to becoming a dual being, developing the "other" in the unit of self. She is often still obliged to do it.

It will create, I believe, first annoyance, then disbelief, and eventually a deep rift between Black Woman and the world when society tells her, this woman with her peculiar history of transcendence, to play a role, to become some two-dimensional illusion of femininity the way it still instructs her white sister to do. This black woman has lived deeply beyond such caricaturing and she will not seal off those depths easily, if at all. If only enough work, experience of the world, and influence are available for but half the black population and these are given to men, as they no doubt will be, then her struggle against capitulation will not be any mere resistance to her "place" as domestic creature and pin-up doll. It will be the outrage of probably the most psychologically developed American among us. Oh, there are infants among them; there are those who preen and those with empty heads. But this history is recent, and a black American woman bears it all in her unconscious, just as I bear my Pilgrim and pioneer Western and landowning, slave-holding great grandmothers in mine. She is what she had to be and do as we all are; and what she had to be and do has made her strong and adaptive, not retarded—or delinquent. We shall see. We will hear of her outrage.

Many have said to me that the Movement carries more for them than equality with white people, that it carries something particular for women. This may become some terrible, wrenching battle of patriarchy and matriarchy. If both forces die, they can only die into *humanity*.

There is a great need for Negro men and women to reestablish relations, for Negro men to find economic and social strength and a natural position of dignity in society. The need of these men and women for time and peace, for freedom from harassment and perpetual deprivation, is great and is one of which they all seem to be aware. The trend, obviously, is in the direction of reunification of black society, the bases for which are black marriage and black family. Negro women have unique talent and empirical knowledge among American women, and they are too dynamic a social force to be forgotten and trained regressively for mere housewifely living. Many want and will accept that life at least for a time, but most, I believe, will be driven to take a larger, more demanding and creative position in their communities. To a woman who, over many decades, is used to being paid in cash for her labors, however meagerly, even volunteer work is not quite the answer.

Besides, intelligent, mature, experienced, responsible women are desperately needed at the highest levels of influence in American society, although that society is not yet willing to admit that a serious part of its ailment is their absence.

Well, down here in St. Marys County the patriarchal mask is assumed at present by the Church. By that mask, the Virgin and her mythological ancestry are obscured. The black man here has a sort of stature, rickety and illusory, perhaps, but he is accorded something by the women that I do not see elsewhere. They, like Gussie, seem to stand about as a kind of Greek chorus, in praise or lament or condemnation before the sometimes absurd drama of his life. But he is, strangely, the subject. I still believe that is because he shares his gender with God, Jesus, and the priest, who are not familial but sacred figures—not Protestant. They have the power not of morality but of magic. And the priest has the added power of white skin.

Back at the store the lean, alert, proper white fellow who owns the place asks me what I am doing in these parts; he has heard (word travels fast down here) I am writing a book; something about Negroes? Yes, the women. He gives me a stern look, understanding of all such subjects. "I expect you find a lot of difference." "Difference?" "From one to another." "Oh, yes, of course. Just as one would with any people." "I mean from old to young," he says.

Yes, a great deal. The old evidently still "keep their place" with him. The young have begun to boycott his store, I heard. I turn to go out, despising him when I ought to ignore or pity him. An old black man has slipped quietly, deferentially in the front door and is shuffling—actually shuffling—toward the door of the Negro poolroom. The light there is not so bright as that in the white poolroom. The table is the old one, worn out by white trade. But this storekeeper serves both. A game of pool for a Negro, in fact, is cheaper than a game of pool for a white—a subtle condescension essential to an economy as false as this.

The station manager started to beat on the rest-room door. He tried the knob, then looked at me incredulously. "Get that nigger girl outta there! She's not supposed to go in there." He banged again. "Get outta there! This is for whites. Can't you read?"

"No, I can't read. Sorry. I just be a minute."

The man, by this time, was ready to drop. He turned back to me, and I automatically put out a hand to stop his fall. His face was like an old saw. I tried to control my own fear and irritation. "It's all right. She won't do any harm. She'll come right out."

He was ashen; his chin trembled. He turned away, faltering. His helper was now fussing with our tires while the manager himself went into the booth and came out with a tire iron. I stood near the car. Bethel started the motor just as Edna ran across the lot and got in. Bethel told the boy not to bother with the tires and never mind the gas. We started off but got only about twenty feet, just to the road. Both back tires were flat. Bethel swore violently. Charity sighed. Louise wore a look of weary chagrin.

"Why, that stinkin' . . ." Edna shouted.

"Shhh! You just be quiet now!" Charity silenced her.

I got out again and approached the attendant who still had the tire iron. I put on the irate white matron act for him: "How long will it take this . . . *help* of yours to repair his damage to these tires? I think we've cut one of them."

Strangely, they both rushed to the job in absolute silence and obedience. They must have thought all along it was my car and these women my servants. They could not conceive of any other relationship, I suppose. When they finished, Bethel roared off without even a nod, leaving them dazed.

Finally we began to laugh. Bethel looked in the mirror at Edna, who glowed. "That's all the big shows I want from you while you're in my car, girl. You just hold your water till we get there."

We arrive late but are the first of the staff at the conference grounds. The dining room will not open until morning. It is about ten P.M. and none of us has eaten since late lunch.

"Mr. Miller will fix us something," says Louise. "Let's get in these rooms first and then go down there."

The island here, like the mainland, is stalked by huge trees, magnolia, pine, and cypress, which are hung with moss and blanketed in mild, dampish air. The birds seem heavy in flight and larger than those in other regions. The moon is wet.

I share a room with Louise and am glad of the chance to get to know her a little. Most of the time she is guarded but given to sudden bursts of candor. It is difficult to observe her: the general constraint and look of compassion are about all I can see in the very black face. Other expressions are too controlled and tend to disappear into the blackness, anyway. She is the blackest person I have ever seen. She could be pure African. It fascinates me. Louise is comely and gentle. She has a sturdy, neat, peasant body and moves with a deliberation not unlike Charity's. Her straightened hair is worn in a simple chignon fashion. She wears a variety of cotton-knit dresses. She goes bare-legged and wears simple black flats.

We toss our things on the beds and turn on the dormitory furnace. Charity and Edna have a room that connects with ours through the bath. Other staff members and the participants will come later tonight and early tomorrow.

These are large frame buildings; the rooms have pine walls, very high ceilings, and high narrow windows and consequently are somewhat dark. A school for Negroes during Reconstruction days, the place has six or eight buildings of this general, sturdy frame construction with wide verandas; flat tree-covered lawns lie between them. It looks like a plantation, romantic and antiquated. The big bobolinks are numerous, and only one among a dozen other native birds here. The place is now a general conference grounds for conventions and workshops of the sort we are attending.

After settling in our rooms, we drive to Miller's café a mile from the conference grounds. The island is hooded with a low murky sky in which there is only a general dimness of light from the moon. The darkness under these heavy trees is formidable. Now and then, on this short slow ride, we pass a body moving along the edge of the road, and I sense the value of black skin for night-time obscurity. Most of the inhabitants on this island are Negroes and most are very poor. They grow their own vegetables and catch fish in the channels. Many of the women work on the mainland for white families.

Mr. Miller has gone to bed; his little cabin behind the café is dark, but Louise doesn't mind rousing him. He comes, long-legged, slow, humble, and gracious, into the greenish glow of the café sign and lets us in. We sit in the bar in the eerie light of beer signs while he rattles the kitchen awake, makes his fire and finds us a candle. No sense in turning on the lights at this hour. Folks might want service; the police driving by might wonder. Wonder what? Just wonder. It is better to avoid encounters with them. We, plainly, are family. Louise and Charity know him well.

He has some hopping john left from supper which he heats for us, also a little corn bread, some okra, and a large platter of the fried shrimp for which he is famous. We drink beer and gorge while Mr. Miller leans against the counter in his white apron, talking gravely with us. Edna, happy again, eats noisily and moans. Charity and I, too, are ravenous. Louise, I note, assumes a small-daughter attitude with him. Her voice sounds almost childlike just now.

The little café is like a cave. Mr. Miller's voice is nocturnal, slow and meandering; he seems weary. He is not young, maybe in his early sixties. "We glad to see you back," he says softly. "Been quiet for over a month. You let me know the day befo' and I fix you up an oshter roast."

That, apparently, is traditional for this group. The staff prefers this to any other conference ground because of the oyster roast.

When we leave I look quickly over the grounds. In the deep channel behind the place, small oyster and shrimp boats are docked for the night, rocking in the smeary moonlight. The lawn is grassy right to the stone wall of the channel. I see the large old barbecue and a few broken pieces of outdoor furniture under the trees.

Business here, Charity explains to me, is very unpredictable, and the conferences help Mr. Miller greatly. He has lost some white trade that used to come over from the mainland. That could be, Charity says, because he has let the building run down a bit or perhaps it is retaliation: a few Negroes have begun to boycott some local white businesses.

"But you watch," she says as we leave, "some of these women at the workshop will be over here helping him out with the dishes and serving; maybe even cook. It always happens. We come over for a late snack and some of these farm women will go right in there and take over his kitchen." She laughs. "They can't understand a man in the kitchen."

"Lotsa women around here would like to move in with Mr. Miller," Louise laughs. A dependable and solvent Negro man is not to be dismissed, even if he is aging.

Back at the dorm Louise and I unpack and hang our clothes in the long narrow closet, take a chest of drawers each, and discuss the beds.

"You like it warm?" she asks tentatively.

"No. Do you?"

"Yes." She laughs a little. "I like to sleep by the furnace."

I am relieved to have the bed by the window. It seems we are to sleep all night with the furnace blasting away through the vent near her bed. The temperature outside cannot be lower than sixty. We decide that the temperature on her side of the large room will not be seriously affected if I keep the window open slightly by my bed. I give her my extra blanket besides, a heavy red wool. We are both content.

But before we undress, others begin to arrive: some staff from the organization and a carful of participants from Mississippi. Some of the latter are just spectators, three young radicals—a Northern Negro girl and two Southern Negro boys—but with them in a station wagon are four Mississippi women who will take the teacher training. Two of the women are young, not over twenty-two, both very black, both pretty; the other two are middle-aged. The radical three are attractive, casual, hip, and independent looking. They greet me upon introduction with stiff nods and very little voice. The others are more gracious, even interested in my presence here.

Louise gets them settled in the two dorms, and then, as we start for bed again, a lone elderly figure arrives by taxi and stumbles into the sitting room dropping a heavy bag that the

white taxi driver would not carry up the steps for her. Charity
pays him with a scathing silence.

We greet the woman, who stands at attention in a vaguely
military way and announces breathlessly, "Avis Hall, Ascension
Parish, Louisiana," like a runner bringing news to field headquarters from behind enemy lines. She is fairly scented with the
secret-mission atmosphere.

She is in her mid-sixties, solid, heavy, stooped, an ugly, shy,
even browbeaten-looking woman with large loose open lips and
dull eyes in a head that, because of its thin hair and receding
hairline, appears from the front to be bald. A chronic desperation
and dull resistance mark her expressions. She smiles and nods
shyly, saying "Yessum" to everybody. We all shake her hand and
swarm around her. She has been three days and three nights on
seven different buses and, among other things, is punch drunk.
Her money is gone.

"That what they give me to get here run out after my supper
yesterday. Haven't et today—jess some crackers."

Louise provides sandwiches and coffee, which are always
brought for this kind of emergency. Mrs. Hall settles in her room
across from ours, a four-bed room that others will share with her.
She returns to the sitting room, sits stiffly on the couch, and
devours her rations. We crowd around her. Charity speaks
gently.

"We were wondering about you, Mrs. Hall. You had the
longest way to come by bus of any. We should have sent you
more money. I'll see you get more for the trip home and maybe
we can find you a quicker way back."

"Yessum." She nods, mouth full, desperately weary and confused, a little elated even so. Her eyes slide from one face to
another and down to her hands. "I never been outta my parish
befo'. Got a little mixed up on the bus ride. I think they sent me
down outta the way some."

Louise sits very near her. "But you got here, Mrs. Hall. That's
the thing. We're very proud of you coming all that way."

All at once huge tears form and fall over the dull face. "That's
a hard trip," she murmurs.

She has slipped out of her shoes and now fumbles for them

with one inept foot. She wipes upward with the heel of her hand, catching tears at her nose and cheeks. Someone offers her a Kleenex. She has come on the bus all those days and nights from a rural area in Louisiana; she is equipped with a broken suitcase, a very old and rusty country school education, and a raw spirit for the chance of it, the hope, the last curiosity perhaps, to learn to teach illiterate people of her area to write their names and to spell words like bread and rice and soap and vote and president and constitution, civil rights and black and white and love and FREEDOM.

Why? I stare at Mrs. Hall's heavy face. She has endured much pain; that is evident. The trip and the week's living are free. There is a chance to make a little money at the teaching. And there is experience. She was to have come in a car with four others but all backed out at the last minute. She asked for bus fare to come alone.

"Yessum," she repeats wearily, "that's *some* trip."

Sunday. Cars and taxis arrive all day. Our building fills up, and the sitting room is crowded with the somewhat shy women who make tentative friendships and keep an eye cocked for clues, for directions.

One of these is Mrs. Mindy Adams. Mrs. Adams is one of those pretty, fat, tidy farm women who radiates health and wit. She seems perpetually engaged in controlling laughter or at least smiles. The laughter begins inside, deep, and grinds and wheezes up to the voice like a force of water under the earth. It is convulsive, hilarious, and yet not exactly loud when it finally is emitted from her chubby brown glowing face. Her whole being bursts with it. She wears steel-rimmed glasses; a few white hairs curl at her small neat ears. The sweetness and joy of her face are so magnetic that everyone clusters about her, all ages and sexes, without knowing what has drawn them. Automatically there is a circle around her chair in the sitting room after our noon dinner. She says little and laughs with a control that seems to take everything she's got. I have felt elated all day merely because of her presence. Even Charity, with her profound equanimity, is infected.

Mrs. Adams is about sixty-five. She lives on a farm in rural Alabama with her husband, a much older man. Her three children are grown, married, parents themselves, and all live in the North. She visits them at least once a year.

She smells soapy. Her simple homemade cotton print dress and her white orlon sweater, the single-strand necklace of white plastic beads are all poignantly clean, new, and decent. She dips Peach Dream snuff and chews tobacco, packing her jaws several times a day, and totes about with her a polished-looking mayonnaise jar that is wrapped in a soft thin chiffon scarf. She manages to spit into the jar with great finesse and secrecy. It is not evident to most people that she has anything in her mouth except laughter and a set of fine square white teeth touched here and there with gold work.

Two young girls sit near her, making woman-talk. It is warm and sunny today; birds are madly busy in the huge trees outside. I can smell the sea. I feel tempted to run out the door into the woods for a walk but cannot tear myself away from Mrs. Adams. The furnace blasts away although the front door is open. I have turned it off twice today but finally I get the idea that someone here is more determinedly cold than I am hot, and so I'm resigned to it.

Mrs. Hall comes in and sits beside me on a couch. Two fellows from the other dorm have just left after making dates with Palma and Bobbi, the two girls. We are all women alone now. Mrs. Adams looks at Bobbi.

"That your sweetheart?"

Both girls laugh loudly, Bobbi almost hysterically. "God, no! We jess met him. He over in that other building."

Mrs. Adams laughs, wheezing, and deftly spits into her jar. Mrs. Hall cackles a dry laugh and says:

"Don't git you a sweetheart too fass. Take a long time to know a man."

"That's *right!*" says Mrs. Adams with conviction. She says it often, a congregational affirmation. I learned this morning that she is a Sunday School teacher and missionary. I know she has loudly affirmed some shouting preacher down there in her country church. One can tell that she loves the Lord invincibly like most other Negro women.

We get into a kind of anecdotal conversation about men. Palma tells how she outmaneuvered a fellow in a car one afternoon in Jackson. "He took after us and we couldn't shake him off for a whole owa! I jess had to run him into a ditch or somethin' to git rid of him, I knew that. My sistah was cryin', she so scared. That's the kinda smart stuff I hate from a man."

Mrs. Adams shakes her head, troubled but amused. She chuckles, totally lost in the story. At the end of the story, the stranger properly run into a ditch by Palma, Mrs. Adams emits a loud laugh; and as it tapers off she reaches for her jar.

"Can't never tell about mens," says the stern Mrs. Hall. She has sat through the story in total sobriety, her mouth slightly open, her head forward, concentrating. "See that eye?" She points to a dull bruise on her right eye that I had not noticed before. "Man give that to me. My own husban'." She shakes her head and becomes teary. "He *mean!*" She rallies, girds herself with anger. "He come at me with a fire poker! Like to kill me!"

We express horror. Mrs. Adams winces under a threatening laugh.

"Don't say!"

"Oh, yeah," says Mrs. Hall. "He be the *meanest!* He's old, see. Jess mean and old. He git dronk and then he like to argle like a nigger. Can't *nothin'* stop him. He come on me with the poker but he trip ovah somethin' and caught me in the eye with his elbow."

Mrs. Adams lets out a gleeful yelp and tears up. We all grin, trying to hold back, but Mrs. Hall notices little. She relives the terrible scene intently, staring ahead, trancelike. Then she looks around. "You git you a man likes to argle and you got you some trouble. Cause you can't git out without you has some money. I owns the place but he won't let me sell it. I'm goin' try to sell it off next year. I got me a cow I'm goin' to sell when I git home. I sell my cow, then I can go. I say: 'You be lucky you see me in this world, cause I'm goin'.' He don't think I do it, but I'm goin' one of these days." This is the blues, pure and simple. "I'll sell that cow and git. Now I had me this bus ride, I know the way, see. You got to git out a little. This is the bess trip I ever had. I never saw so many nice peoples in my whole life." She is close to tears.

Mrs. Adams bats her eyes and withholds her mirth but the pain is terrible. She is bursting with the vision of the drunk old man aiming with a poker and connecting with an elbow. Hers are not tears of commiseration but of pure amusement. She says, however:

"That's *bad!*" Clearing her throat, she sneaks a spit into the jar and settles back in her chair. She has a great quality of availability—nothing pressing to attend; time is a wound-up skein in her lap, domesticated. She creates on all sides an atmosphere of pleasant surrender to being, just as Charity, by her own nature, elicits work, compassion, forgiveness.

Later, as Mrs. Adams and I walk to supper together, she says softly.

"I didn't mean to make fun on that old Miz Hall, but them *old* mens, I tell you, they the *debil!* Like my neighbor say, she say— 'All them *old* mens wants to do is fill you fulla that old hot piss and make you friggid!' Heeeeee!" Finally she can let it out. We howl together like two old shrews.

"Well, I tell you, bein' married ain't no easy job. You take jess housekeepin'—hit's tough on you."

"Do you think marriage is hard for most women, Mrs. Adams?"

"Mos' ain't goin' say so, but they know it. Hit's tough. Mens is the debil, mos' of 'em. You know—you say you'll marry and stay there till death? Well, you gotta do *somethin'* to stay there till death; you gotta take some hard words and some everything to stay there like you said, till death, and keep that man at you side. That's right! Hit's *tough!*"

"You think a man has more freedom than a woman?"

"Well, in some cases he do and then some he don't. Jess like— you take owa laws here in the Southland—there ain't no laws much on no colored woman and no white men. But it's on the colored man and the white lady. You know, you see all these colored women and white men makin' all those babies? But you never see that on *their* side. They mostly don't care *what* they do.

They don't want a colored ova in their race, yet they'll jump ova in owa race and look what they do! And you see, we have to take all that. That's the reason this upstir is up now! Say: 'I gots all the insurance myself and you none at all.' And you know that's not right.

"Well, that's why I say a colored woman have mo' freedom in some things than a colored man here in owa Southland. But it look like it changin'. We do see the light a little mo'. We have mo' insurance; we have mo' priblege to say. Heap o' things we was feared to say and we don't be feared anymo'."

Tuesday. The young radicals, including Carol, the very attractive girl from the North, have been charmed by Mrs. Adams and now monopolize her company in the dining room. They all laugh loudly at their table, and I feel sure everyone in the room is devastated with envy. I am. What a great woman!

Because of the presence of these radical youths there is a stratum of acute antiwhite tension here. They act openly against me, and the three other whites here, unless I encounter one of them alone. Then the gentleness and politeness that seems native to all of them comes through.

They spend much of their spare time passing the new militant line to the younger participants, who seem cautiously interested. Louise is tempted by them and occasionally will blurt out a reaction to a conservative speaker that reveals her own upheaval and confusion about integration. Mississippi, the tall thin one, plainly enchants her.

Today Louise gave her two-hour lecture and discussion on household management and marketing. It was excellent, although she let the discussion stray into a kind of witch hunt.

There are two white girls here, quite young, who have taken upon themselves a private good-works project in Alabama. They are from California. One is married, seems sensible and intelligent. The other is single, childish, sloppy, and sentimental. She speaks in a babyish manner and obviously annoys some of the others in classes merely by opening her mouth.

This, in any case, is the hour of judgment and we are trapped. Somehow we are suddenly attacked from three sides by angry youths from Mississippi, Carol, and a few of their fellow travelers. Carol turns on the babyish white girl and shouts:

"Why don't you work on the Alabama *whites*, for God sake? What are you doin' with the Negroes? They're not sick! The *whites* are sick!"

And as quickly turns on me: "What're you doin' here? Why are whites always hiding with the Negroes?"

"Because," I say defensively, "they're nicer, I suppose."

Charity, beside me, keeps silent. She should bring the meeting to some kind of order but she waits, evidently believing the confrontation to be necessary.

My retort confuses Carol and she turns away, scowling. The little white girl do-gooder has rushed from the room, tearfully. The other, more stanch, sits blushing, apologetic but dignified. "Well, we're learning, too. We've obviously made a lot of mistakes."

Mr. Wellman, a former preacher from South Georgia, stands, raises a hand, and tries to bring order. He appears to be trying to start a prayer or a song, but he is out-shouted. The Mississippi youths are now standing, shouting at a moderate woman from Charity's office who defends the white visitors. Pandemonium. I try hard to control my anger. The accusations are biased but I know the validity of the anger. Carol is right: the healing has to be done elsewhere.

We recess and come back calm, sore, determined to transcend the battle.

Louise sits on the grass under a tree, idly, an open book unattended on her lap. I join her, breaking into her well-earned solitude a little dubiously. Both of us are still ensnared in that angry encounter of the morning. She resents me, yet she seems to like me. Also, she envies me somewhat. I feel awkward but compelled to join her. We burst into a crazy rebuttal:

"Well, I'm glad they said what they did."

"So am I, Louise. But everybody has a lot to learn. Those kids from Alabama . . ."

"Who's working on *whites*? Most whites are making more mess than helping."

"We're going to flounder, too. I can't punish myself for my

ignorance anymore than I can anyone else. I don't care how many mistakes it takes . . ."

Her face slams shut. "I don't care either. Just don't make them *at my expense!*"

What am I costing you, now, right now, Louise? My very presence is an unsolicited burden to her: the life I have lived; the clothes I wear, which, though modest, are of a better quality than hers. She and Beulah have been staring at my clothes for two days. They have asked me about my background: my education, my travels, my work, my pleasures, all in falsely casual asides. "You've *done* so much!" Beulah said last night, in wonder as if at something too bizarre to envy. Experience. That is the great lack and the tragedy—that these wonderful people have not been able to move about, see the world, change their atmospheres, breathe an alien air.

Mississippi and a young male guest suddenly appear. The guest, Willie, squats beside us. Mississippi stands, tall, lean, condescending, but gentle. Louise is fortified by their arrival.

They plunge in.

Yes, but you whites got to learn it, *hear* it, Baby, that you gotta go home. *Yes.* I mean, we different. *Yes.* We know something else. *Yes.* See, when I bring up my son, I'm goan tell him who the enemy is. I want him to know who the enemy is. *Yes.* What about this book you writing? What about *white* women? *Well, there are hundreds of books written about white women, Willie.* None about black? *Not precisely. And nobody black is writing it.*

"And that," says Mississippi, with philosophical irony, "is the great tragedy."

"Yes. But when *she* writes it, hers will be something else and in no way inhibited by this one."

Willie perseveres: "So you whites had you a black mammy and you love your black brothers and sisters now. And you never goin' to forget that black mammy. You owe her somethin' now. You 'ainliated' from white society."

Silence. Louise winces, hoping I won't correct his pronunciation.

Willie: "Ain't that right?"

Jo: "Yes, in a way that's right."

Willie: "Listen, Watts is America, see?"

Jo: "Yes, so is Beverly Hills."

Willie: "See, that's the way with you whites. You got to answer. Yes but, yes but!"

Louise sits relishing it all in silence. This attack obviously satisfies her frustrated need to confront whites. I agree: we whites have an answer. Many do not listen well. I pull up a few pieces of grass and hold them in my hand. Willie squats facing me. Mississippi looms, gently bitter, over me. Louise waits.

Willie (pleasantly): "You know, when my friends and I get together we jess . . . set around. We run around the street or jess set and be quiet or watch the folks or something. Maybe we drink. But we jess bees together, see?"

Yes, I see. I do not tell him that I do the same. He sees mine as a busy, ordered, proper, and blind existence—logical, unquestioning. See what you must see, Willie.

Dusk. Supper is over. Evening meetings about to start. Black bodies, men and women, moving slowly, head for the recreation rooms. Every meeting begins and ends with the circle formed, the hands locked, and "We Shall Overcome."

Willie comes across the wide lawn from the opposite end, a paper in hand.

"Here's something; you can read it. I like you to read it." Serious, friendly. "It's a kind of Bobby Dylan type of song sort of thing."

"Thanks."

It states in ballad form, obviously, but passionately, how he would like to burn me. *We have found you out.* It is familiar. I hear a tune. Willie waits in an old car near the recreation building as I read it and try to recall why it is familiar. Then I go to him. "Didn't I hear it sung somewhere?"

"No. I just wrote it a few days ago."

I keep it, return to the porch, read again. I listen. Yes, I heard it forever ago, not the words, not the unknown tune, but the idea. I heard it when I was a child, that about burning, wanting to burn; before he said it or his father said it, a long time ago, I know that I heard it somewhere, perhaps with ancestral ears; I hid it and saved it. Did not heed but heard it.

But Willie does not burn me. He writes an anguished song about it and delivers that to me instead of fire.

Louise is conservative, stoical, stubborn as a wall. She falters, hovers between the young radicals who dazzle her with their blunt courage and their willingness to be angry and heartbroken, and the alternative of moderate action, nonviolence, a hope for integration—between them and Charity, one might say. She tries to understand me. She has observed that when someone pleases or charms me, I laugh. She is cautious, wondering if the laugh is condescending. She studies my face, my style. In the night, when one of us gets up, the other watches. She is invisible in the dark; only a pale nightgown passes through the room; to her I must look ghostly pale and bloodless in the dark.

Mississippi was once shot in the neck by white police and nearly died. Louise was once beaten in a Mississippi jail. Why then are they not on the same wave length? It confounds her, perhaps. She is struggling. She would like to be radical, but her history, her personality, and her very body are conservative.

Late one afternoon I find her, curled, solemn, reading on my bed where the window light is good, the deep red blankets wound about her; their color is of living rich blood. One must be willing to feel pain all the time to feel all the rest. Louise is in pain and it presses her down; it collapses her suddenly. She will disappear and go somewhere to brood. But I note that, although I figure in some way in that drama of pain, minutely, she will still lie on my bed, wrap herself in my blanket and her own, too. I see these two blood red blankets sheltering Louise and I am glad one of them is mine.

She has a boyfriend who is not faithful to her. In Atlanta one night before we left, he took Edna out, made passes at her. Edna knew better, but she is restless and lonely, so she went out with him again. Now she despises him. She self-righteously tells Louise: "Don't trust him. Don't let him push you around." Edna, a very wise young lioness, advises Louise, who is less convinced about her own living than Edna, more bruised, more humble, more complex, less spontaneous therefore.

Louise tells me about Johnny B.:

"He has a little church in the country. He's a preacher, just in summertime. He was married once and got divorced. He has a little girl about nine but he doesn't see her very much because her mother has another husband and she doesn't like Johnny to come around. Oh . . . he's like a bad boy or something. He just needs to do a little growing up."

The tone is sentimental and maternal. Bethel says Louise is slavishly available to Johnny B., that he can come to her apartment any night he wants, however late, no matter what he has been up to, and Louise will take him in.

Charity says Louise was in love with a white boy two years ago and very broken up when he left her. "She's too easy with 'em. She puts up with so much."

I look at Louise and wonder if she is discriminated against by men because of her deep blackness. Probably that still operates. In any case, "a good man nowadays is hard to find," seems to describe her problem. Her tenacity and stubbornness are forms of aggression that alarm many people. Only a paternal man could transcend them, I fear.

We go late, after the meeting, to Mr. Miller's. As predicted, one of the older women is helping him in the kitchen. The long table in the back room is occupied by a mixed group of the young and old, but mainly by the older country women. Mississippi and Carol are with them; when I enter, they rise quickly, move to a private table and stare bluntly and sullenly at me, Whitey. I ignore it. The women are very elated tonight. The workshop is exciting; they are making friends, seeing a new world, eating someone else's cooking.

"Learning so much, Honey!"

"Set down, Sweetheart."

"Here, have you some shrimp."

Rock and roll music. Edna, high hips bound in a beautiful pink tweed skirt, dances with one of the staff, a married, very light-skinned Negro fellow from Michigan named Charles, who has a pretty, shallow, baby face. Mississippi watches with mild amusement. *He* has a beautiful face, elegant, deeply black, bony, sad. Edna turns everybody on. We drink beer. Bethel and I share a plate of shrimp and engage in minor harmless gossip. She rolls a scornful lip at the sight of Charles flinging Edna about the room.

"I don't like him. Lotta men from the North I don't like. I can't see it. They not even polite."

Charles seizes Edna and drags her off to a corner, laughing. She breaks away and says, loudly, "Okay, Charles. Watch it!" They laugh together, and she swings back to our table.

Charles and I dance.

"You're not bad, Jo."

"You're not bad either."

He whispers suddenly, "You going down to the beach with me tonight?"

I laugh. "No."

"Why not?"

I don't explain.

He clamps his mouth shut and stares over my shoulder. All at once he presses against my ear. "Okay, then," he whispers savagely, "you've got to persuade Edna to go with me!"

"*What?*"

"You can talk her into it."

"You must be kidding!"

His face is cold and flat, like the bottom of a pan.

"Well, will you?"

I laugh, amazed. "Of course not. Do your own arranging."

Charles is cold now when he sees me. He will join forces with the radicals when they speak first. Alone he is fearful, tentative, pouty, condescending to most of the women who work with him.

Bobbi and Palma spend a lot of time in our sitting room talking. They have heard that I'm staying on the island after the workshop for a few weeks.

"Oh, I love it here! I jess wish I could stay ovah longer!" Bobbi's face has a look of anguish when she becomes intense, which she often does. She is very passionate, will stand up in a workshop meeting and tell, with angry primitive gestures, a story of how the civil rights group she worked with in Mississippi paid her less than the white student who came there to do the same kind of work. Her large, protruding, very white teeth are bared when she talks. Her gestures are jerky, swift, stylized, very much like those of a primitive dancer. Her limbs are long, very thin—even stringy—and powerful. Her back is absolutely straight; her feet are long and pointed. Now and then she will break into some kiddish act—a running game of tag, a crazy dash at a tree to embrace it—and then her limbs fly in all directions. She looks to be pure African. Her intensity and integrity are a marvel to the group. She is nineteen.

I offer to keep her and Palma here with me after the workshop but cannot pay their way back home. Palma, who has been involved with one of the middle-aged men on the staff, says suddenly, eyes popping open in discovery, "I . . . listen, I think I can get us the money fo' the bus home!"

She will ask her friend, obviously. I hope they will stay. I have rented a large, very simple but comfortable apartment, the only thing I could find, over a Negro family's grocery store, and we would each have a private room.

Bobbi suddenly gives me a ferocious hug. "I gotta stay! I'm gonna stay! We'll git the money, Honey. We goin' to git the money." I feel very badly not being able to offer it.

They seem ready to weep with excitement. The air is so emotionally charged that we are all ready to laugh and cry most of the time now.

Thursday. A very proper and pale Negro woman from New York arrives by plane and taxi to conduct the workshop on family planning, which means, of course, birth control.

I go upstairs before class to arrange a private talk with Mrs. Adams and find her and her roommate dressing.

"Come on in. We be ready in a few minutes."

Mrs. Adams stands at the ironing board in her bare feet. Her portable spittoon is on the floor beside her. "Jess lemme git the crease outta this dress."

The roommate, a huge young woman from Alabama who has

eleven children, no husband living at home, hypertension, and possible heart trouble, sits on her bed trying to write a note home to her children. She has tried every day but cannot delineate this great volume of what's happening to her and all the others.

Indecisive and nervous, she sits staring, chewing her lips.

"Tell 'em we goin' to fry them oysters tomorrow," advises Mrs. Adams. She laughs then, because the idea of an oyster roast is beautifully tormenting. She spits into the jar and wipes her mouth carefully with a handkerchief.

We walk to the class together, gathering up Mrs. Hall on the way.

The speaker, very chic and beautiful, is fortified with huge charts, cases of samples, and a thick stack of notes and figures. The class is full, not a member missing. We break up to find seats. Mrs. Hall sits beside me, eager and tense, her tablet open, pencil poised. She gives me a nervous smile.

The radicals arrive late with hastily made cardboard anti-birth control signs around their necks and are greeted by a few laughs. Mrs. Adams, sitting just in front of me, laughs. Why not?

We sing, someone prays, and the session begins. As the speaker clears her throat, Mrs. Adams rises and says in a clear, firm, but not loud voice:

"I don't believe in birf controls!"

The radicals look alert, smiling, chuckling. Beulah, who is a kind of monitor this session, wants to let her speak.

"Why not, Mrs. Adams?"

Sweetly, Mrs. Adams explains herself. There is not a trace of anger, merely conviction. "Use to be they was always tellin' us—'Have a lotsa babies, have a lotsa babies!'—cause they wants a lotta work done on the land. Now they tellin' us—'Don't have no mo' babies'—cause they don't want so many colored peoples goin' up to vote! No sir, I don't want no birf controls!"

The radicals rise in a body, shout, cheer, run to kiss her, slap their heads in gleeful amazement, and generally fall apart. Most of us laugh, but it is plainly their triumph.

"Beautiful! Beautiful!"

Mrs. Adams smiles, chuckles a little, and keeps her cool.

The speaker holds up a hand. "Well now . . . let's just consider a moment . . . just a moment . . ."

A new wave of laughter and cheers drowns her voice.

Mrs. Hall rises from the seat next to me and says, commanding immediate silence by her mere stance, "I jess wants to say, I owns fifteen chillrun, eight of 'em in the grave, and I love all my chillrun; they all good and I'm not sorry I had erry one of them chillrun." She sits but Beulah calls her to her feet again over the new uproar.

"Here! Wait a minute! Let Mrs. Hall finish. Listen here, Mrs. Hall—you say eight of your children are dead?"

"That's right. I owns seven living."

"Well, Mrs. Hall, wouldn't it have been better if you had only had seven children or five, maybe, instead of so many that some died? If the mother has another baby before she gets her strength back from the last one, then that baby might be weak. It might not live. If you could plan your babies, space them out . . . why then . . ."

Mrs. Hall stands firm, solid, patiently enduring a totally absurd and inscrutable commentary.

"I'm not sorry I had me them chillrun, not any. They was all good, dead and alive. If the Lord don't want me to have them chillrun, then he don't give 'em."

Shouts and cheers. The speaker is flushed and annoyed now. In front of me next to Mrs. Adams sits Mrs. Berry, a delicate, refined, antiquated little brown bird of a woman in lavender sheer with lace cuffs and a high neck bound in black ribbon. She is a retired Southern lady schoolteacher, a black version of a Tennessee Williams character with a straight back and a pure nature. She is just short of elegant, well-educated in the classical style and dedicated to nineteenth century ideals: to modesty, charity, and moral conduct. She writes poetry, and although she is now very old, has been ill, and finds it difficult to walk much, she attends all these workshops. Charity says she comes because she is lonely, but somewhere along the way she may put what she learns to use.

During the fracas and shouting, Mrs. Berry sits in silence, shaking her head, stupefied by the absence of decorum.

Finally, just as order is overtaking us, Mr. Wellman rises and says, "Now, I just want to ask you people here—now you may think I'm just an old man with no education but I was once a

preacha and I got me a good education in nineteen six at the
seminary—and I want to know: just how many peoples in here
believes in God?"

Charles waves an impatient hand. "Oh, that's not the point just
now, Mr. Wellman. This is a workshop on birth control . . ."

"Well now, wait a minute, wait a minute . . . Just where does
life *begin?*"

"Let's hold the questions now for a minute," calls Beulah.
"Let's give our speaker a chance to get started."

But the interruptions continue. Finally it becomes evident that
the majority of the group believes birth control to be a method of
abortion and has not heard that it prevents pregnancy. They are
dead set against even hearing about it.

Beulah clears up the issue sufficiently to let the frustrated
speaker begin again. Evidently the speaker is used to lecturing to
obedient audiences. I look carefully at Mrs. Hall and see a fine
thin sweat on her neck and forehead; on her tablet is written in
large shaky letters the name L O R D, and nothing else. The
speaker hastens to begin while there is a breather, and with short
explanations, proceeds to hand around samples of the various
kinds of birth control equipment: plastic spirals, tubes of jelly,
diaphragms, pills in cardboard packets. The country women,
Mrs. Adams and the others, take them in dubious sobriety,
"Looky this thing, Honey. How you gonna keep a baby from
coming down with *this* thing?" They know now that these are
preventive measures, but they are mothers and still think graphi-
cally of babies being implanted, taking human form, and de-
scending to the light of day through the indefatigable life urge
which is not easily deterred except by God. Mrs. Adams squeezes
out a laugh at the sight of the plastic spiral gadget, holding it up
and giving it a slight swing, "What they doin' with this crazy
little thing?" Mrs. Hall receives from the woman on her left a
tube of jelly, gives it a woeful, suspicious scrutiny and hands it
on to me with embarrassment, not so much at the subject implied
as at the possibility of being duped once more by the establishment. There are laughs of scorn and incredulity. The younger
people are politely amused.

Beulah continues to interject little comments to remind them that this is preventive material. Mr. Wellman continues to ask the people around him in stage whispers—just where does life begin?

Our lecturer is now pouring it on. She has regained her composure and is deftly circulating material and explaining it at the same time. Now suddenly she brings out, to face the audience, a large cardboard placard on which the female anatomy, shoulder to mid-thigh, is drawn in the medical-text fashion and in cross section. Silence. Attention.

The refined Mrs. Berry has not ceased to shake her head in amazement, but now she adds a "tch tch" and lowers her gaze; this is the final straw. Mrs. Adams, on the other hand, is totally engaged. She clears her throat and spits silently into her jar. Beside me Mrs. Hall can no longer give attention to fools; her head is slightly bowed, her hand moves on the tablet. Some of the women have taken a few notes. Mrs. Hall merely adds the name of JESUS to LORD, in large jerky printed letters, and fortified, looks out the window.

The anatomy chart has been viewed by all.

"This," announces the speaker, "is a cross section of the lower half of the human female anatomy." She is unaware, evidently, that the idea of a cross section is in itself new enough to stall a befuddled mind.

"There are three orifices in the lower body of the female."

Mrs. Adams grunts an affirmation, shifting the wad of tobacco slightly in her smooth golden cheek. Mrs. Berry gives a defeated sigh and meditates, eyes on her hands.

"These orifices are," here she points carefully with a pencil, "the urethra, the vagina, and the anus."

"That's *right!*" shouts Mrs. Adams loudly.

Amen! Charity, across the room, smiles broadly.

At the end of the two-and-one-half hour session we wander away to the porch and terrace. The excitement lingers. A few women tentatively exchange the idea that it might not hurt a woman to hold off between babies long enough to "git up her blood a little." "Spacin' out you kids" is not a bad idea really: nobody is asking you to give up children altogether. Life, Mr.

Wellman agrees, is not, by this means, being extinguished. But as to explaining to an ignorant neighbor back home how she can achieve these advantages? Well, no one got quite that far. The seed has been planted. These are fertile women. Something, if only a relaxed mind about it all, will surely bloom there.

Our speaker frantically packs her gear and manages, as if by more magic, to get a taxi from the mainland within twenty minutes, and is whisked away from this mainly rural company like some interrupted scientific insight from the mind of a farmer. Nobody mentions her, although the subject dies more slowly.

Oyster roast tonight. A fire of coals is made in the old barbecue, and a huge lumpy metal cover is placed over it. The oysters are tossed on top of this and lie there darkening, spitting and casting off fabulous odors. The long table is covered with newspapers, bottles of hot sauce, cans of beer, soft drinks, and paper plates. There are collanders of fresh French fries brought from the kitchen every few minutes. We crowd up to the table. Charity, who wears a slightly formal hat for some reason, exudes a well-being just short of ecstasy. Edna is being fed by two young men who obviously are hypnotized by her open mouth. The men officate. Johnny B., a charmer, draws me to the pit and says, "Come on, Baby. Git you some oystahs. Don't be shy," and loads my plate. I look up into the eyes of Mississippi and get the idea that Whitey is not supposed to dig this thing. He waits on the periphery of the crowd, sad and cool.

There are three passionate women inside the hot little kitchen with Mr. Miller, all in white aprons. He seems swamped by their fervent presence. While they dispense his fried shrimp to those who dislike oysters, they laugh, chide Mr. Miller for his monasticism, dazzle him with flashing gold-toothed smiles and their kitchen efficiency. The kitchen is too small for all of them, but the women dodge about like Turkish dancers and manage not to collide.

Mrs. Hall sits in the back room with a few others who do not like oysters and crowds. Of oysters, the blunt Mrs. Hall merely says, "Too slick."

"I heerd," says another, "that they does a harm on the woman organs."

"The food good here," says another. "I hates to go home cause we don't git this kinda food home." She laughs. "I tired o' my own cookin'."

They talk for half an hour about cooking and eating and conclude, as usual, by talking about men.

We stay there late, reluctant to end our first real party. Willie gets very drunk and, passing our table, lays a gentle hand on my shoulder and forgives me my whiteness. I smile at him but he doesn't look at me. He wanders slowly through the door and passes out in someone's car outside.

Johnny B. drives Louise, Edna, Morris (a young Georgia boy), and me back to the dorm. Edna taunts him for flirting with other women, for pretending fidelity to Louise.

"You nothin' but a two-time liar. You watch out, Louise."

She has had too much to drink. Her voice is painfully loud. Johnny B. careens down the dark road arguing with her. Louise sits next to him silently.

"That's the kinda coward-man always end up with some prostitute or somethin'! Just don't say I didn't tell you, Louise."

"Aw, shut that up!" Johnny drives off the road onto a flat lawn, puts the car in neutral and leaps out. He flings open the back door and tries to drag Edna out. Morris holds her back. She screams. Louise screams at Johnny B.

"I'm goin' spank her butt! Her daddy oughtta spanked her butt ten years ago!"

Finally we separate them and finish the ride in sullen silence. In the dark Morris seizes my hand and kisses it, then lets it go, staring straight ahead like a zombi. He told me yesterday he would not attend the banquet because he knew he would cry and men are not supposed to cry. He is twenty years old.

Edna stands talking loudly to Louise in the hall, rousing some of the women who went to bed early. Finally, Louise gets her to bed and comes in to undress in the dark. She sighs. All afternoon she sat on a sofa in the television room with Johnny. They seemed happy and close. "I think I'm going to let him loose for a while," she says tonight. "Men . . . I don't know. They *need* so much."

Friday. Workshop ends tomorrow. Tonight is the farewell banquet, and Mrs. Hall has been chosen to speak on behalf of the participants. Deeply worried about it, she spends many hours sitting on the side of her bed near the window, staring out, muttering. She does not make notes; she troubles her mind for the language. Some of us have offered to help her but she prefers to go it alone, which is a very touching thing to see. She thinks slowly, striving for honesty and clarity. She accepts the honor of this chore with more confidence than I would have thought possible.

We spend the afternoon in the library looking up reference material on famous Negroes. The assignment for our last class is to write one or two sentences identifying famous Negroes, such as Harriet Tubman, Sojourner Truth, W. E. B. DuBois, Charlotte E. Ray, Mary McLeod Bethune, Nat Turner, Charles Drew. Astonished, they read about these black people who found stature and power in America, some a century ago. Aaron, a young Mississippi boy with huge sorrowful eyes in a smooth, shining, gourdlike head, looks across at Mrs. Berry and says, "Listen to that man! Colored man stand up there in the govermen' house and tell all them white senators what they oughtta do!" and shakes his head.

Painstakingly, and with pride, they copy the facts in their notebooks.

Why did we all have to wait for adulthood to hear of these great Negroes?

Mrs. Mindy Adams neatly deposits a bolt of tobacco juice into her jar and slips it under her seat again. In tidy script, she has made a few notes about Harriet Tubman and the Underground Railroad, but her attention is not as profound as that of the others. She sits quietly, musing and smiling, unperturbed. She has learned a lot, enough, and she knew a lot already. She sits. Now and then she reaches into her pocket for a corner of the sandwich she made last night in the snack bar. Sandwich-makings of cold meat and cheese are served every night after our evening classes. There are three large hot meals a day, but nevertheless most of these people, especially the country women, never fail to eat again at about ten P.M. Mrs. Adams and her roommate will each take as many as four big sandwiches back to their room at night. Mrs. Adams is not "dirt poor," as she calls it. She has never known real hunger. From her size one understands that she is a big eater. Also, she has been a hard worker. "Farmin' is tough. That's right! Hit's tough!" An observation, not a complaint.

Later, when we are alone in the lounge, she talks.

"I have three chillruns in Massachusetts. Two boys and a girl. And I has about nine grandchillrun.

"Well, yes, I tried to bring 'em all up, my own chillrun, to obey, but you know girls is a heap different than boys. You can't control boys all the time like you can girls cause when they get up some size boys gotta *go!* But your girls they *will* stay home with you *some* times. I say boys is harder than girls. They'd go—yet, they'd never go and be out all night; they'd go to a certain time o' night and then they'd come in. I never did worry 'bout them bein' out all night in different rowdy crowds and things like that.

"Oh, yes, I had my husband with me. I and him raised 'em. He's a farmer. The boys farmed with him when they was at home, but then they left home and—well (wheezy laugh) I didn't much blame 'em—I'da left myself if *he* hadn't been there. But look like he juss lo-ove to farm. But he claim that this be his lass year to live and he gonna set down too and quit all that work cause you know farmin' ain't no easy job. He say he goin' to retire and I hope he do, cause I don't feel like it no mo'.

"Yes, ma'm, a man oughtta help with the chillrun. Cause they's both of 'em's chillrun. Course, you know, a man can't help that he's not workin' like he should. A man know he should be workin' and heap o' times he jess can't find no work but he can help in the house. Oh, yeah!

"You know, chillrun is work! I mean . . . Is you got any?"

"No, I haven't."

"Well, you may come along some time. Don't give it out." She gives a yelp of laughter and then lowers her voice confidentially, "Lemme tell you, I was married *nine years* before I owned erry chile. That's right! *Nine* years. I jess *knew* I wasn't goin' to have no chillrun and then I come up with my first chile—my little girl.

And from then on—jess one right after another. I owned those five chillrun after I got started."

"You had *five?*"

"That's right! But two passed. But that's why I say—don't give it out. You may come along." She spits into her jar and re-covers it with the scarf.

"Yes, sir, I grew up in a big family too. They was eleven head of us chillrun. And then, after I was nineteen years old, my mother she died, and left some real little chillrun—Ooooo, she left 'em from six months old on up. I was the oldest so I had to care for those little ones till they got big enough to care for theyself. My father, after a while he married again. And then I married out cause I had a pretty good stepmother to see 'bout those chillrun.

"Yeah, I was close to my mother. But it look like I lovéd my father the best. He was jess really good. You know how they's some father chillrun and they's some mother chillrun? Yeah, that's right!

"I think the best thing my father and mother did for me was they didn't allow me to do jess any and everything. They didn't allow us out all time o' night. And they believe in we goin' church and doin' good things like that. But all these rowdy things, noooo! They didn't believe in that. Well, once I got grown I was jess as proud of it as I could be: they didn't let me do all that."

"Mrs. Adams, do you think a woman can live a full life without children?"

"Oh . . . she can but it's better for her to have some chillrun if she can. Oooo, she don't know how she will enjoy her life with some chillrun! They jess comfort, they happy and it jess make for a happy home. Chillrun do."

"Do you think a woman can live a full life without being married?"

She gives me a skeptical look and breaks into a spasm of laughter full of innuendo.

"Ooooo, I don't think so . . . I don't believe that, cause you know it's quite nachul . . . naycha's goin' take its coass." This is intimate talk, almost whispered. "But I say they jess have to

protect theyself, you know . . . They don't hafto jess go to an
*ex*treme. But I don't think you can really live that life. Cause
that's due to a woman . . . and a man, naycha is. Now if she
don't get naycha, if she don't do *nothin'*, then she age, she get
sickly, she bees puny, rough lookin'. But when they say: 'Oh, my,
she *so* fine,' I say: 'Huh uh! She is *not livin'*. No!' Cause naycha's
due to a pusson. And, you know, if they don't get *naycha,* if
naycha don't take place . . . early . . . well then if you go out
and tinker with the thing, you might *look* bettah, but you don't
have to go to an *ex*treme. You know how to do anything in a nice
way. You don't have to go jess lay yourself out! You know how to
take care of yourself in a nice manner and go ahead home. That's
right! And then you know how to not have *every one*. You take
you one stiddy boyfriend or somethin' like that, and go along
with it. And not just have this one and that one and the other. I
don't approve o' that!

"Well, hit's good fo' a woman to work. I'd ruther work. Soon as
my kids got up some size, I worked fo' a white lady and I loved it.
Hit's good fo' the chillrun. They oughtta work too and learn how
to not sit down and depend on somebody else to care fo' them.

"Hate? Well, I'll tell you, hate ain't good. Now you take us
here—we jess like a family. I don't have no hate in me. I could
get out there and treat *any*body right, jess like I'd wish fo' 'em to
do me. Ain't nothin' I got that bees so good for me that I wants to
vie . . . with a pusson. I give him what he need, if he ask me.
Cause the Lord made all us equal. All us sprung out from the
same pusson! Adam and Eve is the father and mother of the
whole generation. We came a different color but all us created
equal."

About the Bible she says with great feeling:

"I like John. Matthew. The resurrection of Jesus. I likes to read
it. We've got an organization. I'm owa missionary teacher. I jess
goes in the Bible, one chapter to another, fo' how we ought to
live. And how John was baptize in the wilderness—strainin' mens
to come to him. See, John was the fo'runner. Befo' Jesus Christ.
He was sent to make the way straight befo' him.

"He was out there preachin' mens ought to repent, and baptizin'. But he say one comin' after he whose shoes he wasn't

worthy to loose, would baptize 'em with the Holy Ghost. And that was Jesus Christ.

"I like that part. You know all those people—the Pharisees, the Sadducees and them—come down to the Jordan to see what was he baptizin' and he looked up and saw Jesus comin'. He say: 'I'm not worthy.' Jesus say, 'Suffer it to be so.' And after Jesus baptize, straightway he went up out de water. He went in the wilderness and stayed forty days and forty nights. You know the Bible? Oooo! I *love* the Bible."

"How would you feel about a woman preacher?"

Mrs. Adams laughs, reaches for her jar. "Oooool! I don't know about no woman preacha! Ha!" The picture breaks her up. She unloads her jaws into the jar again and sits back. "Women preacha! I don't know *what* they is. Coass, they say they gets out there and preaches! I don't know. It jess don't sound like no man preachin', I know that."

"How about a woman doctor?"

"They *real* good. We have a woman doctah down there near Selma; she's a real good doctah."

About friends she says: "Well, jess to take a man fo' a pussnel friend, like I does a woman, I haven't ever did that. I guess fo' a woman, a woman is a best friend cause we mostly can say anything to each other that we couldn't say to a man. I and a woman, we can 'scuss it together.

"Well, a man is stronger in his body, but women can beat 'em thinkin'. And plannin'. I mean it's jess between the pussons. Womens don't mind goin' out ventin' theyself but mens, look like they has a fear on 'em, some of 'em. But womens jess goin' stick and hold out there to their point. They don't have that fear on 'em much to do so."

"Is that just a woman's nature, do you think, or is it that the world makes it easier for a woman to do that?"

"Well, hit's jess her naycha but hit's the world makes it easy too, cause mankind mostly gives to a woman, a woman has a higher honor."

About love she says:

"Love is a thing that grows. If you go to another and you treat that one the right way, why you know that creates love. It's jess like they say 'Kind words creates love. Kind words turns away wrath.' The Bible say mostly li'l chillrun is love, anyway. He tell it: 'Suffer li'l chillrun come unto me.' You know, someone ask, 'Who would be gooder than a king?' and he took a li'l chile and stood it in the midst. Jess like I and you—I want to do big things and you want to do big things. We try to do the biggest thing, you know, to git the praise? But he say, 'Less you come as this li'l chile, you can in no wise see the King.' Well, that's the way—A li'l chile, he don't know, he's jess out there. That's the reason I say if anybody don't love a li'l chile, well I don't know *what* they is. Cause a chile, they don't know hate till they get all this teachin'. It's teachin' that cause peoples to hate. But if we wouldn't do this hatin', jess be one, it wouldn't be no greater love. The Lord would bless us, you know that. It'd be mo' bless. It wouldn't be all disaster. None of this business would have to be demonstrate.

"Oh, yeah, my chillrun love each other. They didn't have no confusion for each other."

Later she tells me: "I tell 'em, I'm a citizen of A-merica. I bees a citizen of Alabama but fust I bees a citizen of A-merica. I wasn't boan no place else and I never been no place else. That's who I am.

"Well, all we that went up to regiss, they say, 'Oh, no! You don't regiss today.' We regiss, though, lass August when the Federal regiss come up. Cause those white peoples wouldn't let us regiss. Turn you down every time. It was bad on us. Those was some bad peoples. Oh, yes, ma'm! I goin' vote soon as the time come, on May 3rd. I'm goin' try to vote the bess I can so we can have decent legislators. Decent gov'ment. Cause we wants a gov'ment fo' the peoples and by the peoples. A gov'nor put in there for *one* set, he not no gov'nor fo' the peoples and neither by the peoples.

"If somebody give me a hundred dollars? Well, I don't know what I'd do with that hundred. I'd take it and try to fit it in my budget and see where would it do bess. And then, I'm not no rapid spender, anyway. Heap o' times you needs money fo' sick o' lotsa things and if you spend rapid, you goin' down empty."

Mrs. Adams has hospital and burial insurance so that she may be "put away decent." She is an Eastern Star. She likes to belong to organizations. She looks forward to teaching. Life on the farm is lonely if you don't keep busy.

"What I has is my cats and my dogs. But my cats, I don't know where went all my cats. I say I think foxes is gettin' my cats. . . . And you know, every time I gets myself a good dog, somebody takes that dog! You can't have a pretty fine dog and care 'bout it. Look like something happen to it. I got two now. I had plenty of 'em round when my chillrun comin' up.

"In my life—? Well, there won't be no real freedom in my life cause I'm too old. But my chillrun and they chillrun goin' to have it. I knows it. I be ready if the Lord wants me cause I done lived mos' my whole life already, but not my chillrun. Noooo! They got somethin' comin' and I see the light fo' it. That's what I pray and that's what I know.

"I don't care what those kids sayin' 'bout white peoples. I saw 'em come down there to help the regiss, all those white chillrun, all summah long, and *still* some of 'em helpin'. I don't care *what* they say—they plenty whites took a risk to be kill for we and I won't nevah fo'get it. *Nevah!* We all one. We got to work and stop all this killin'. That's all!"

She signs off, spits decisively, and rises to leave the room. She is tired of talking and sitting still, and I need no explanation. She simply leaves my presence. But her physical departure is incidental; one is accompanied forever by the impact of her spirit.

Bobbi and Palma come to report their unhappy news:

"Can't raise fifty cents around here. We have to go home in the car we came in."

I explain my own dwindling funds and they understand. We go long-faced to Mr. Miller's before supper to toast one another with beer, Sprite, and Pepsi.

BANQUET

Bethel goes to the airport on the mainland to meet our main speaker—a well-known Negro preacher who has a humorous and passionate style of delivery. Banquet time and no Bethel, no speaker. Patiently we wait at our tables, having delayed dining for over an hour. We sing, we are nervous. The food shrinks. The cooks fret. Mrs. Hall is still in her room working on her speech and will be summoned the moment he arrives.

Finally Bethel stumbles in looking harassed, gritting her teeth. She whispers with Beulah and Charity. A few heads shake. The speaker is freshening up at the dorm. The tables are being served now, and the talk becomes animated again. It seems that the Reverend had to stop at the airport for a three-course meal; he was hungry and could not wait to get to our banquet for his supper. Bethel sat with him, angrily submissive, stewing in her hatred of martinets.

"I shoulda figured that one. He just *has* to show his power. Shhhht! That's no power. I wonder can he even *do* it anymore."

His speech for which we have waited one hour and twenty minutes is quaint, long-winded, now and then funny, and repetitious, but the group gives him silent respect. He is a leader, he is black, he makes promises to them. In his peculiar way, he is sincere.

Mrs. Hall stands and makes her offering, that over which she has suffered for three days.

"We come from all the places—country and city, all over the South and some North. We friends together here fo' brotherhood and the Lord bringing us to freedom. All the peoples that made this meeting be bless. They's too many to name. But we goin' home and tell it and carry love where we go and don't matter what they say or do, we goin' vote and we goin' learn and we goin' have freedom, deep in my heart I do believe. We thank all the teachers and all these kind peoples."

We applaud. We sing: Mississippi loves freedom; Alabama loves freedom; Georgia . . . South Carolina . . . California . . . We applaud the cooks; the conference directors; Beulah for monitoring, for singing, for listening to troubles; Charity for everything. We applaud Bethel. We sing and clap and tear up like babies. Mrs. Berry stands on shaky birdlike legs and, in a brave cracked voice that was trained by an elocution teacher back when, delivers her impassioned poem, "Black and White Together," which traces the history of our crimes, failures and terrors, and ends:

> Break not the clasp, now
> Black and white
> Hand in hand go forward
> To that Sacred Freedom Land.

A white woman visitor sobs openly. Next to me young Morris bites his lips, rolls his eyes up, widening them to tighten the tear ducts. He hasn't eaten a bite. He has scarcely moved. What a bath! I am wrung out. Finally Johnny B. stands, says something inanely funny, and starts singing. The country women rock in their seats and clap, flinging their palms wide apart after each contact, rolling their heads back, throats open as if praying for rain. Amen!

A car carrying Bobbi and Palma departs late in the evening. Bobbi dives out twice and seizes me.

"Lemme hug you one mo' time! I wish we could stay."

Charity, Louise, and I wave them away, everybody tearful and full of promises to write, to send pictures, to remember. The rest of us repair to Mr. Miller's for final celebration.

The Reverend, having had his airport steak supper and refused the banquet food, is now hungry again. He sits at the head of the long table, officiating over several women who drink Cokes and eat shrimp, Bethel among them. I sit down next to Bethel, and suddenly Reverend says:

"Bethel, go git me a orange drink!" It is an order, a snap of royal fingers.

Bethel freezes; she is humiliated, stunned. The women look away. I harden myself as if to pass on to her a resistance I fear she cannot muster. She is not a confident woman. She is kind. She hates scenes.

Silence. Then with great aplomb, she looks up at the door where Morris has just arrived.

"Morris, would you mind bringin' an orange drink to the Reverend?"

Reverend, his chops shiny from buttery shrimp and French fries, knifes her a look, and continues to gorge. Bethel and I exchange scornful glances. "They think," she whispers, "they strong if they got some woman runnin' for 'em."

"Don't you dare wait on him!" I say it as a joke, now that it is safe.

"Honey, you saw me get outta that, didn't you? Never again! That airport mess was my last dance with him!"

We go back to bed around midnight, leaving the younger group—Mississippi and his friends—to dance all night.

Dawn. I drive Mrs. Hall in Bethel's Lincoln to the train that will take her, with one change and a short layover, home in sixteen hours less time than the buses. She stands on the platform terrified, never having been on a train. I ask a Negro porter to watch out for her. I kiss her cheek and she weeps, clutching at my arm. She steps backward and knocks over her cardboard suitcase, hastens to rescue it. It is wound with heavy twine but would never withstand the baggage car.

I would give an eye to keep Mrs. Hall from returning home to that old man who "gits dronk and likes to argle like a nigger."

"Don't you forget now, you're going to sell that cow and get some money," I say.

"I'm goin' sell it, I *clare* I will! I'm goin' git outta there befo' that old nigger *kill* me."

She climbs aboard and waves pitifully. She was one of sixteen children. Her brothers and her father beat her. She worked in cotton and cane for thirty-five years, sun-up to sun-down, a life three hundred years old; she tended her little brothers and sisters, slaughtered hogs, made sausage, canned beans and okra and tomatoes, learned a primer by heart, married an old widower to get out of hell and got more hell. Is she bound to all that, body, soul, and mind, or can she sell her cow and get out?

The coach that bears her away, despite all cases fought and won, is segregated. Blacks only. The one ahead of it is full of whites.

Edna goes home to try it again with Leroy, determined (but not convincingly) to win out over his matriarchal auntie. Charity is amazingly light-handed about the problem, believing, I suppose, that they can and must deal with it themselves.

We take Edna to her bus, her excitement faintly impaired by separating from Charity, whom she obviously loves with a child's sincerity and possessiveness.

"Now don't you do it by fighting. That doesn't work," Charity advises.

"Listen, I'm going to let old Leroy do the fighting. That old cat woman is *his* trouble. He's beggin' me to come back. I told him I was havin' fun. Oh, yeah! I got him all squirmy."

I leave to give them last minute privacy, and when Charity returns to the car she wears a smile of capitulation.

"I think they'll be okay. She's good for Leroy, keeps him on his toes. Oooo, she's a character!" She laughs deeply. Edna breaks her up. "All that talk! She's just a baby, but she's going to be a good woman. I'm prayin' for them. That Leroy has to get his life straight pretty soon."

My hopes are with Edna, but there is something tragic and certainly classic about the tenacious last attempt of old Auntie to hang on to what has been her only family and her only authority. Where will she go? What life will she have now if they leave her or she them? At least she will not be financially disabled by it.

I stay on the island for ten days, using a rented bicycle to wander the quiet sandy roads and talk with any woman who is willing. Evenings I ride a mile toward the village to be fed by Mrs. Willard, dietitian for the local school. She lives alone in an immaculate, feminine, cheery little house with a scrubby, rambling, highly fruitful garden. She has made all her curtains, slipcovers, tablecloths, quilts, pillows, and braided rugs as well as most of her own clothes and all the white uniforms she wears to work. She cans the fruit and vegetables from her own garden and never has to buy frozen or canned food in winter. She loves her work, has been in her present job for sixteen years.

"We have four cooks because it's a big school. I supervise, plan the menu for the week, and do the ordering. We try to use as much local produce and dairy food as we can. I'll buy from a

Negro farmer before I will a white over in town. You can see the value of it. That Negro man's children are in the school, and anyway his prices are reasonable. And I want to give the business to local people. Our population is 85 percent colored. I tell them they ought to raise prices to meet the school budget—you know, what we'd have to pay from town—but they stay under those prices for most products. This way I can give the children more greens. They always have a raw vegetable with lunch unless we have a cooked one. Now, today we had hot dogs. We have those every Monday. We have relish with them and then they get raw carrots and celery, milk, popcorn and Jello. Tomorrow we'll have tomato soup and cheese sandwiches, raw carrots, and milk and a cookie. Wednesday we have a hot meal—meat loaf this week. See, I'll use leftover tomato soup in my loaf, and leftover raw carrots. These cooks we have are all used to working with very little; they have big families most of 'em and they know how to spare. We'll have green beans and bread and butter and a piece of fruit. Always give 'em milk. I try to see to it that the county gives plenty of free milk to the poor children. I would say about one in ten of our children right now is getting a free lunch and I am sure there are some more who need it and won't say so, even won't ask for free milk. Or some, you know, never had milk and don't like it, don't miss it. I talk to them and tell them a little about nutrition. We have a better situation here than most places because we worked very hard over a long time on the county to give us a good food program. I think this is why we have a pretty good school record—because the children are well fed. Now, I notice that when some of them come back in the fall after bein' home all summer, they are run down. They don't eat as well at home as at school, in some cases.

"One thing about island people though, coast people, see, is that they get fish. They can always fish and that's very good food. We have very little fish in the cafeteria because I know they all get it at home so much. In spring they'll get some fruit at home too from the orchards and wild vines, so I'm not so worried about that as about the other things, meat and milk and all that."

She serves me supper for one dollar, which she says is a very fair price. Every night we sit down together for an orgy of homemade, home-grown, home-canned, home-churned delicacies that are as ruinous to character as they are nutritious to soul and body. This woman spends the whole day cooking but still loves the rare opportunity to cook for guests at home.

The kitchen is huge and eternally established by the presence in it of great gleaming appliances that seem to give Mrs. Willard deep content, even in the mere opening of their doors.

"But you see I do a little cookin' for sale. I make cakes for wedding parties. I cater a little for people on the mainland. Last week I did up two big hams and a five-tier cake and about fifteen pounds of potato salad. I get a lot of orders for oyster stew." She smiles, pleased and shy. "I have a name for my oyster stew."

Mrs. Willard is a small, dainty, slightly plump woman, her face round and pretty, her eyes deeply set above high shining little rounds of cheek. She is in her early fifties and was once a beautiful girl. She wears her white uniform and shoes all evening, looking starched, spotless, and trimly fit, corseted probably, for her waistline has vanished in these kitchen ecstasies. She has never wearied of cooking, planning menus, or of eating. Life is simple, most of it pleasurable, and goes something like this:

Rise early—five-thirty or six A.M.—regardless of the day, the weather, the season or the past. Pray. Bathe. Straighten the house. Drink coffee slowly while watching news on television. Eat a light breakfast—hot bread, one egg, maybe. Cut flowers, pick fruit. Smell the morning earth. Dress for work. Walk down a country road to work, about two miles. Work until three P.M. Walk home. Rest. Sew, garden, cook. Dine early—maybe five P.M. Read papers, magazines, watch television, visit a friend. Read the Bible. Pray. Retire at nine-thirty.

Weekends? Church? No church. I am intrigued, for in this she is almost unique.

"There was a big scandal, you might say, in our church. Baptist. That was my faith. Oh, I still believe but I don't go to service anymore. There was a young girl here, a poor family but good church people. She was their only child. Well, she turned up pregnant a few years ago and what did they do to that child? They put her out! That's right, they put that child out of her church. She was fourteen years old. She named the father of that baby but they didn't bother him. Oh, no! Not the boy, only the girl. That boy's up there prayin' yet. He has a new wife and they both go up there to church every week. He was eighteen when he got that girl pregnant and he never claimed that child for his own, never gave her a cent of money. I know the families. Why, if that had been my boy I'd see to it he claimed that baby and gave it a name and took care of it. But not those people. They better off than the girl's family, too.

"Well, her people sent her up to some kin in Virginia and she's there yet. Like to broke the mother's heart. You see, in a place like this, so countrified and so few people, well that church is the whole society. You put a girl out of her church and she loses all her friends; she's in disgrace.

"I grew up in Charleston and it's not like that there. But these country churches, my, they are so narrow sometimes. Well, I couldn't go back. I stood up and told my people; I said, 'You preach Christian living, you preach the golden rule and the teachings of Jesus Christ, forgiveness of sins, and you call this girl up for the whole sin and leave the boy free of his half. I see more wickedness here,' I told 'em, 'than ever will be in that girl's life.' And I never went back. You'll never find me in a church again.

"But I would say I'm more religious since I left the church. I mean it! Church is not the only place to get religion. I think the educated people are beginning to question the church. Not religion but the church. See, as you have it here in the South, I don't know about the North, but here the church is all a man's domain and the women really don't have much say. They do a lot of work, they cook for picnics and socials, and they raise most of the money and they kind of keep the church going, but when you get to policy, the men have that all tied up. They don't want a woman in any kind of power. You take some of these country preachers, they are *so* ignorant, you wouldn't believe it. They don't need any education. Now, not the Baptist especially, but some of these little country churches only have twenty or some folk in the congregation. My, there's a lot of ignorance. And the Baptist church I would say is definitely segregated against women, even if they say different."

"Do you have some idea of why that is?"

"Well, for one thing, that's the only place a colored man can be strong. He doesn't have any power any place else. This Movement is changing things but it will be many a year before you see a colored man with influence, generally speaking, in this world. So he'll swing it all into the church where he can order all the people around and put down the law the way he wants. I can't see it. I was brought up more liberal than that. My folks were liberal-minded people and they got me an education, my sister and three brothers, too. But I see that most colored men have to get their power off the rest of the colored people because the world won't let 'em work it out in the natural way."

"Do you feel that you influenced the church any by your speech to them and by leaving?"

"Oh, yes. I used to cook for them a lot!" We both laugh. "Don't let anybody kid you about that, colored people love to eat and they want good food, they know what good food is. I hear people say colored folks live on starchy food and don't eat too well but they don't bother to tell that those people just can't pay for anything else. When they can pay for it, they eat good food. Well, they miss me for that and then, I think they did give it a little consideration after that. But it's too late. They already ruined that girl's home life. She's probably better off in Virginia. She's in a good school there now."

"Where's the baby?"

"Her auntie's taking care of it, I believe. I know that baby is living around with some of her kin."

"So you took exile from the church in protest along with the girl, in a way."

"Well, I don't think of it being protest so much as just—well, I just gave up the church. That's what it was to me. I quit church. I wouldn't go to *any* church anymore. I don't need it. I have my religion and my Bible and I'm doing just fine."

"How about your social life?"

"I lost a few friends but I am glad to know which ones weren't too good a friends anyhow. My *real* friends, I still have. The Porters, down where you're staying—they are my best friends, very good people. She doesn't go much either, you notice. But he goes regular. She has heart trouble now."

I find it hard to rise and leave, being stuffed, groggy, and intrigued with Mrs. Willard besides. She is the first Negro woman I have met who seems to have retired, not only from church-going, but from involvement in the world around her generally. And that, in this totally rural community, may be merely a matter of having left the church. She expresses little interest in civil rights or local politics, social problems or education. She seems genuinely content and fulfilled.

Her relationship with her son is still the major one in her life. She writes to him three times a week and stays in touch with his local friends. He has been in the service three years and in Vietnam for seven months. She says she does not worry about him. "He's in the Lord's hands. It's all up to the Lord." But she prays for his safety.

"God bless you," she says unaffectedly when I leave her at night.

I ride home in the deep black of night with a flashlight in one hand. No street lights. Most houses are far from the road. The moon is misted over. Occasionally someone walks the shoulder totally obscured by darkness and will greet me softly, "Hey . . ." and pass. The tranquility here multiplies with nightfall; a rapture of silence and soft air grips the world. Even crickets' sounds are remote. There is a quelling of time, a sense of profound pause. I ride as if into eternity and not toward Mr. Porter's driveway of sand and crushed oyster shells. On the way I pass the little praise house—sitting in the middle of a dry field—a white frame, one-room churchlike structure where, keeping to a custom as old as slavery, the people gather one night a week to sing and shout by the light of a big stove fire or a few candles. Most slaves were not allowed their own churches, and their religious passions were stifled in the decorum of the white churches of their masters. But they contrived to build praise houses, sometimes in old abandoned shacks in isolated parts of the plantations, or perhaps now and then even in caves, for their own kind of religious service and pageant. They invoke the New Year, Christmas, and Easter this way, even now, although the custom is dying. Most of the people are now stoking the fires of Puritan righteousness in middle-class churches and let it go at that. Charity speaks with pride and love of the ceremonies in praise houses. She lived on Johns Island many years ago and was in them often.

In the daytime I continue to cruise the island on the bike.

Mrs. Reedy is raking leaves in her yard.

"Come on in. See my house. This my honeymoon house. My husban' built it ten years ago. My money and his labor."

It is a cement-block house with wide rooms and a profusion of small treasures—pictures, medals, china figures, impaled and framed butterflies and embroidered mottos, diplomas, antimacassars, plastic flowers—that must take dedicated maintenance. All is tidy and waxed. She recounts for three hours the incredible saga of her life—an amalgam of Little Match Girl, Liza, Abandoned Bride, Tarnished Bathsheba—a saga destined to elicit mirth, compassion, admiration, and utter disbelief. She was adopted from an orphanage and brought up by an ignorant white family who loved her but used her as a servant from the age of eight. She was taught to sew, play piano, cook, clean, garden, and tend babies, and was given all the basics of elementary education. They died together, the foster parents, and left her their farm in Kentucky, but she was too ignorant of the "ways of the world" (she uses such phrases) to realize what it meant. She left home with a sort of knapsack and went in search of her lost brothers and sisters. She found her oldest sister at "death's door" and sat beside her in her last hours, grateful to God for their brief reunion.

She is a tough cooky. She has a round, humorous, bold and good face, a peasant face. She is tall and stalwart but beginning to settle with age. Her head sprouts four short runty braids like spokes of astonishment. A frequent expression of stagey madness gives her an absurd and wild charm. She is either a fabulously creative liar or an indefatigable deathless mutation of humanity. She has lived through anything you can name and tried all work, all fun, all risks, and most places.

"I married a no-good man but I loved him and when he went off from me I took sick. I lay sick, near death's door for near onto two month in the hospital. I come to and first thing I heared was that man's voice! I thought I was dead and gone to heaven but then I figured they wasn't going to hear *his* voice in heaven so I muss be alive or else in hell.

"But he was down the hall hurt from a accident and there we was, both laid up in the same place. We got back together for a while but with a no-good man you cain't go far. You gonna hafto quit sooner or later. And we quit out in about a year.

"Oh, I worked. I had a gospel group. You know gospel music? You *do?* Well, girl, looky here."

She pulls me to the small upright piano over which is hung an award from a music society for her outstanding work as a leader of gospel singers; also there is a framed letter from President Harry S Truman thanking her for the special street-corner concert of gospel singing during a rally for him.

She opens the piano, sits, and sorts through some sheet music. "Looky here. I wrote this. See, that's my name, in my first marriage. I had twenty-five gospel songs published."

She proceeds to play and I to sing, with her cracked and perfectly pitched alto voice in harmony; the piano is struck with strong blunt syncopated fingers: "I'll wear a white robe in my heavenly home!"

We sing four songs. Between the first two I hear applause from the rear of the house and look down the long hall to see, just off the kitchen, a curtained doorway. The curtain is half open and beyond it, in what appears to be a tiny alcove, is a bed. I see the end of the bed on which are two skinny black ankles and two long wrinkled old shoes pointed upward.

"That's *him.* He's takin' his ress. Come on, girl, *sing!*"

We get a beat going as Mrs. Reedy attacks the piano savagely to drive me on. Our voices are now loud and sure; her harmony is fancy and embellished with devastating crescendoes. It is thrilling.

"You sing pretty nice," she honors me. "I could teach you gospel." Her own singing is extraordinary.

Afterward we enter her bedroom where she displays a large collection of pictures made of butterfly wings, some of them her own work. "Made money on these in the depression." Also displayed are samples of fine materials on which she has applied her own metal-stud or bead designs, very elegant, professional work.

"I went to a school up North one time that taught me this. I made dresses for high society. Got me one hundred and fifty dollars a dress from high society white ladies. They knew me all ovah the South and some North in those days. But I doesn't do much now. I sews a little for some peoples over in Charleston."

She reveals a graduation dress, pink embroidered organdy, being made for a young white girl in Charleston.

"Oh yeah. I does a lotta different work. I saved my money and paid cash for the materials in this house. *He* built it," she repeats, "and I put up the money. This house goan lass for a hundred years. Come on, lookit my kitchen."

The rooms are all very wide and light, with plenty of windows. The kitchen is yellow, sunny, and radiant with clean surfaces, impeccable paint, and shimmering windowpanes. The curtain at the door of *his* little nook is a bright-blue flowered cotton. His long creased old shoes still protrude there below the old-man ankles. Mrs. Reedy sweeps to the door and flings aside the curtain.

"This a lady stayin' up to the Porters."

He grins; he is skinny, old, devilish-looking.

"Howdo, Missy. Gimme some mo' music, Mama."

She throws the curtain back across the door.

"No! We all thoo now!"

Outside on the front lawn she leads me to a small cement-block structure that resembles a crude square mausoleum or a war bunker or an air raid shelter. It is like her, somehow. She opens a padlock with a key on a string around her neck and invites me into a small soft-drinks stand with a wide wooden shutter that swings up and out to make a roof over the counter.

"Hot times come, we sells a lotta drinks and ice cream. Here, have you a ice cream."

She thrusts at me, with awkward generosity, a chocolate Popsicle.

"Thanks. Do you and your husband run this stand all summer?"

"Who, *him?* *He* don't run nothin'. *I* runs it." She becomes, suddenly, a little wild-eyed, fired by what seems to be mock rage, an irresistible act.

"*I* built it and *I* runs it and *I* keeps the money and he don't do nothin' but lay in there nappin'." She whirls, tosses her head in an animalish derangement. It is comic and she knows it, but the subject is serious and she knows that, too. She knows that I know. She knows, like a good actor, what she is up to. She thrusts out her chin; her eyes flame. She flings a hefty brown arm.

"Men eat shit! That's what I tell that old leg back there. Eat shit! I say—'You nothin' but shit and don't try to come git *my* ass cause I paid fo' my bed and I'm keepin' it to my *own*se'f.' Shit! I had all I want from these mothas."

"Doesn't he help out anymore?"

She bangs her shop shut, and we stand on the dusty drive together, she, continually waving an arm toward the house and tossing her round head with its four stiff, random little braids—a spiked, jack-o'-lantern of a head. Her tongue fusses at a wide space between two front teeth. Then all at once she grumbles quietly:

"Oh, he's gittin' old. He want me to bring his supper in there to bed. I puts it out on the table and he come sniffin' after it like a houn' dog. I say: 'Why don't I put yo' supper on the floor? You jess like a doag when you eats.'" She sucks at the tooth. "Shhhhhht! He want my money to spend on some black ass he can't even use."

Several women fishers talk briefly with me:

"My husband died so I and my boy fishes. We does all right. We savin' fo' he to buy a boat."

"It be a little mo' nice roun' here now cause some white peoples will talk to you nice. Used to be they would pass you over without not a word to greet."

"The civil right come here and now the men has a little mo' work pay. But The Man still got you undah his dollah! Don't want to confuse with The Man. It a long road to the grave. Bettah you live peaceful and keep you loved ones. You live good, you see many generation."

"When I am home I feel wonderful free. But if I goes over, I gets a tough pain on my heart fo' the way the peoples is turnin' from the Lord. I like to love my neighbor and do he good. All at home. This my home place. I be set to die on here."

"I think a colored woman have a hard life, but it bettah than a man's."

"The world is all jess chillrun and come wisdom, we goin' turn out good."

WASHINGTON

Yesterday in Mississippi an all white jury acquitted eight white men for beating school children with pieces of iron pipe. The courts aren't the answer.

I still agree with Stokely in some things but not all. He told the young people at Miles College in Birmingham, Ala. that if they want to send you to Vietnam demand that you be trained at West Point Academy. I feel that is right. They send them to a fort for two months, then on the firing line and back home a box of cold meat. He knows where to use his inflammatory strategy.

I have a front-page article and picture of Mrs. [Lurleen] Wallace. It's going to be very hard for you to believe how sorry I am for her and how my heart feels when I look at her picture. I was in Montgomery when she stood beside her husband declaring her willingness to campaign for the governor's position. She was just out of surgery then. She was so pale. I said to myself, "That demagogue wanting power is going to kill that woman." And now it is about to happen. I do feel extremely sad and wish I could talk with him. Maybe I'll do my old way—writing him a letter but I feel that it is too late now. It should have been done at that time.

Charity is referring to a habit of hers of writing notes of advice to her friends and associates, usually to indicate to them some habit of behavior that is doing harm to others and destroying their own effectiveness. She says she finds it more valuable than talking to the offender personally at first. Usually, after reading her note and pondering it, the recipient will seek her out to discuss the matter. She says that men take this sort of advice and criticism from her with far more equanimity than women do, but she has written notes to women too and continues to do so where she sees a need.

I am amused and somewhat appalled at her audacity. Only a woman as humble and available to the same sort of criticism as Charity is could get away with it. Once she wrote to one of the high officials in her organization who was throwing his weight around and pouting over the general lack of regard for his stature. She made the mistake of dictating the note to a secretary in the office, thus allowing it to become public information within a few hours. I had to laugh at her innocence when she told me of it.

"Charity! You didn't! I would have been furious at you. Wasn't he?"

She smiled. "Well, yes, he was. And I don't blame him. I should have known better but I just didn't expect that girl to tell it all over the place. I thought she would keep her mouth shut. I guess I wasn't being very smart."

But the significant fact is that the man took it from her, called her into his office and talked humbly with her. He even thanked her for bringing him to his senses. I have met him and seen some of those same overbearing qualities in his personality, but one has to admire his courage. He would be difficult to reach, especially by a woman. Charity has great skill in these matters in spite of the rather blunt approach. She says she definitely believes that her note writing is the kindest way of approaching another. Evidently she is famous for it. I sensed at the South Carolina workshop a certain resistance to her authority and what might be taken for self-righteousness. But she is much loved and respected. She is wise. One cannot live with her for even a few days and doubt her humility. I note that the young field workers

often touch her for a little money, and although she has heavy
financial responsibilities and is always a little hard up, she never
refuses them.

She also writes:

> Lately, traveling in Mississippi and Alabama, I have seen some
> of "Life's Unrealized Possibilities."
>
> 1. Negro pickets guarded by Mississippi's state troopers.
>
> 2. A 100% Selective Buying Campaign in progress.
>
> 3. Negroes registering in large numbers.
>
> 4. Negro school teachers taking an active part and marching
> every night to the courthouse.
>
> 5. The National Council of Churches sent in $600.00 for
> medical assistance for beaten children.
>
> 6. Judge Clayton speaking out against the beating of the
> children.
>
> 7. The F.B.I. holding a hearing and having the children point
> out the white offenders.
>
> 8. 170 Negro children in the two formerly all-white schools.

Washington. Mrs. Purdy and her family hold monthly
round-table meetings to discuss problems and advise and comfort one another. She and her two oldest children—one in college,
one in high school—all have more education than Mr. Purdy,
but he is a perpetually supported, perhaps now and then even
propped up, head of the house. Her income in city education is
better than his as a factory foreman. She had great advantages as
a young girl: private schools, upper-middle-class comfort, secure
family, modest wealth. He had none of these. But she wisely
looks upon her background as limiting, too.

"I never heard of race trouble. I never associated with whites
but I thought it was because we didn't care for them or they . . .
oh . . . just lived in another world. My mother never told me
the facts of life. My sister had to tell me what my first monthly
period was all about. Law!" She chuckles discreetly, waving a
thin hand. "What would I have done without my older sisters?
We were like babes in the woods. When I married I didn't know
anything. Not a thing . . . My husband had to be like a father to
me for a long time. He's not educated but he knows a lot. I tell
him he is a good man and a wise man."

And she leans gently toward me to whisper, "We just have to keep it to ourselves when we find we know more or we can do something better than a man. My children have respect for their father and I never let them tear him down. *Never!* But you just have to support a man in that way. You see," just in case I am ignorant of the fact, "a Negro man has been broken down and he's got to be supported and . . . built up, you know? I don't mind that. My family is very close. My son in college still comes to his daddy for advice.

"One time my husband had to come home and tell his family—in one of our meetings—that he had been insulted by a white man. It was six months before he could tell it and I didn't know a thing about it. But he finally decided he had better tell us because it was just digging at him—he couldn't forget it. And his children were so sweet about it . . . well, he just broke down and cried. Couldn't help it. It meant a lot to him. That white, just an ignorant type, called him nigger boy or something. You know how they do. Oh, Law!" She whispers again, "You've got to give them a lot. You've just *got* to make them feel strong at home."

"Do you think a Negro man is aware of this protectiveness from his family—I mean, isn't it possible that sometimes he can be made to feel lame by it?"

"Well, if the children ask his advice and come to him for permission, you see, then he knows that he's the head of the family. The more he has to decide those things, the stronger he becomes. We train our children to do two things: make hard decisions and devote themselves to helping others. They all spend their summers in social help programs of some kind—through the church or some other organization."

I am impressed and say so. "Do they miss the vacationing their friends enjoy in summer?"

"A little. But we give them three-week vacations and we reward them. Now my daughter is crazy about foreign countries and travel so we are going to let her invite a foreign student to live here and then she can become part of an exchange program when she's a senior in high school, maybe go to live in France with a family or something like that. She is earning that privilege by working for others. But they don't always get paid for it. They learn that the reward is in the work itself."

She is active in a program that fosters community work for children and gives me literature describing it.

Mrs. Purdy is a beautiful, slender, light-skinned woman, a tropical beauty who wears soft flowered clothes and a red blossom in her hair. Her daughter is very tall, and though not so beautiful as her mother, has the same elegant bearing, grace, and modesty. She is already a polished, efficient, and mature young woman but one wonders if she has ever had a spontaneous moment in her short fifteen years of life.

Mrs. Purdy dismisses the idea of Black Power with, "There is only one power and that is in the hands of the Lord. I don't like to hear talk of any power. It all sounds like war to me. But I do believe that love between black people—I mean a community feeling—is essential.

"Black business, black leaders—Congressmen and Senators, Mayors—of course we must have them. We Negroes need them. But revolution—no, that's too costly."

Mr. Purdy emerges from the rear of the house to have tea and ice cream with us and then takes me home. I am grateful that he will hold my arm to help me down the steps and I wonder if it comes naturally or if he had to outwit that insane taboo against a black man's touching a white woman. Driving me home, he talks rather personally about the lives of Negroes in Washington.

"It's an international city and that is good for the children. They going to meet mo' types. But it is a race-minded city. The big percentage are Negroes and most of them are poor but the money here doesn't go to improve the life of the citizen. It goes to building up the government buildings and making a good show of the capital. The poverty here will shock you."

He is an obscure, sober man but has a sturdy virile quality. He immediately elicits protectiveness, at least from a woman. He is too gentle, too modest. The radical blacks would brand him as a Tom after a one-minute scrutiny. But they would miss the point. Whatever his past, however modest his present, he is a man and needs to make little noise about it.

"I don't want my children to know too much comfort," he says. "That's the problem in America. I am glad they live here so they can see this mess because I want 'em to work on it."

Mrs. Purdy says that enormous time and money is expended

by Washington Negroes toward improving the lot of the local poor but that it seems to "slide down a drain and disappear."

"Mainly we need for whites to stay in the city and keep their children in city schools and not turn this place into another black ghetto."

"Hasn't that already happened?"

"Yes, but it still could be remedied, I believe, if we could get the funds to improve the schools. And fix up the slum buildings because most of the poor people would stay here and live decently if they had a little help with the schools and the buildings. There are a lot of transient Negroes here."

I ask in many streets, "Would you leave this neighborhood if you could?"

"Well, I sure would if I had any place to go. But if they fix my house, I'd stay cause my chillrun is all in school here now."

Another says, "I ain't goin' nowheres. It's jess as bad ovah there as here."

And another who sits eating a piece of bread on the steps of a tall sagging brick structure, which lacks half its windowpanes:

"Listen, you know somethin' about Washington? I kin *walk* to the White House. Thass how close I bees to the Pres'dent of the United States what don't know that I and my chillrun is hongry. He let me trick in the streets to feed these chillrun! My husban' done went off cause he can't find no work. He's a house painter but he don't have work. So what I'm goin' do but hustle to feed these kids? Shit! This gov'ment don't care. If they care, Baby, they goin' to prove it by comin' to fix up these awful places. They do all that talkin' but they don't even fix up these broken houses so we can live like peoples and not some hogs or somethin'. And they can come ovah to git these mens and put 'em to work. I mean *steady* work and not jess some day work. These mens can't run aroun' town on no buses all day. It cost money jess to look."

She finishes the bread and rises, gesturing over her shoulder at the house, the lower half of which is hers.

"See that mess? The kids put out the windows with a ball. But if they made a place for the chillrun to play round here, they wouldn't hit balls in the street."

It is true that in Washington, as of this writing, the play space is one-third to one-half below the minimum in any American city of comparable size.

"I got one chile ovah in that Junior Village. That place a mess too but at least he's eatin'."

"What do you think of the schools your children go to?"

"I don't know because I never saw a good school myself and I don't know how good a good school is. But my chillrun don't study much. We too crowded up. My only one that studies, she goes to her grandmother's place where it's mo' quiet but that's a long way. My little ones can't go that far. Only my twelve-year-old can go."

Hot muggy evenings. Streets full of wanderers. It rains but the outdoors is still more pleasant than the indoors. Two small black boys fish on the bank of a canal. Their little sister removes the fish from the hook and puts it in a bucket of water, squatting there, playing with it until the next is caught and unhooked. At nightfall, they scoot home, lugging the heavy bucket between their spindly black arms.

"How many'd you catch?"

"Uh, seven."

"No, eight, man! Eight!" His brother corrects him.

The little girl says, "These fish fo' my mama. She goin' cook 'em up."

They stagger away, dashing across the boulevard where traffic is still heavy, the bigger boy, who is about nine, holding the shoulder of his little sister's dress with one hand and the bucket with another.

Howard University, eight P.M. The campus lights are dim. The trees drip. The air is cooler now but heavy. A freshman girl meets me at the entrance to the dorm and leads me through a kind of underground passageway to the room where I will meet with eight girls, hand-picked by the house mother from seven different Southern states. They arrive on time. Everything is very orderly. They were obviously selected from the most respectable of middle-class students but still are far less concerned, I discover, with appearance, comfort, dating, and all the rest of that than the girls in Louisiana. They are serious students, majoring in career fields.

"How are you going to establish yourself in a career and still carry out your plan to marry and raise children?"

"Well, I'll stay home and get my kids started. Get them up to about three years old and then I can go out to work."

"How old will you be, approximately, by the time you get two or three children to that age?"

Henrietta shrugs. "Depends on when I marry. Maybe thirty-one or two."

"Yeah, but Henrietta," says another girl, "that's really not the best way to do it."

"Well . . . for me it is because I'm definitely going to have children, after I've been married a year or two."

"But I think you have to work first because I think that's why women don't go on with what they study in college. They get pregnant too soon, before they have experience working. I think you ought to work first and then you don't find it so hard to get back. I mean, if you're going to study law you can't get in when you're thirty-two or something."

"Oh, that's not so old!"

Abby, a premed student, serious, plain, very intelligent, says, "Well, I'm not going to marry. I mean until I'm in practice. I'm just not thinking about it. In medicine you have to be dedicated to that first or you don't make it, that's all, so I have to think about marriage a lot later."

The others imply, merely by glances, that if she had more sex appeal her attitude would change.

Margie says, "Look. Negro women all work. We don't have very many women who don't work. It's not hard for me to imagine working and having a family at the same time."

I explain that I am not concerned with mere working but with careers in special fields for which most of them are prepared to or already training: law, medicine, social work, psychology, teaching, fields that require varying degrees of higher education and much dedication.

"Will you be marrying men in professional fields, too?"

Probably. None is willing, except Abby, to deal with actual details of managing career and family. None sees the late beginning or the interrupted career as a problem.

Life at Howard?

"It's changin' fast. I been here two years. I see a lot of dissatisfaction. Used to be a kind of . . . oh, mild interest in civil rights. Now it's more Black Power and pro-Black everything. Isn't that right?" she asks the others who agree. But there is at best a vague sense of what is happening in Howard college politics and what might be called the rise or strengthening of a radical group of students. These particular young women are not as deeply concerned with the local scene as with a broader one. And more than politics they stress social problems and their own relationships with others.

Considering the most serious problem in a woman's life, Sherry says what I have not yet heard so clearly defined by a Negro woman:

"The most serious thing is upholding the image of femininity and womanhood that we have in America and here at Howard University today. That's really serious even if most girls don't take it that way."

She feels the pressure greatly, more than the others who reluctantly agree with her. She is the oldest of the group, seems more mature and womanly than the others.

"What's the source of this image, Sherry?"

"Well, men. But then women get it and pass it on to their children, their little girls. And then you got a lot of it in the magazines and in the ads . . . oh, just everywhere. I mean, you know, if a girl is going to start wearing her hair natural—and some of 'em doing that around here now—well, that's not just identification with African ancestry like they say. I mean, it's just probably because her boyfriend or somebody that's giving her the word wants it that way and that girl's going to do what he says, to be the kind of woman he wants her to be."

"I don't think that's always why, Sherry. I agree with you about some, but a lot of these girls—I mean here in Washington anyway—they've already been to Africa and they changing their names some of 'em and all that. That doesn't always come from a fellow's influence."

We talk of Negro men generally.

Most believe Malcolm X to have been a great man, but they associate him vaguely with violence, which they abhor. One girl states, "I believe as Christians we ought to forgive sins and he was a real sinner at one time, but I can't go along with *any*thing that separates the races like Black Power cause we have to make it together in this country if we going to make it at all. Now, I really believe that."

Another: "But we didn't suffer all that Malcolm did and I think he was a really great man to come out of crime like he did. You could call that salvation."

Henrietta's hero is Martin Luther King, Jr. None of the others names a revered public figure.

Men and sex and marriage are serious concerns. Marriage is a more natural state for a woman, they conclude. Some looser relationship would serve a man better, perhaps.

They are eloquent upon the matters of sex education, pre-marital sex, and birth control. Two are Catholics and definitely reject birth control. A third, not a Catholic, punctilious and naive about the subject, states that a person who is married is supposed to be mature and that she has always believed that a mature person is supposed to be able "to control things of that nature" and that "self-control is the best control."

She is answered by a few winces and wry shrugs but no verbal challenge. One girl recites, from recently studied texts on economics, the economic prognosis for "our nation if we continue to breed at the present rate." Another is informed, through sociology courses, of the figures on infant mortality among the poor, mainly Negro poor; of the conditions in which poor children in large families must sleep, eat, and study.

The discussion never becomes hot, never quite personal among them. They are polite and respectful of one another's positions. Yet the two or three who take definite stands on these subjects are the most articulate and informed. Suddenly I wonder:

"Are these things you discuss with your roommates and close friends or do you deal with them only as academic subjects?"

Frances laughs. "I think what we talk about with other girls is mostly fellows."

They laugh, except for the premed student who endures their folly with a devastating serenity.

Birth control wins out as a social necessity and inevitability despite three stanch objectors. Premarital sex is a private matter and up to the girl involved. Sex education is essential at about junior high school age, maybe earlier, in both the home and school. Marriage without love is fake. Women endure where men are flighty and romantic or downright irresponsible. A good man is a rare thing, better perhaps than a good woman.

Television is important for educational purposes but a bad habit of frustrated housewives and abandoned children. Violence is a matter of faulty social education and lack of love. Love is the answer to most ills. Mothers are more likely to teach and give love. Work is the salvation of man. Women are better in social than political fields of influence. Men do not gossip and divulge secrets as easily as women. All their concerns are with social problems, health, science, and education rather than with philosophy, art, nature, etc. They read for school courses and outside reading is usually for "escape." I find little interest in literature and art.

The trouble with the world is greed and a failure to love. Also money, says Karen. "Something wrong about money that I haven't figured out yet but if we could just go pick up our food and clothes and our needs, without giving money, then maybe we wouldn't think so much about it."

"You're talking about communism, girl!"

They all laugh.

What's the future of America?

It is hopeful. It is great. But it is trouble, trouble, trouble as long as racists have power.

How to get them out of power?

"Get the 'good' people to run more for office and work harder."

I roam the campus again, during the daytime. The most animated young women I see are those who appear by dint of dress, speech, and hair styles to be part of an avant-garde society. The others are not dull but are evidently more modest, timid, or downright repressed than the former, who are, incidentally, usually in the company of several male students.

A brief conversation with Sandy, a girl reputed to be one of the most radical on campus:

"Most black women livin' in the dark ages. Sex isn't the point anymore. Any black woman that doesn't use birth control today is either very smart or very stupid. You see, if she's a radical, she may protest curbin' the black population. But if she's only thinkin' about herself, then she better use it and try not to end up like her mother ovah in that wrecked-up neighborhood where everybody's got ten kids and no husban'. Depends on where you stand, you dig?"

"Most radical men won't mess with whites now at all. But the women still do. I mean it can't harm *me* to talk with *you* and it might do *you* some good.

"Dope, I don't approve because especially for blacks they have to be sharp right now.

"Women can do what men can do except for certain heavy work. All this stuff about men and women—that's not where it's at. Black people got to get together and make a new thing together. *Together,* see? Nothin' a white can do now but move ovah. We need leaders but we gettin' 'em. They all young. They *got* to be young. It's only the young that haven't been messed up by white power. That's the power of Stokely. He's got it straight. Yes, I loved Malcolm X.

"I may go into law school. Haven't decided. Or I may not graduate. If you want me to be frank, I'm beginning to think in terms of no more school. I mean, it seems kinda stupid to turn outta here all fixed up to move in on a white world that—like I just don't belong in and—I mean, it just don't speak to me, see? You go through Howard, you got to come out half white, the way I see it. But that's goin' to change very fast. So I may stay. I haven't decided yet. I'm just beginnin' to think, see. I was raised as a darkie and I'm not all *cured* yet."

The tone is effusively sardonic.

"No," she says thoughtfully, staring over my head, seeing through and beyond me, "we can't go all the way without whites. That's not the issue right now. Most whites have been just as messed up as everybody else. But some—a few—can see it like it is. Just a *very* few." She smiles ironically, shaking a head of bushy natural hair and two large thin gold loops that hang from her pierced ears. "I haven't anything against anybody—really—I mean, I'm s'posed to be radical but I'm not really *mad*. It's just that I think this is *my time* now and I'm goin' take it. Anybody'd be crazy not to take it. And that ties me up with my own thing, see. I just don't care about anything else right now but takin' what my mother and my grandmother oughtta have had and they didn't get it. That's where I'm at just now. I guess you have to be selfish if you in my position right now. I don't know—sometimes I feel pretty confused."

Suddenly she is embarrassed because she had given me the straight word. Her voice has become not only "level" but faintly wistful. We smile at one another, and she turns away as if to don again hastily the tough armor of the psychologically hip. She waves me a vague farewell and hurries away.

Somehow, in roaming this campus, I have a sense of underground rumble, of something about to happen. There is a feeling of division among students. There are such disparate groups, in style at least. The eight girls I talked with live on an entirely different plane from that of Sandy. Will they come out of Howard half white?

Washington, D.C., where the sick are still enduring long waiting lines at D.C. General Hospital to be interviewed by social workers who determine if they are poor enough to be admitted. As if anybody *not* poor enough would wait.

Washington, D.C., where less than one-fourth of the elementary schools have an official library.

. . . where 90.9 percent of the students in public elementary schools are Negro.

Where do the white residents of Washington, D.C., send their elementary children to school?

The U.S. Riot Commission Report says:

> Because this rapid expansion of Negro population [in cities] has been concentrated in segregated neighborhoods, ghetto schools have experienced acute overcrowding. Shortages of textbooks and supplies have developed. Double shifts are common; hallways . . . have been adapted for class instruction . . .

Slowly the big cities of the South are inheriting the pattern—an exodus of whites to suburbs and an intensification of the Negro population in the central city. Public schools in Atlanta and New Orleans already reflect this trend with well over half the school population Negro.

ATLANTA

BACK TO ATLANTA as if to home. Charity has left her winter clothes in Charleston at her new home and now travels lightly, one of the few charms of traveling in hot weather.

"But," she says philosophically, "travel is easier this year. I used to find a lot of empty seats around me on the airplanes and trains and that has passed. Being old and being a woman makes it a little easier. They'll sit next to a Negro woman before a man. They even talk a little. But I never tell my work. I say I'm a missionary." She laughs a little. "That seems to please 'em. I'm being a good colored woman and staying out of race troubles."

"They" is an adequate title most of the time for Mr. Charley, Miss Ann, Whitey.

Charity has been praying with great zeal that Marshall Kornegay, Grand Dragon of the Ku Klux Klan, will follow his recently publicized impulse to retire. And also she prays many times a day for Mrs. Lurleen Wallace. About the Klan she says:

"You read that about their debts? See, that's where you get 'em every time—economically. They don't care if the world laughs at them or if they are found out for all their evil. They only care about their money. You hit 'em there and they break up fast. That's what those legal defense fees are doing to them now that we finally got some court action against them. Twenty-three thousand dollars they had to spend already."

Charity's convictions about the power of economic pressure are recent ones, more emphasized now than when I first met her.

In a new small black straw hat with a soft white flower, and a black cotton suit, she goes to church with the Mennonites today. She attends different churches from time to time but more often her own Christian church.

I go alone to Ebenezer Baptist to hear Dr. Martin Luther King, Jr., and afterward, in the basement over coffee and cookies, I meet him and his family. They are beautiful. We talk for half an hour or so, about the Movement, about mutual friends, and they drive me back downtown; but I have no time with Mrs. King except a later phone call. She leaves on tour in two days.

Yesterday the Klan marched through a very poor Negro district here. This town is headquarters for the Student Non-Violent Coordinating Committee, Southern Christian Leadership Conference, and other groups dedicated to civil rights; and yet the Klan boasts that its biggest membership is here.

"You see how many police they had out there?" says Charity. "That's the only reason some of those Negro people didn't gang up on those Klansmen. It's hard to believe, isn't it? American people so full of hate.

"Well," she consoles herself, "they finally got equal pay on municipal jobs. They been paying the Negro city workers less than the whites all this time.

"Now the mayor says twenty-five thousand jobs are waiting for educated people to fill 'em and yet they don't improve the schools so they can turn out educated students. They never learn. Sixty percent of the school children in Atlanta are Negro but there are fourteen white schools and only nine Negro. See, that's the picture in the most liberal city of the South."

"Charity, I have only a week left!"

"I'm going to put off my trip to Tennessee until you go."

If there is any end to her generosity, I have seen no sign of it. When I tell her I am to meet Sarah T., a radical civil rights worker in Atlanta, she says:

"Oh, she's going to talk to you? That's good. She used to hate white women and wouldn't speak to 'em. That shows she's growing."

Sarah is twenty-five, has a master's degree in English from Spellman College. She describes herself as a "careful radical." She was married two years ago and has a baby son who is named after a well-known African leader.

"I know what it suggests when I say that my mother is keeping him while my husband and I work—that we're living in the same old matriarchal style. But nowadays all these grandmothers can say that they're bringing up their grandchildren so the parents can work in the Movement and it sounds better . . ." She laughs ruefully. "And . . . it *is* better."

"In this organization I'm a sort of coordinator of finances. I decide what we can spend for what and usually I have to tell them that we can't afford it no matter what it is!" She slowly relaxes and levels with me, but her pride is exercised perpetually, a kindly warning to me. Talk of marriage opens her up.

"Well, I've found out there's no answer, really, for a woman who works in a career and has children. Like: my baby knows who his mother is, I think, but it's his grandmother who's giving him the food and that means something very special. He's getting more of her . . . uh . . . nature than he is of mine. He's learning to live with *her*, not me. But I hope I can stay very close to him. I take him on weekends and spend a lot of time with him. And he's crazy about his daddy already.

"Sometimes I worry about it, though. My mother is a very special woman. Very powerful."

"Did she influence you as much as your father?"

"Oh, more, I think. She has so much social conscience, for one thing. I remember when I was little—our house was on the escape route for Negro men on the prison chain gangs. You know, Negroes used to be really brutalized on the chain gangs not so long ago, and they escaped when they could. It's still pretty bad for Negro men in prison. Well, my mother always kept a suit of men's clothes in the house and a package of things—a little silver money, matches, names and telephones, maybe of certain preachers around the South who would help—you know?

"Once or twice I remember a lotta commotion in the house and whisperin' and a strange man in the kitchen in the middle of the night.

"She took a big risk. Didn't matter what he did or who he was—he was a Negro man off the chain gang and if they caught him, they'd beat him to death. So she helped him escape.

"But my daddy was very angry about it. He was afraid we'd all be killed if they caught us. So, see, she's a strong woman and she *could* influence my son if I'm not with him enough. She's good but he *is* my son." We laugh.

"But marriage is funny. I can't really figure it out. Like, it is so hard to find a strong man that I think sometimes the only reason I married the man I did was cause he was the only fellow I met who is stronger than I am. I mean, I love him but we aren't very much alike."

"You think it is essential that a man be stronger than his wife?"

"In a certain way, because women are *so* strong. Negro women, anyway." She laughs guiltily. "I mean, you know, a man has to be *powerful* to handle a woman. We're smarter. There's no question about that. We are. And Negro women can be pretty hard on a man. I mean, white women don't do so much of this as far as I know, but we *fight!* We scream and fight. Lotsa Negro women beat their men!" We laugh knowingly together. "I notice that Jewish women can do that. They scream and carry on. But white gentile women are more . . . uh, cool."

"Maybe they're intimidated."

"Well, to be honest, I think a lotta white women are screwed up terribly, but . . . that's their problem. I don't worry much about them. I spent three years hatin' white women so much it nearly made me crazy. It came from discovering how the whole world had this white idea of beauty. See, the western world concept of beauty is *your* kind of beauty, not mine. You can't find my African kind of beauty—I mean thick lips and kinky hair—in a picture anywhere except a little bit lately with fashion models. But the ads and all that—they still think in terms of narrow noses and light skin and straight hair. Most Negro women straighten their hair and they're going right on with it. Bleaching cream still sells in the stores. And I mean, I just hated that so much that for three years I wouldn't speak to a white woman.

"And then I realized what I was doing to myself. I was losing my self-respect and even losing my looks. I finally had to work myself out of it. I had to find a new sense of my own dignity, and what I really had to do was start *seeing* all over again, in a new way. That's one thing Negroes are trying to do now—to *see* differently. That's hard!"

"Do you think whites are also trying to see differently?"

She deliberates. "Yes . . . yes, I think they are. They don't want to, but some are really trying."

"What do you see as the future of Negro people in America?"

She gives me a wry smile and drops her eyes.

"You wanta know what I really think?"

"Of course."

"I think we will disappear. Because as we are now, we aren't Americans because we aren't white. And, even though I support Black Power and believe in it, I know it is just a temporary necessity for Negro people to get some independence and dignity and catch up to the level of whites. Like, high school education for Negroes is the same as eighth grade for whites, even today. Well, all that is going to change by Black Power pressure, I think. But the more equality we get, the more we are going to fade into the big group. We are too small to stay Negro.

"I mean, look, we are 'something else.' You know that?"

"Well," I am reluctant to agree, "I'll accept your belief, at least."

"Look, everything we need is the very thing that is going to make us less something else, and more what you might call white. And then, just physically, we will intermarry. The trend now is to keep black people together but that won't last either. We will intermarry and very few of us are very black anyway. So, as a psychological type and also a physical type, we are going to get into the big American soul and disappear. There's no other way to go if you stay in America.

"So, in a way I'm working for the extinction of the African type in America because I want black people to have their own businesses and hold high political offices, but I know that when they do, they are going to become more and more a part of the American character. And the black soul is going to die in the middle of the white soul."

She says it softly; it is a dirge.

I consider it. "Don't you think though, that that is in a certain way the fate of all humans? I'll be outlived by the world, by life, it will absorb me and transcend my existence and my individuality. One becomes a part of the nature of the world and very rarely is there a person who remains an individual force and gains immortality by becoming something that happens to the world. Very few individuals or groups have enough impact to remain inviolate from the big digestion of man's evolution and history."

"That's right. But see, I got this double life—as a human being and also as a special group outside the main group."

"Yes, I see."

"And to know that Negroes are going to vanish here is like knowing that your family is going to be wiped out. Because your white identity isn't going to be wiped out here; that is, not for a long time. You are a minority in the world but by the time the majority can wipe you out it will be a little whiter. It will *have* to be a *little* bit white just to get its hands on the wealth that it needs to wipe you out. You see what I'm saying?"

"Yes," I say, "but I guess I see it as the history of humanity and nature, and as a way of saying that mutation is the only means of refining the species. Probably all distinctions of color and type, perhaps even what we know as the biological types of male and female, will be altered and perhaps appear to perish in the process of our evolution. The process inevitably kills off something that one, in his time, finds precious or something by which one defines himself, such as black, white, European, female, or whatever."

"Well," she says, "that's true. But for Negroes in America, because our life was always threatened, we feel very frightened by the idea that Negroes will disappear in America. Because it's very heroic that we are still here at all."

"And yet you believe Negroes *will* disappear and you allow yourself to face that belief?"

"Yes, I do. I have a feeling of . . . well, of death, but it strengthens my feeling of life, somehow. My son has something to do with that, too."

"Would you say that you have acquired the tragic view of life?"

She smiles. "Definitely. But I just never gave it such a dignified name. Ha! That's good. You *gave* me something." She is slightly shocked.

Ah, Sarah. You are, at twenty-five, more whole than most of us at eighty.

"Well, you gave me something too, Sarah. Thank you."

We talk for two hours. I do not want to leave but I know that her work is urgent. We talk about the disappearance of the last American peasantry, which is mainly Negro. We talk of Christianity, which she thinks is an alien religion for Negroes; Christian practice allows for very little ritual action. "Action is necessary to Negroes. In church service, I mean."

We talk about literature, which, she confesses wistfully, she has forsaken. She rarely reads anymore. She likes the French existentialists, especially Camus, and senses that that is already a dated sort of taste. She is one of the most thoughtful women I have talked with, more honest and self-knowledgeable than the others, except for Charity.

Midnight. Charity and I are wide awake. She is somewhat depressed again, explaining as a cause that Governor Lester Maddox has returned to his erratic segregationist stand after the relative restraint of the election period.

"He's using the public school system to fight the Federal Government," she says scornfully. Any blow to education is a blow to the heart in Charity's case.

Yvonne and I walk to the Neighborhood Center and suddenly see Mrs. Ferris on the opposite side of the boulevard, moving unsteadily up the block.

"Look! There she is. Mrs. Ferris!"

"Wait, Yvonne. Don't call her. She looks drunk."

"You think she could be?"

"Yes, I think she could be!" I say it with annoyance and she gives me a look of reproach.

She crosses the street, leaving me. Mrs. Ferris, whose drunkenness is now flatly obvious, talks with her a little. But in a few minutes Mrs. Ferris wanders off, dismissing Yvonne with a vague wave.

"What'd she say?"

"She said she's been sick. But you were right, she is drunk. I wonder if she drinks all the time? What do you do about people who drink?"

I shrug. What you do about people is Yvonne's burning question. I want to ask if she has ever considered leaving them in peace, but it is a cruel idea.

"Probably another poor woman who is Negro could help her better than a white," I say.

"Maybe so."

I watch regretfully the disappearance of the young, powerful, if momentarily deranged, body of Mrs. Ferris, whom I am never to meet.

. . . Stays in bed all day to keep her baby from falling out . . .

She carries, for me, the spirit of a wild creature who, I hope, will elude all benefactors if they must try to reform as well as feed her.

Last week the Polish store owner hit a young Negro boy while driving his old Dodge down our street. He has been desperate ever since the accident, terrified, in fact. The boy, our neighbor Mrs. Waldo's son, has a broken leg and is in the Negro ward of a hospital across town. The little store has been closed all week. The poor Pole, Mr. Lipsy, visits his victim twice a day and sits, mournful and pale, staring at the poor child until both are wretched.

Mrs. Waldo says, "That Jew's feared somebody goin' to burn

his sto' but he don't know the colored folks doesn't do that kinda burning. A *white* will burn his sto' if anybody goin' to burn hit."

There is only time for a quick visit with Mrs. Sigh to give her the snapshots I took of the family. Pregnancy may be the price she pays for peaceful relations with her husband. He is still sober. Mrs. Sigh's expression has not altered with her condition, unless perhaps to become slightly more phlegmatic. The bare walls of stained shredding wallpaper, the punishment of ugly, small, crowded square rooms, the irritant of ever-present other bodies, perpetually broken windows and ailing plumbing, the musty smell; endless, unrewarded work, the small ominous failures of children in school, in the world; the unvaried unbalanced diet . . .

Mrs. Sigh's life is stalled and sinking under the weight of all that. Phlegmatic she is, therefore.

Where will they put the new baby? No doubt they will simply hold it, pass it among themselves like a sacred but unsolicited object until it can move on its own power and by then one of the older children may have left home, may even have found work and have a few dollars to share.

The conception of a child is so magical that the world submits to it no matter what the cost. The idea of conception and birth evokes great awe. Yet knowledge of eventual deprivation through hunger and illness does not move the world sufficiently. One's whole impact upon the world is in those conundrums of birth and death. Magic.

"Charity, can't somebody talk to Mrs. Sigh about birth control? Maybe Joy? [A resident of our house.] She's a nurse."

"Maybe I can get her to go over to the clinic with me. I'm going to see what I can do. Having babies is killing that woman."

She sighs, adding one more chore to the list that is too long to keep anywhere but in an agile mind.

Lee Ann walks around the block to our house and delivers, with conviction, a handful of hastily pilfered pansies from the garden of a neighbor.

"For me?"

"Yeah. Cause you goin' away."

"Thank you very much. They're beautiful. Can you come in?"

"No. I got to go back. Beeboy have a splinta in he foot. He hurt."

There is always news in a big family, always drama. The currents of pain and pleasure pass among its members as electricity through the wires of a house; the whole house is fused for all versions of life from a single illumination to a total blackout.

So that is our last exchange: a small girl brings a stolen gift for me because flowers, like all works of art, belong to everyone, no matter who plants them. I must leave the South. Charity and I talk until two in the morning but that does not stop time. She mentions retirement again:

"I'm really tired this time. I want to get home. I have a good woman doctor in Charleston who's going to give me some new treatment for my allergies."

This is the first I have heard of her allergies, although I have complained of mine several times.

"Well, I get used to 'em and forget about it, but they're bothering me again."

She rolls up her thin hair in the few curlers and creams her face wearily. She is very communicative tonight, utterly present and available; yet I feel that we have parted already; as if our friendship was scarred that night of the stormy ride down to Baton Rouge when, as she so summarily put it, we were both full of private obsessions. And I tell her what Sarah said of Negroes: "We're something else, you know that."

"Do you feel that way about Negroes and whites, Charity?"

She smiles.

"No. I can't remember sometimes what color a person is. We're all children struggling out of darkness. We got to love each other, even if we think we can get out of it. And we have to forgive. *Everything*. That's the answer I get from the Lord no matter what question I ask."

Charity rises early and without announcing her intention, goes down to fix a big breakfast for me before I catch my plane.

Once she chided me for my reluctance to accept favors from others. She didn't say so outright but hinted that it was a hostile or perhaps egotistical fault. I thought at the time I was merely reluctant to allow her any more generosity beyond our traveling together, all the time she spent with me and the many people I met through her.

But today, upon seeing her up early and in the kitchen to cook for me, the old defensiveness rose again and I took the gesture awkwardly. I saw suddenly that, like Sandy, the hip girl at Howard University, I was not all cured yet. I could not bear the sight of Charity making any special effort, especially cooking, for me, because service from a black woman was once a fixed concept. I have allowed myself those generous gestures I could afford toward her, but a fear of this old pattern sometimes forced me to reject the same show of friendship from Charity.

But Charity, if she was ever tainted, *is* cured. She knows not only what she is doing but what I am doing also. She directs one of the boys to bring down my bags. She calls the Negro taxi we always use and tells him when to come for me. She gives me a quick, piercing glance and a simple command:

"Sit down, Jo, and eat."

A Silhouette

WHAT DID SHE TELL, THEN? Did she tell it like it is?

She was willing to say "Mens is the debil," and "The trouble with the world is too many poor people," and "We've got to get these Negro men on their feet"; to declare publicly a hundred times over her faith in the Lord, her belief in education, equality, integration, and brotherly love; to pronounce and demonstrate her capacity for forgiveness. She was honest enough to say, "I don't lie to the Lord, why'd I lie to you? I drinks." To say, "It can't hurt *me* to talk to *you,* and it might do *you* some good."

The impression left is of a formidable woman: a worker, a believer; one who is patient, enduring, full of wit. A fortress. A matriarch by default. Someone had to mother that estranged white South and try to bind that sundered black family. Negro society is no more matriarchal, no more addicted to her healing power than the South itself. Scratch the surface of the American character, for that matter, and you will find that sanity has gone underground to bide its time in the being of the woman, the other half. It has never occurred to the white male powers of the

Western world that their lethal games, besides terrifying and depressing women, also bore them to death. She waits, she works.

The South still exalts white womanhood and loves black womanhood; the one position is false, the other true. She is necessary. She is loved and hated.

The image of the worker persists and dominates. Charity has not retired. There is too much to do. The murders of Martin Luther King, Jr., and Robert Kennedy wounded her deeply. She grieved, and she continues to work harder now, with even more conviction. It is still men who are murdered and murderers. "We got to get to 'em" she says. But *the thing* is happening.

"Last week," she told me recently, "every Negro teacher in the county came to our meeting for stating grievances to the school board. Last year you couldn't get half of those teachers to attend. The white officials came too and they listened for a change. Even the look on their faces is different."

Charity seems to understand that, although the cost is high, as long as there is movement there is life. She has an ear against the pregnant body of the future. In spite of murder and chaos, she hears life. She is reinspired.

Mrs. Martin Luther King, Jr., Charity tells me, has taken initial steps to organize the women of America toward ending war and poverty.

A worker. Yes, the impression is fixed and one becomes increasingly convinced that Black Woman will not retire. The current is upward and out: slow, ponderously difficult, but sure. A few falter, a few stagnate, but they are rare. Sacrifices are great: Sarah, who said, "I think we will disappear . . . we are going to get into the big American soul and disappear . . . I have a feeling of . . . well, of death, . . ." that same Sarah is already dead of cancer at twenty-six years of age; and most of that brief adult life, whatever its sense of impending death, was given to work for equality and dignity for her son.

But in most cases, Black Woman is alive and on the move.

"It's just that I think this is *my time* now," Sandy said, "and I'm goin' to take it."

Mrs. Clury said, "Black Power means Negroes having a few

choices, making their own decisions. I can make mine because I already have Black Power. I'm economically independent and if I don't want to die in some general hospital, I don't have to. I can *choose*, you see."

Memories of that great stagnant lake of poverty remain, too. Often intelligence and imagination are devoured by the disease of poverty, and the poor black woman cannot make a contribution or benefit from experience on her own level. She is busy surviving. She knows the trouble of the world to be its poverty, that greed and indifference cause it.

Black Woman is a worker, a woman who, although poor, can imagine and approve of women in almost any work or role except that of preacher. A woman whose modesty does not seem false; who can say, "Naycha is due to a pusson," and "No, I never knew my father. My mother was not married."

A puritan where life is concerned, but not in regard to sex.

A church-goer, imbued with classic Christian values.

A neat, unself-conscious, often beautiful, woman who still has her hair straightened to fulfill an ideal not of her own creation, an ideal that denies her original West African beauty; who still buys bleaching cream; who talks of "good" hair and light skin. Once, not so long ago, she was purchased in batches by merchants who then bartered her for tobacco, rice, or indigo . . . she recalls her grandmother who knew "slavey times."

A woman who in scorn will call her man a nigger, who still too often goes to the back door of a white woman's house to mop her floors and tend her children for ten or twelve dollars a week.

A woman who traditionally has been a federalist but, although still so inclined, is beginning to dicker with and challenge the state and county white power structure.

A woman who takes, at any age, great sober pride in going to the polls; who watches the news and a few soap operas on television; who seems to enjoy her food, good company, the presence of children; a woman who rarely fails to describe her mother with love and admiration.

A woman who is loved, needed; who is sometimes sacrosanct, often exploited; who endures.

She is still the only person in the South who speaks to all Southerners.

These are the impressions.

The facts and figures, although not definitions, provide a kind of silhouette.

The United States Department of Labor prepared a paper on Negro women in the population and labor force and found a few hopeful and many bitter facts concerning their lives in the United States in 1966.

About 52 percent of the Negroes in the United States are females. About two-thirds of those are under thirty-five years of age. The Negro woman is young.

She has, on the average, slightly more schooling than the Negro man, although that gap is closing. In March, 1966, the median years of school completed by the Negro woman eighteen years of age or older was 10.1. The Negro man completed 9.4. Both had two years less schooling than the white man and woman.

In 1966, more than half the Negro women in the United States over eighteen years of age were married and living with their husbands. About one-third were widowed, divorced, or separated. Only 15 percent were single.

Her family, having 4.4 members, is larger than the white family which has 3.7 members. In 1966, there were 4,426,000 Negro families in the United States, and one-fourth were headed by women. Approximately 4 out of 10 Negro families were living in poverty. But when the black family was headed by a woman, 61.8 percent were living in poverty! That is more than twice the percentage of white families headed by women and living in poverty.

The more education a Negro woman has, the higher the wages she receives. Those employed are most often in the thirty-five to forty-four-year age group. She earns less annually than any working American, and that has been her fate since at least 1939. She is more apt to hold a professional, managerial, or clerical job than a Negro man is; and yet the cruel fact is that in 1966, 59 percent of employed Negro women were doing private household or other service work outside the home. And this is why her annual wage continues to be low. She not only engages in the lowest paid, most menial work, but also work that is least often covered by any sort of security, such as the Federal Fair Labor Standards Act or a state minimum-wage law; neither by health insurance, nor overtime, nor vacation coverage. The United States Social Security legislation makes no allowance for work or income lost during childbearing. In seventy other countries in the world, these provisions are enacted in law.

In 1967 nonsupervisory jobs engaged 2,604,000 Negro women, over half of whom had no coverage of any sort. Minimum-wage coverage of private household work is practically nonexistent in the United States.

And so, like Ivy Demerest, Black Woman moves from one household job to another seeking higher pay and better general conditions. Expecting nothing in the way of legal protection, she relies on the chance of finding compatible and sympathetic employers, "charitable" employers, one might say; and her ancient inferior position becomes more deeply entrenched. Last month, however, Ivy joined a group of women in her county who are hoping to organize a household workers' strike to establish a minimum wage of $1.25 per hour, a figure which is lower than the national minimum-wage requirement. In Mississippi virtually all domestic service jobs pay less than $1.00 per hour. Ivy will no doubt lose her new eighty-cent-an-hour job with a white family when her activities are discovered.

This Southern domestic worker is the nearest thing among Negro women to the random, outcast, free-floating Negro man. No provision beyond the whim of her white employer can guarantee her a raise, time out for illness, or even steady work. Her bargaining power, such as it is, is in good work performance and in the old military technique of unpredictability—in a kind of caprice and false aloofness that often intimidate white employers who are desperate for good servants. With Negro employers she has a little better time of it.

"It's happening," Charity said. In three years these figures have changed a little in the Negro woman's favor. Opportunities for training have increased slightly. The President's Commission on the Status of Women published a report in 1965 stating that "a major means of entering the secretarial field is through graduation from a recognized business or secretarial school. Many of these schools, however, do not admit Negroes. Yet they are granted licenses to operate and have such advantages as tax exemption and indirect federal funds through veterans programs."

But the results of investigation of such malpractice—a tightening of inspection and the implementing of old laws—often have little effect in the case of a Negro woman such as Ivy Demerest, who, intelligent and energetic, could benefit from business training and would like to have it, because there is only one such school in the entire county in which she lives and that is expensive. And besides, it has a long history of segregation, which, as she puts it, "isn't about to break up for another hundred years because they aren't going to let all those white girls go just to get one or two colored girls in there. And they might couldn't get a job when they get out anyway. I doubt if they have more than two Negro girls working as secretaries in this whole county. See, it's still tight. They don't have the idea yet that we can dress up nice and speak good and get in that office on time and smell right and all that. I wouldn't want to work in a white office anyway, and not too many Negroes have business in Mississippi."

Ivy is in her early forties now. It is doubtful that the slow developments, even when they reach her area, will dramatically alter her life. Probably she will work for some white woman until she is old, and then? "Less hope by then I can get a little retirement or something. I can maybe take in a boarder. I don't think much about it. I'm busy. I got good health. I'll make out."

But old Negro women are the poorest of Americans, and in that, ironically, they share the lot of old white women. The aged in America are lonely and poor.

The President's Commission recommended to the President in 1965 (1) unionization of household workers to establish decent wages and hours and standards of working conditions, and (2) facilities to help those who are qualified or desire further training to move to better employment opportunities. They especially stressed the need for broadening the programs of the Manpower Development and Training Act to create a stronger vehicle for the preparation and placement of Negro women workers.

But, typically, direct action involving the least bureaucracy comes from private organizations. An organization called Women in Community Service (WICS) was formed by the National Council of Catholic Women, the National Council of Jewish Women, the National Council of Negro Women, and the United Church Women; it proposed to do a total job of continuing community service for every girl who expresses interest in the Job Corps. WICS and the quiet organization headed by Mrs. Clarie Harvey of Jackson, Mississippi, which calls itself Woman Power, Inc., are very effective, and the former can probably take as much credit as the government for the few women who have found better employment through the Job Corps.

The crucial point made by the Status of Women Commission was that the type of guidance usually given to Negro youth limits their view of job opportunities. High school guidance counselors, when not openly prejudiced, are often ill-informed and reticent about the idea of advancement for Negro youth. They often hold misconceptions of young Negroes' capabilities and project these onto the youth.

Negro communities themselves have a far better understanding of the needs of black youth than any other social group, obviously. The need for the aspirations of parents to be supported; the need to stress upward mobility for young Negroes; the need for handbooks, films, specific information, training in such simple matters as learning the city and its transportation system, learning to write checks and bank money, securing loans at reasonable interest rates, reading contracts, asking for scholarships, have all been stressed by civil rights groups and militant black leaders. "Black is beautiful" is a hopeful cry. The huge, complex, rural citizenship education program of the Southern Christian Leadership Conference has done immeasurable work in these areas and most of that work has been done by Negro women field workers whose labors and accomplishments remain totally unknown to the general American public. This organization alone is changing the nature of American culture and specifically changing the literacy statistics in a very dramatic manner.

Every new experience opens a horizon, even the simplest. It is happening and the black people of this country, in this author's opinion, can take the credit for making maximum inventive use of the slow unimaginative offerings of their governments, state and federal.

The President's Commission on the Status of Women, in summarizing its findings, stressed the special difficulties of Negro women. Their problems, it declared, cannot be dismissed lightly. Miss Dorothy Height of the Commission said:

> Negro women have the same problems and hopes as other women, but they cannot take even the same things for granted. If the Negro woman has a major underlying concern, it is in the status of the Negro man and his position in the community and his need for feeling himself an important person, free and able to make his contribution in the whole society in order that he may strengthen his home.

Yes, the dignity of Negro men and the security of her children surely preoccupy her. These problems are complicated vastly by the fact, too, that the person she most needs and wishes to see flourish is her most severe competitor in the labor market today—Negro man. He is now entering fields that she has traditionally dominated: teaching, social work, nursing, office and managerial work, personnel.

The Negro family picture changes so much more slowly in the economic sphere than it does in other areas that the Negro woman is still very often an essential wage earner, even when the Negro husband and father is employed. A study of Atlanta Negro high school students revealed that, where both parents were employed, only 43 percent reported the father's income as the principal means of support. Yet, 67 percent of the mothers in such families were employed in low status occupations (defined as domestic workers, operatives, common laborers, etc.), which means that the income relied upon from her could be a pittance—anything from twelve to fifty dollars a week.

But she perseveres. She works, she fights to get to the polls to vote for a leader rarely concerned with her dilemmas. She is only beginning to discover the profundity of the prejudice against her in her native land. As late as 1965, she, being a woman, could not serve on any jury in Alabama, Mississippi, or South Carolina. In Alabama, Mississippi, and Georgia divorce is granted on different grounds to men and to women with the favors going to the former. These absurdities seem to trouble her more now than they do her white sister. Being black, she knows the put-down in double force. And we will not continue forever to witness her composure and patience. Studies of the riot participants in major Northern cities report that many Negro women took an active and not merely supportive part. That this will be true of the urban black woman of the South is debatable, but not beyond imagining.

She still dies of stress diseases and of the remnants of early neglect, and dies five years sooner than her white sister. The most common form of serious mental illness from which she suffers, as do all black people, is paranoid psychosis (an exaggerated sense of persecution). She has less medical care than her white sister and more need for it. She has less money than anybody and getting her and her family of four or more children up to an annual income of $3,335, as Michael Harrington pointed out in a *Saturday Review* article of July, 1968, is not going to put them "in the private-housing market, give them access to a decent school, or even provide them with clean air."

If the United States withdraws from its war in Vietnam and spends those billions on tax reductions for middle- and upper-income families instead, then Negro woman, mainly poor, will feel scarcely a ripple off that big splash.

American welfare, the stingiest welfare system in the Western world, does not reach but one-third of the poor in the United States, and those whom it does reach are kept in poverty by it, with no choices, no privacy, and no dignity. In 1967 in the state of Mississippi, for example, a dependent child was given $9.30 per month for food, clothes, and books. The national average payment is a mere $31.61 per month.

Thus, with poverty and the status of Negro men her main concern today, what does she see ahead of her? And in what spirit does she face what lies ahead?

She seems to have hope and she puts faith in work and the

Lord. How she works! As if laying up grain against future famine. She prods the slumbering American conscience by her dedication.

Late in 1965, Marian Wright, a graduate of Yale law school, became the first Negro woman to pass the Mississippi state bar examinations. She practices there as a civil rights lawyer, deeply involved and underpaid by clients who, in the main, have never seen a lawyer nor heard of a woman in that profession. She is one of six Negro lawyers in Mississippi representing 900,000 Negro citizens. This gives her a theoretical clientele of 150,000.

In 1968 Shirley Chisholm of Brooklyn became the first Negro woman elected to the U.S. House of Representatives.

Constance Baker Motley, former President of the Borough of Manhattan is now a Federal judge.

Mrs. Grace Hamilton continues to sit in the Georgia legislature, the only Negro woman there.

Two Negro women are state senators: Verda Welcome of Maryland and Barbara Jordon of Texas.

Yvonne Watson Braithwaite, as assembly woman in the 63rd district of Los Angeles, won her office over considerable opposition to her as a female, she states, by people who said it was time for the Negro male to arise.

Cora Brown, a Negro woman lawyer in Los Angeles, a former state senator, says that current emphasis on the Negro male image in leadership is bringing about a kind of discrimination in reverse against black women.

Ethel Maynard, Democratic member of the state legislature of Arizona, foresees a great future for Negro women in politics.

Dr. Clotilde Dent Bowen, a physician and psychiatrist, is a colonel in the United States Army.

June Franklin of Iowa, Victorina Adams of Maryland, Daisey Elliott of Michigan, Lena K. Lee of Maryland, Rosetta Ferguson of Michigan, all these Negro women and many others are moving into influential political and social positions, and through mass media thousands of young hopeful and perhaps timid black girls in America are seeing their faces, learning of their work.

The question is not has She, Black Woman, the fortitude and imagination and intention to emerge as she should, but against what odds? How much sacrifice can black families continue to make for the most ambitious member who, like Lee Ann Sigh, will get an education and probably find a profession?

And having made it, will she get into the "big American soul," as Sarah predicted, and disappear? Lose her blackness, her identity?

This author cannot presume to answer. Like Mrs. Mindy Adams, I see a little light. But I am no longer impressed by a *little* light. Until women in America are understood as the missing and desperately needed half of what we call our power, our soul, the half that has untried, daring, and wise solutions to offer our ailing world—until she makes herself thus understood, she will have to pretend to be solaced by that little light.

That black women could at this moment lead white women in such an emergence, I have no doubt. They have known total repression, abuse, hopelessness, humiliation and endless labor. They know the human race, Americans especially, by way of the back door. We must seek them out and aid them and listen to them.

We must.

Ojai, California
January, 1969

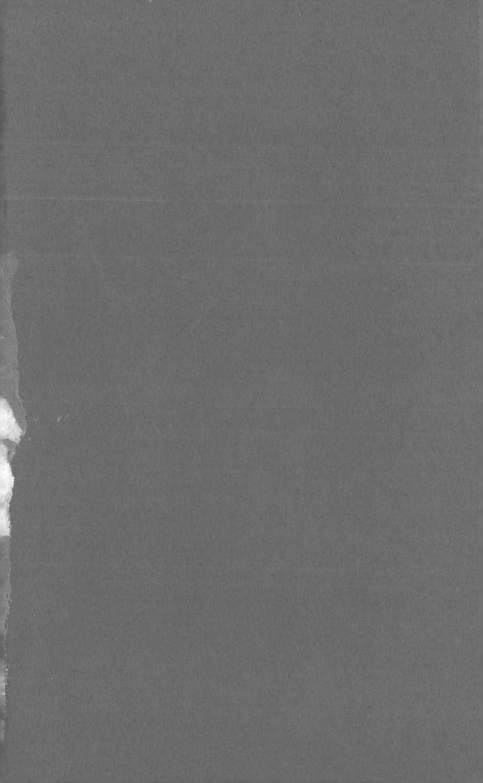